HOW
CAN
THESE THINGS
BE?

A PREACHER AND A MIRACLE WORKER
BUT DENIED HEAVEN!

Dr. Bill Hamon

DESTINY IMAGE® PUBLISHERS, INC.
P.O. Box 310, Shippensburg, PA 17257-0310
"Promoting Inspired Lives."

This book and all other Destiny Image and Destiny Image Fiction books are available at Christian bookstores and distributors worldwide.

For more information on foreign distributors, call 717-532-3040.
Or reach us on the Internet: www.destinyimage.com

ISBN 13: TP 978-0-7684-0903-1
ISBN 13 EBook: 978-0-7684-0904-8

Previously Published by Christian International Publishing
P.O. Box 9000, Santa Rosa Beach, FL 32459
Previous ISBN 13: 978-0-939868-14-8

For Worldwide Distribution, Printed in the U.S.A.
1 2 3 4 5 6 7 8 9 10 11 /18 17 16 15

Contents

Introduction

During my 60 years of ministry, I have known of and worked with a problem that has been a source of much confusion and wonderment in the Church. How can ministers of Jesus Christ build great works of God, and even demonstrate miraculous ministry, yet be practicing major sins? This is not exclusive to any particular group of ministers within Christendom. It has been found among ministers from Catholics to Charismatics, in denominational and non-denominational churches. In this book, we will discover the cause of the problem and answer the question "How can these things be?" We will define what sin is from God's viewpoint. Can a Christian sin? Can born-again and baptized Christians sin enough to cause their names to be removed from the Book of Life? Christians and people in the world have many questions on this matter.

How can Christians and ordained ministers with major sins in their life seemingly be successful—like pastors building great congregations; evangelists conducting great crusades with thousands being saved; prophets prophesying true prophetic words; teachers teaching great truth and apostles working great signs, wonders and miracles. All of these things happen within Christendom around the world. How can these things be?

Many have urged me to write this book for several years. This is the year I've felt God wanted me to write the book. The content of this book will affect people in different ways. For some it will bring comfort, within others it will activate the reverential fear of God, but all will be enlightened and challenged to fulfill the scriptural admonition to, "make your calling and election sure." This book will not get involved with the centuries old debate between Calvinism and Arminianism. Each of these doctrines has their strong and weak points, benefits and problems.

A certain group of scriptures can make it look like anyone who professes any acknowledgment of Jesus Christ or embraces Christianity will go to heaven regardless of their lifestyle. Another group of scriptures can make it sound like many who confess to be Christians and are doing great Christian works may not make it into heaven. We will use and thoroughly evaluate all of these scriptures in determining how these things can be.

One of the key scriptures that will be thoroughly evaluated is the statement Jesus made in Matthew 7:21-23. "Not everyone who says to Me, Lord, Lord, shall enter the kingdom of heaven, but he who does the will of My Father in heaven. Many will say to Me in that day, Lord, Lord, have we not prophesied in Your name, cast out demons in Your name and done many wonders in your name? And then I will declare to them, I never knew you, depart from Me, you who practice lawlessness."

We will deal with the 10 M's -manhood, ministry, message, maturity, marriage, methods, manners, money, morality and motive. For years, I have used these 10 M's to determine true and false ministers. How many M's have to be out of order before a person becomes a false teacher, pastor, prophet or apostle? We will use many biblical characters and scriptures to give us answers and examples of God's thinking and judgment on these matters. Hopefully, by the time you finish this book, you will understand God's thinking and determination on these types of ministers and will be able to explain to others how these things can be.

As I was finishing writing this book, I discovered the following vision that Steve Hill received from the Lord. It spoke of so many of the things that I cover in my book that I felt it must become a part of the introduction to the vital truths that so desperately need to be made known to Christ's 21st Century Church.

The Spiritual Avalanche That Could Kill Millions
by Steve Hill

"This is coming to you from a man who has just passed through the valley of the shadow of death. Since my close call with eternity just a short while ago ... everything has become clearer. I can hear His whisper. Unabated obedience has become my mandate. That is why I'm writing this word from the Lord.

A few days ago, after enjoying quality time with Jesus, I was surprised by an alarming vision. I saw a massive, majestic mountain covered in glistening snow. It reminded me of the Matterhorn in the Swiss Alps. Its peaks were sparkling white, and I was amazed by God's attention to detail. It was so realistic I wanted to go skiing! But I sensed that there was more that the **Holy Spirit** was about to reveal. As I closed my eyes, I was in a winter wonderland bustling with thousands of vacationers. The ski lodge, condos, hotels and cabins were at full capacity at this popular resort.

Day quickly turned to night as the skiers, snowboarders, and sports enthusiasts were settling in. Anticipation grew as the snow began to fall. Everyone headed to bed believing tomorrow would be a day of sheer enjoyment on freshly covered slopes. For an avid skier, the exhilaration of being the first one to race down a new blanket of snow is a dream come true.

Throughout the night, winter storms dropped several feet of new snow on the slopes. The night ski patrol was put on full alert. Their mission was clear. With the potential of killer avalanches, they took to their posts.

I began to weep as the **vision** continued to unfold along with its spiritual application.

The ski patrol operated like a well-trained platoon. Some boarded helicopters manned with small bombs; others jumped on snowmobiles loaded with handheld explosive devices. What seemed to be a strategic group of sharpshooters were stationed at the base maneuvering anti-tank weapons aimed at the snow covered peaks. They fired their weapons at strategic points in the "avalanche zone" to force avalanches before the snow accumulated to a life-threatening depth. Left unchecked, the accumulation of heavy, dense snow packed on top of lighter snow could easily slide down with incredible speed and force, resulting in enormous damage and loss of life.

The Lord began to speak. I trembled. The fresh, new snow represented the **false teaching** that is steadily falling on the ears of the body of Christ. It has been, and is, a heavy snowfall. The skiers represented believers and non-believers, trusting the resort for a safe and memorable experience. As Christians, we have been warned to be sober and vigilant (1 Peter 5:8). However, the present, awe-inspiring teachings have lulled many into a deeper sleep.

The layers upon layers of snow have been steadily covering the solid traditional truth of Christ. The truth is that foolish teaching in these days will become so fashionable even the most dedicated believer could become deceived (Matt. 24:24). It's happening before our eyes. One spiritual leader said the other day: "You guys are old-fashioned 'holiness,' we are modern day 'grace.' You live in bondage while we can do anything we want.

Pastors and teachers worldwide have succumbed to **heretical teachings** including universal reconciliation, deification of man, challenging the validity of the Word of God including His judgments, and even lifting any boundaries, claiming His amazing grace is actually "amazing freedom." You are free to live according to your own desires. Sound familiar? "They had no king and did what was right in their own eyes" (Judges 17:6). These popular self-proclaimed ministers of the **gospel** are covering the "slopes" and will be held accountable for the spiritual death of millions.

Just as the ski patrol did in this vision, those who are aware of what's happening must take swift and accurate action. Their weapons of **warfare** must be aimed at the peaks and the 'avalanche terrain' to dispel the lies. Apostles, prophets, evangelists, pastors and teachers must be willing to drop spiritual bombs, fire anti-heresy missiles, and even drive into the danger zones armed with explosive truth to confront this potential avalanche. The generals of this generation must leave the war room and put their years of experience on the front lines.

Friend, I humbly encourage you to heed this vision and take it before the Lord. I've written it just as it was given. My responsibility is to share with the body of Christ His words to me. The ears that hear and the hands that obey are out of my control. This is not just **Steve Hill** telling a story. Most of what the Lord shares with me is personal and remains in my heart. But I sincerely believe that this is a warning for this hour.

Satan is 'snowing the saints', but it can be stopped. In the vision, I heard explosions. I saw dedicated Christian soldiers scrambling to do anything it took to bring down this avalanche before devastation occurred. One of the most powerful weapons we possess to combat this onslaught is the tongue. Let God set yours ablaze by preaching ALL the words in RED. If we take action now the result will be a tearing down of **false teaching** and a remaining layer of solid, God-given, biblical instruction that will save the lost, heal the sick and strengthen Christians to do the true work of the ministry."[1]

On Sunday, March 9th, 2014, Steven Hill, one of the greatest American evangelists, passed on to his eternal reward. This was one of Steve's major visions and messages before he departed to heaven.

On September 22, 2014, my wife, Evelyn Yvonne Hamon, went to be with Jesus just one month before this book was finished and published. She was lovingly known as Mom Hamon by thousands around the world. She was the love of my life and co-labored with me in ministry for 59 years. She left a legacy of 3 children, all ordained ministers, 11 grandchildren, and 14 great-grandchildren. Her reward will be great.

[1] Hill, Steve. "Steve Hill: The Spiritual Avalanche That Could Kill Millions." *Charisma News*. Charisma, 11 Dec. 2012. Web. 09 Oct. 2014.

Chapter 1
God, Man and Earth Relationship

THE AGE LONG QUESTION:

During the 20th and 21st centuries, there have been hundreds of ministers within Christendom who publicly were successful ministers, but privately were committing serious sins. During my 60 years of ministry, I have known of numerous ministers from Catholics to Charismatics who have been very successful pastors. Others have been great evangelists preaching to tens of thousands in great crusades with thousands being saved and healed, signs wonders and miracles with demons being cast out, and great deliverances being wrought among the people. Nevertheless at the same time they were committing major sins such as, adultery, fornication, drunkenness, and homosexuality and about every sin mentioned in the Bible. Some began teaching strange and false doctrines that were contrary to the fundamentals of the Christian faith. Many continued in Christian ministry and were very successful in the eyes of man, but at the same time they were workers of iniquity and lawless because they were breaking some of God's moral and doctrinal laws.

The age long question continues to be asked throughout Christendom and around the world, "How can these things be?" The purpose of this book is to bring some answers to this question of the centuries that has caused great confusion, anger, discouragement and reproach to Christ's Church, the Body of Christ.

THE KEY SCRIPTURE TO UNDERSTAND:

The key Scripture that is the topic of our discussion is Matthew 7:21-23. Jesus had been teaching about the fact that narrow is the gate that leads to eternal life and only a few enter that gate and continue on to receive eternal life. However, broad is the way that leads to destruction, and there are many that follow that path all the way to *hell*. He warned them about true and false ministers and trees that produce good fruit and trees that produce bad fruit. Jesus stated that the trees that do not bear good fruit would be cut down and thrown into the fire. Jesus then made the statement that we all quote quite often. *"Therefore by their fruit you shall know them."* And Jesus follows that statement with our key scripture:

> *Not everyone who says to Me, Lord, Lord, shall enter the kingdom of heaven, but he who does the will of My Father in heaven. Many will say to Me in that day, Lord, Lord, have we not prophesied in Your name, cast out demons in Your name, and done many wonders in Your name? And then I will declare to them, I never knew you; depart from me, you who practice lawlessness!*

UNDERSTANDING GOD AND HIS PURPOSE FOR MAN:

Before we can bring a clear understanding and proper application of our key scripture and answer the question concerning "How can these things be?" We need to bring insight on the following.

First, we need to know who God really is and what motivates Him to do what He does. We need to derive a better understanding of why God wanted the human race. What does the Eternal want to accomplish in the mortal race of mankind? What overall plan does God have in His mind to fulfill His purpose for creating man on planet Earth? If you ask the average Christian, "Why did God create man? Ninety-eight percent will give the same two basic reasons. God created Man to worship Him, or God created man for fellowship. The main reason Christians in past centuries developed this concept is because they thought of God as being alone and lonely in eternity. For that reason, God wanted someone with whom He could fellowship, and they would worship Him, so God created Man. But before man was created God had an unlimited number of angels for fellowship and the Seraphims worshiped God continuously saying, *Holy, holy, holy, Lord*

God Almighty." The Cherubim and the trillions of Angels co-labored with The Eternal in governing His eternal universe. So why did God want a whole new race of a different kind of being called "Man?"

Worship and fellowship are two of the eight major reasons that God created the human race, but there are six other reasons that are more meaningful to God than these two. So we first must know the real reason God created man and His overall purpose for man not only during his time of mortality but also *"according to the **eternal purpose** which God accomplished in Christ Jesus our Lord."* Eph.3:11.

Second, since God is the Alpha and the Omega, the Beginning, and the End, He knew when He would begin the human race and when He would end the time of mortal humanity. God knew that man would sin, and Christ would be sent to earth to become a mortal man in order to be slain on the cross as the Lamb of God. Before even the foundation of the earth was laid God planned and purposed for Jesus to be crucified. This was not only to provide redemption for mankind, but also to provide an opportunity for God to demonstrate to all of His creation His true nature and being. Jesus came to earth at the "appointed time" but in God's eternal purpose Jesus Christ was, *"The Lamb slain from the foundation of the world."* Jesus would then birth the Church for it was planned from the foundation of the world. *"God chose us (the Church) in Christ before the foundation of the world."* Rev.13:8; Eph.1:4.

God planned the creation of man and His purpose for mankind when He created the universe. The Almighty Eternal God exists in the **NOW** and His now consists of eternity past, the present, and eternity future. God is eternal which means He is at the beginning and end of time at the same moment, for in God's realm there is no time as we have on earth. God is not only everywhere present, all powerful and all knowing, He is also timeless. Our God has always been, He is and always will be the "I AM". This is almost impossible for mankind to comprehend, for we were born at a certain time which was our beginning. We live in a world of a 24 hour day, making weeks, months and years. All mankind is born, lives and then dies. In the natural all things have a beginning and an end, therefore for natural man it is hard to think of a God without beginning of days or end of life.

Jesus Christ is the same as His Father God. He declared to John in Revelation the first chapter; I am the First and the Last. I am He who was alive on earth, died on the cross to provide redemption for mankind, and now I am alive forevermore. Christ was in eternity past, came to earth and took on a human body, resurrected that human body after crucifixion and now is alive in that body seated at the right hand of Father God in eternity future. Yet Eternal God chose to create a creation in His own image and likeness called mankind to bring forth a sufficient number of the mankind creation to fulfill His eternal plan for creating the Human race. We will discover what it takes to become one of God's types of mankind and what it takes to get our name in the Book of Life and not have our name blotted out. We will discover what causes God to say to certain "Christian" ministers, depart from Me you who practice iniquity! I cannot give you entry into my heavenly kingdom.

THE GOD OF THE BIBLE

God is not a foreign being or an alien to mankind and planet Earth. God made for Himself a mankind body from this Earth in His own likeness and image. God made a man and named him Adam. Man was the first being ever made in God's own image and likeness. God walked and talked with Adam in his Paradise Garden of Eden on planet Earth. Earth has been the center of all universal activity and heavenly interest since man was made from the dust of the earth. In God's heavenly world of Cherubim, Seraphim and Angels, all of God's eternal creation lives and functions to fulfill God's will and His plan for man on planet Earth. Since God created mankind in His own image and likeness, the human race has been His main interest and activity.

MAN'S HOME IN THE UNIVERSE:

Mankind's scientist and astronomers tell us that man is just a finite speck of dust on planet Earth, which is but a grain of sand in relation to the vast universe. Evolutionist wrongly theorizes that man evolved into his present state accidentally upon a planet that somehow came into being. The astronomers give us the following information concerning earth. It is a round planet approximately 8000 miles in diameter and 25,000 miles in circumference. Its position is that of the third of nine planets that orbit around the sun. Its orbit is at an approximate distance of 93,000,000 miles from the sun. It makes a complete orbit around the sun every 365 days. Man's home star (the Sun) with its nine planets is called the Solar System. The Solar System is located 28,000 light years from the center of the Milky Way Galaxy, which has a diameter of 100,000 light years and contains about 100,000 million stars, (Light travels 6 billion miles a year making the distance across the Milky Galaxy 600 Quadrillion miles). If man could travel at the speed of light, it would still take him 100,000 years to just travel across the Milky Way Galaxy. Outside our galaxy, there exist billions of other galaxies. One group of scientists today thinks the universe has no beginning or end. But another group of modern scientist thinks that whatever its size, the universe is getting bigger. They say that stars and galaxies are getting farther and farther apart as if they were exploding outward. It is almost impossible for the finite mind of man to grasp the size and dimension of our Milky Way Galaxy, let alone the idea that there are multimillions of galaxies. The universe seems to be as infinite as the God that made it, with no beginning or end.

GOD'S HEADQUARTERS FOR MAN:

Who then can tell which galaxy is the center of the Universe? No one can tell the positional center. But the Bible does reveal that the center of universal interest and activity is Planet Earth. As small and insignificant as Earth is in relation to its size and natural position, yet God chose this planet as the place where He would take the substance to make the body of His masterpiece creation in His own image and likeness. The Bible reveals that earth is the place God chose to make His footstool where His feet would walk. He first walked and talked on earth with Adam in the Garden of Eden. Then at God's appointed time He came to live fully in the body of His Son Christ Jesus. God walked on earth in the body of Jesus for thirty-three years.

Earth is the place where God chose to demonstrate, teach and reveal to all His earthly and heavenly creation His divine nature, and previously not understood the motivational heart of love (agape). In God's eternal plan, He chose planet Earth as the place and a mortal mankind body as the means of revealing at Calvary that "God is love." All of God's creation had no way of knowing what motivated God to do all that He did. Although God's whole core being and nature is divine love, He had no way of revealing and demonstrating that until He created the human race on earth. Divine love cannot be demonstrated by doing service or giving of things or the creation of heaven and earth and mankind. God-Love can only be made known by sacrificially giving of oneself. God had to have a being capable of suffering, bleeding and dying in order for Him to demonstrate His core being. Creating man on earth with a body that could become mortal and suffer, bleed and die was God's method of providing a way for Him to give Himself sacrificially. Also creating a male and female human with the power of reproduction was necessary for He planned to take on a human body through this process. Jesus Christ became the only human body that God fathered. Jesus became the only begotten Son of God. Jesus was the human body of God on earth. Colossians 2:9 says that the fullness of God dwelt in that one human body.

Mankind and Earth are central to God's eternal purpose for the whole universe. Man and the death of Jesus, the Lamb of God, was planned from the time that God created the universe and laid the foundation of the earth. Though man fell and all creation was cursed to natural death, yet Jesus came to redeem all that pertains to man, and planet Earth. God's universal, eternal plan is to redeem all mankind who will believe in Him, and bring them and earth back to their original unified position with God and Heaven. Then again, in all reality, Heaven will be God's throne and Earth His footstool. Jesus' **ruling** and reigning with His Church Bride on Earth then become central to God's endless activity throughout eternity.

THE CAPITAL OF THE UNIVERSE:

The earth's location may not be at the center of the universe, but in God's purpose and eternal activity, it is the center and the capital.

Most countries such as the United States of America do not have their capital seat of government located in the geographical center. For instance, Washington, DC the capital of the US is located on the extreme eastern edge, yet all national laws, government and authority originates and issues out to the rest of the nation from the smallest and most insignificant piece of land in relation to the 50 states. Earth is the capital of God's world of all universal activities. It is the place where King Jesus and His Queen Bride, the Church will rule and reign over everything. All other eternal plans and activities in heaven, and all the earthly nations are relegated in relation to God's plan for man on planet earth; all nations of the earth are subjugated to God's plan for His nation of the Church.

WHY GOD CHOSE EARTH:

Before we can bring a clear understanding concerning our key scripture (Mt.7:21-23) and answer the question so many people ask; How can these things be? We need to bring more insight in the following areas.

First, we need to know who God really is and what motivates Him to do what He does. We need to understand the nature and character of the God who created heaven and earth and all natural things on the earth including mankind. What motivated God to create mankind and what does He want to accomplish in, with, and through the human race? Since God is the Eternal, and declared to be the Alpha and Omega the Beginning and the End, that means He knows the beginning of the human race and the end of mortal man on earth.

Second, we need to understand that God Almighty knew that man would sin and need redemption for the Word of God declares that, *"Jesus is the Lamb slain before the foundation of the world,"* and, *"We the Church were chosen in Christ before the foundation of the World" Rev.13;8; Eph.1:4.* Jesus was slain in the mind and purpose of God before He created the earth from which He would form the body of man. We need to understand that our God has no beginning of days or end of life. God does not function in, nor is He limited to the "Time" system and dimension in which He placed man. Earth and its time system is the place God placed man to fulfill His purpose for creating him. After man sinned and was cast out of the Garden of Eden, he became mortal, and God decreed that it is appointed for men to die once and after that to stand before God for judgment. Based on typologies in the Bible God has allotted about 6,000 years to accomplish His purpose for mortal man upon the earth.

OMNISCIENCE, OMNIPOTENT, & OMNIPRESENT:

Theologians declare that God the Eternal is Omnipotent---all powerful, Omnipresent---everywhere present at the same time in space and time. Omniscience---Knowing everything past, present and future. God explained His name to Moses as 'I AM THAT I AM". God exists in the NOW, which for The Eternal that means He is in eternity past, the present and eternity future at the same time. When it speaks of God as the Eternal, it means He is at the beginning and the end at the same time. Trying to explain eternity in human language is complicated, for "time" is a human word we use to explain eternity which does not function on earth's time schedule. In God's dimension of heaven and eternity there is no time as we have on earth. Our God is not only everywhere present, all powerful and all knowing, He is also timeless.

Third, we need to know the many reasons why Father God sent His only begotten Son to earth to become a mortal man. Though He was the Son of God the Bible declares He was God manifest in that human body. The Word was God...the Word was made flesh (of Jesus) and dwelt among us. *"For in Jesus dwells all the fullness of the Godhead bodily.Col.2:9. "For in Christ there is all of God in a human body".* Col.2:9LB And Paul wrote to Timothy (3:16) *"And without controversy great is the mystery of godliness: God was manifest in the flesh (of Jesus), justified in the Spirit, seen by angels, preached among the Gentiles, believed on in the world, and received up in glory."*

As we discuss false doctrine in a later chapter, it is essential that we know that any teaching which makes Jesus Christ the Son anything less than God is a false teaching. Jehovah Witnesses, Mormons, Islamist and Judaism make Jesus Christ less than God. That is one of the main reasons they are classified as a cult within Christendom or a false religion in the world. Jesus, in His resurrected body appeared to Apostle John on the Isle of Patmos and declared to Him, *"I am Alpha and Omega the First and the Last. I am the First and the Last and He who lives, and was dead, and behold, I am alive forevermore, Amen."* Rev.1:11, 17, 18. Christ was in eternity before He came to earth to become Jesus the Man. *"I came from the Father and have come into the world. Again I leave the world and go to the Father" Jn.16:28. "And now, O Father, glorify Me together with Yourself, with the glory which I had with You before the world was." Jn.17:5.* When the fullness of time came that was appointed by the Father, He sent forth from heaven His Son to be born of a woman on earth:

> Your attitude should be the kind that was shown us by Jesus Christ, who, though He was God, did not demand and cling to His rights as God, but laid aside His mighty power and glory, taking the disguise of a slave and becoming like men. And He humbled Himself even further, going so far as actually to die a criminal's death on a cross. Yet it was because of this that God raised Him up to the heights of heaven and gave Him a name which is above every other name, that at the name of Jesus every knee shall bow in heaven and on earth and under the earth, and every tongue shall confess that Jesus Christ is Lord, to the glory of God the father. (Phil.2:5-11LB)

MAN GIVEN ABILITY TO COMMUNICATE WITH GOD:

God created man with his own ability of creative verbal communication. This is called talking. My eleventh book is called "Who Am I & Why Am I Here?" It gives eight reasons why God created the human race on earth. The first reason is to provide God the opportunity to reveal to all of His creation in heaven and earth that His whole being is love. God is Love! The seventh reason dealt with God's desire to personally fellowship with man, not as an invisible presence, but visibly walking and talking together with a compatible being like Himself (Man was made in God's likeness). It was God's desire and delight to talk with man, and to share with him His wisdom and eternal plans. God did not create man as a robot but a human being with a free will and mind like his creator God. Mankind was not created to be just an employee or servant but a son, a family, a church, a people capable of thinking like God thinks, performing as He does; love as He loves; and rule and reign with His same motivation, principles, authority and wisdom. God created man with the potential to comprehend and manifest God's character and nature. Jesus Christ created a "New Man" with the potential of being filled with all the fullness of God, and even be transformed into being like Jesus and actually have the very mind of Christ.

MAN WAS GIVEN DOMINION TO SUBDUE;

God gave man a mandate to subdue and take dominion over all things He had created on earth. Gen.1:28. Man was made from the earth, to live on the earth and to fulfil God's plans for man and earth. One of God's greatest delights was to talk over His plans with Adam and Eve. Adam was to be God's friend and co-laborer, a person capable of communicating and relating with God. There was no communication problem between God and man for an undetermined amount of time. In the course of time man sinned, was cast out of his Garden of Eden and lost his fellowship and communion with God. Man no longer had a visual and verbal communication and fellowship with God.

JESUS REMOVED THE VEIL:

The fall of man caused a veil to be drawn between mankind and God. God and His Cherubim, Seraphim and Angels live in the dimension of the eternal spirit–being world, while the descendants of Adam and all earth creation live in the dimension of the natural world of mortality and death. God and His heavenly beings function from the realm and perspective of the eternal, while mankind was relegated to a time zone and natural perspective. God's place of living and functioning was called heaven and the heavenly places. Man's place was called Earth and the natural realm. Man's fallen soul became darkened in a body of mortal flesh. God's Spirit and man's spirit were separated by this veil, thereby cutting off their intimate fellowship and communication.

Jesus came to remove the veil between God-a-Spirit and man-a-mortal. This was symbolized by the veil of the Temple being supernaturally torn into from top to bottom. When Jesus died on the cross He bridged the gulf between heaven and earth. He reconciled man unto God. There is one mediator between God and man and that is the man, Christ Jesus. Jesus made it possible for the spirit nature of God and the natural being of man to be blended into one body. The following scripture phrases reveal this reality; *"He who is joined to the Lord is one spirit with Him"*... *"Your body is the temple of the Holy Spirit who is in you"*... *"glorify God in your body and in your spirit, which are God's"*... *"we are partakers of His divine nature"*. Though man became sinful and separated from God, through Christ Jesus he can be enlightened and become a born again new creation in Christ. Man's spirit is transformed from darkness to light and he receives spiritual life when he is born again by the Spirit of God. He is then to be led of the Spirit, walk in the Spirit, live in the Spirit, be filled with the Spirit, be spiritually minded and manifest the gifts of the Spirit. The new man in Christ is God's workmanship and is seated at His right hand in the heavenly places.

NEW RACE OF MANKIND

Jesus the God–man was the beginning of a whole new race of mankind. Adam was the beginning of the human race. Abraham was the beginning of God's special Israeli race. Those outside the Israeli race were called Gentiles. Jesus came and took Jews and Gentiles and made from both one new creation of mankind and called them the Body of Christ, the Church race. As Israel is God's chosen natural national people, the Church is God's chosen spiritual people.

The Church race people are not hired servants or purchased slaves but family members of the Godhead. They are children of God the Father and Jesus Christ is their Savior and elder brother. The Word of God declares Christ Jesus to be the firstborn among many brethren. Jesus is the prototype of a whole new mankind Creation–in–Christ who are called to be conformed to the very image and likeness of God as manifest in the life of His Son Jesus Christ. Rom.8:29.

That body of Jesus containing the fullness of the Godhead was crucified then buried and resurrected in an everlasting immortal body. The body of Jesus Christ is now the head of multi–millions of redeemed men and women who make up the Body of Christ, the Church. Jesus was and is man's perfect God and God's perfect man. Jesus is the prototype for all mankind, especially those who are going to spend eternity with Him. "There is one God and one mediator between God and man, the man Christ Jesus. 1 Timothy 2:5. Jesus manifested heaven's way of life and truth on earth in visual form with verbal expression. He was the God-Word that was made a flesh and bone mortal human body to fully manifest God to mankind. "In the beginning was the Word and the Word was with God and the Word was God and the Word was made flesh and dwelt among us, and we beheld His glory".

JESUS MORE THAN A PROPHET OR GOOD EXAMPLE

The Old Testament prophets prophesied God's thoughts in human words to mankind. Jesus did much more, everything He was in every word and action was the full expression of the eternal Almighty God. Jesus was more than a prophet. He fully understood and expressed His Heavenly Father. He spoke the whole counsel of God. Jesus spoke only God's pure words. Jesus was the brightest portrayal of God's glory and the greatest expression of Jehovah's personality ever to be expressed in all eternity:

> God who at various times and in various ways spoke in time past to the fathers by the prophets, has in these last days spoken to us by His Son, whom He has appointed heir of all things, through whom He has made the worlds; who being the brightness of His glory and the express image of His person, and upholding all things by the word of His power, when He had by Himself purged our sin, sat down at the right hand of the Majesty on High. (Heb.1:1-3)

Jesus was such a pure portrayal, revelation, manifestation, and expression of God that He could say, "he that has seen Me has seen the Father". John 14:10. Jesus was the walking, talking, living word of

God. His flesh and bone mortal body that expressed Jehovah fully was crucified and His blood poured out for the redemption of mankind. His body was resurrected from the grave and transformed into an immortal flesh and bone body, which is now seated at the right hand of the Majesty on High. That body will not be seen again by mankind until Jesus returns a second time.

THE HOLY BIBLE---GOD REVEALED IN WRITTEN FORM:

Not all that was said and manifest through the body of Jesus was recorded in the Bible or anywhere else on earth. The last statement John wrote in his gospel was "if all the other events in Jesus' life were written, the whole world could hardly contain the books". However, thank God, enough was written to give us the guidelines and standards by which God can be fully known and understood. The Bible rightly understood in the full dimension that the Holy Spirit wrote it is sufficient to give man the knowledge of all he needs to be in his mortality, and into eternity. God inspired the Old Testament and New Testament writers to record the history of creation, God's dealing with mankind and nations of old; His ministry with the patriarchs and nation of Israel, the birth–life ministry–death and resurrection of Christ Jesus, the birth and ministry of the Church, the instructions and eternal purpose of God as revealed in the Epistles and Revelation. All of the known writings previous to Christ and all of the writings that could be found concerning the life of Christ and the Church were evaluated by skilled scholars. There were 39 writings chosen from the old and made into the 39 books of the Old Testament; 27 letters written mainly by the apostles were chosen and are now the books of the New Testament. The 66 books were canonized into holy writ called The Scriptures, the Bible, and the Word of God. The Bible is now the revelation of God in written form as Jesus was the revelation of God in bodily form. It is all the sacred writings the mortal Church will ever need to do the whole will of God. Any new additions accepted as infallible inspired will be counterfeits, false documents which will not bring a true revelation of God as revealed in Christ, but delusions to damnation of the soul. (Such as the Koran which is supposed to be revelations of God to Mohammed; and the book of Mormon, which contains writings from a golden plate found by Joseph Smith and said to be additions to the Bible.)

The conclusion to these truths is that God created man to have visible and verbal fellowship with Himself. That Adam's sin caused a veil of flesh and soul darkness between Mankind and Jehovah. God could no longer talk to man as He did in the Garden, so He established certain men to speak for Him to the rest of mankind. Those voices for God were called prophets. Most of the Old Testament was written by prophets. The New Testament was mostly written by apostles of Jesus Christ. Therefore, the Bible is the only book on earth that is a pure and thorough revelation of who God is and what He wants for mankind, just as the life of Jesus was a revelation and demonstration of God. Now the Bible is the only source on earth for a true revelation of God for mankind. Therefore, Scripture is our only source and final authority on finding the answer to, "How Can These Things Be?

What Kind of Mankind Creature Did God Want?

God wanted a being in His image and likeness that was sovereign in that man would have a free will to choose for himself concerning what choices he would make and actions he would take. God knew when he created man a free moral being with the right and ability to make his own choices; that man could rebel against God and live his own life. But God did not want slaves or mechanical robots. He wanted a living body, soul and spirit human beings. He did not want man to serve him and relate to him out of forced control or out of fear of the consequences if he did not live God's way of life. God wanted man to know him, understand who He is and to love Him, believe that He is a good, holy, righteous and true God. Almighty God wanted man by free choice to choose to relate willingly to God, be convinced that God's way of being and living and His standards of right and wrong are best for mankind. He wants man to be confident that God is the only right way, truth, and life – the only way to be, the only truth to believe, and the only life to live.

Sad to say this is not the condition of most Christians today. Very few believers have matured to the state of thinking and being like Jesus Christ. There was a time in my Christian life when God illuminated my thinking concerning His desire and purpose for man. In my second year of pastoring when I was 21 years old, I visited a church that we were in fellowship with to hear their guest speaker. The minister was supposedly preaching some new revelation about God and His plans for man. His revelation was a repeat of a false doctrine that has been preached within the church in times past. It was the doctrine of the restoration of all things, including the devil, all of his fallen Angels and every human being that has ever lived on planet earth. He took certain Scriptures and applied them to try to make the false doctrine truth by using certain scripture phrases, such as; it is not God's will that any should perish. He used a Scripture that apostle Paul used to explain how that physical death came upon the whole human race because of Adam's sin, but all men would be resurrected bodily because of Jesus Christ. He went on to say, since God is love can you imagine a loving God taking man that He made in His own image, and fallen angels that He had created and casting them into a burning hell to be tormented forever? He emphasized that all would be redeemed; sinful mankind, fallen angels and Satan himself would be in heaven. They would all be there with us who are Christians and in the end we all would be one complete united happy family with God in heaven forever. The doctrine of ultimate reconciliation sounds very loving and humanistic but the fact is the Bible emphatically makes heaven and hell two separate places that will never be united throughout eternity. Only those who believe in Jesus Christ and their names are written in the Lamb's Book of Life will be in heaven, all others will spend eternity in the hellish lake of fire. "Anyone not found written in the Book of Life were cast into the lake of fire." Rev.20:15.

THE HOLY SPIRIT'S PERSONAL CHALLENGE:

As I drove home that night, I was very upset and frustrated with all that I had heard. I was driving home alone. I began to say to myself, if the devil, his fallen angels and all wicked humanity is going to get into heaven, the same as me; a person with a born again experience, living a life of self-denial and not participating in any pleasures of the world, then what profit is there in me living the Christian way of life? If all of them are going to receive all the benefits of heaven, the same as Christians, then what is the advantage of denying oneself the pleasures of this life and sacrificing for the cause of Christ. I made the following statement out loud as I reasoned on the matter, "I might as well go out and live and do as I please if what that preacher preached is the truth". When I said that, the Holy Spirit asked me a question. "Bill Hamon, are you saying that if it was not for your fear of hell or the hope of going to heaven, you would not live the Christian life?" I knew that when God asks you a question, He is doing it to get you to think and analyze. I knew that He was not saying or implying that there is not an eternal hell and heaven, but He wanted me to think about what my statement implied. He then asked me another question. "If I should decree that all the world and mankind is now eternal and everything is to continue to indefinitely function as it is, would you still think that God's way of living is the best for you and the whole human race to live?" It made me contemplate, that if there is not a Hell to avoid or Heaven to gain by living the Christian life would I still live the life of Christ? In other words, was I doing what God's Word said was right and not doing the wrong only to escape hell and gain heaven? If so, then I was outwardly conforming to what God says in His Word has to be practiced in order to make it to heaven, but inwardly I was not convinced that God's way of life is the best way for me to live even in my mortal life on earth regardless of eternal gain or loss. He likened me unto the Pharisees who outwardly conformed to God's commands but inwardly they were only doing it to avoid God's judgments. The Holy Spirit reminded me what Jesus said to His followers, *"Unless your righteousness exceeds that of the Scribes and Pharisees you will in no wise enter the kingdom of Heaven."* That's when I began to receive the revelation and conviction that God's highest calling and purpose for any one of His children is to be conformed to the image of His Son, Christ Jesus. My success and reward in heaven would not be based on how great a pastor, prophet or evangelist I became here on earth, but how much I became conformed to the life of Christ in His thinking, attitude and actions. If I was to have the privilege of ruling and reigning as a joint-heir with Christ then I had to be transformed into God's way of thinking, His attitude and convictions and be convinced that God is just, right and holy in all His ways.

To have the type of man God wanted, He could not make a living being pre-programmed so that he could only think God's thoughts. He could only make him pure and innocent with a free-will and with the potential to think God's thoughts, but also capable of thinking his own thoughts and even those Satan would suggest to him. After man ate of the tree of the knowledge of good and evil he knew there was right and wrong, good and evil, a bad devil and a good God. Even after man sinned he still had God's creative ability through his imagination to create his own thoughts. Every thought man thinks is not always from God or the devil. Man can create his own thoughts without them being God inspired or suggestions of the devil. Man outside the Garden had to learn to choose the Creator as His God and Savior and learn the Lord's way of right living.

How Many Human Beings Did God Want & Need?

When God created Adam and Eve, He told them that He had created them and had given them the power through procreation to reproduce other human beings like themselves. God would not be creating any more humans beings, for He had created them to be the father and mother of the rest of the human race. God then commissioned them to procreate and multiply the human race until they inhabited the whole earth. God had given this command to Adam and Eve in the Garden before they sinned. If man had never sinned, God's plan for mankind was for them to fill the earth with a race of mankind in their own image which was in the image and likeness of God. Adam sinned and failed to fulfill the plan but 4000 years later Jesus would come and start a new race of mankind created in Christ Jesus to fill the earth with mankind matured into God's own image and likeness.

DID GOD KNOW?

God knew that every human being would not relate to him and be the type of mankind creation He wanted them to be. But God also knew He would not need every human that was born on earth to fulfill His purpose for creating man. His purpose was to accumulate a certain number that would believe in Him and be conformed to His image and likeness. His long range plan was to send His only begotten Son Jesus Christ to shed His life's blood to redeem a people to be a new creation of mankind. They would be a special race called out of the human race and would be known in heaven and earth as the Church Race. They would be a body of believers also called the Body of Christ. Apostle Paul compared the Body of Christ to the human body, which is one body, but with many members. It requires millions of members from the mighty muscles to the microscopic molecules to make a functioning human body. Likewise, the same is true concerning the spiritual Body of Christ. The Body of Christ is a real living and functioning Body of true believers in Christ Jesus, who have eternal life. Jesus is the Head of this Body, which is called, designed and designated to function forever. Jesus Christ needs a certain number of members to make His body complete. He needs prepared members to fulfill certain positions and functions. He also needs a certain amount of Overcomer Saints who have been transformed to be like Jesus in all areas of their lives. The mortal human race will continue on earth until Jesus has sufficient qualified members to make His corporate Body complete. When that is accomplished Jesus will come back to earth and remove all that are not members of His Body off the earth, cleanse the earth and its atmosphere with His cleansing fire, then old earth will become new earth where only righteousness exist. Apostle Peter declared that, "We according to God's promise are looking forward to New Earth where only righteousness dwells". 1Pet.3:13.

EIGHT MAJOR REASONS GOD CREATED MANKIND

In my book, "*Who Am I & Why Am I Here?* I take 213 pages to identify and explain eight purposes for God creating mankind on earth. Several of them have been accomplished, but others are still in the process of being fulfilled.

The first Purpose: "God created Man in His image and likeness to fill the earth with a mankind race in His likeness."

The first part of that purpose is fulfilled, but Jesus is still working on the last part.

The Second Purpose: "God created man in order to demonstrate His nature and character of love". This purpose was fulfilled at Calvary where Jesus demonstrated God's love.

The Third Purpose: God created man with free moral agency so that he could be tested and purified until conformed to the image of Christ." The first half has been done, but the second part is still taking place.

The fourth purpose: God created man with the power of procreation in order to fulfill His eternal Fatherhood by Fathering His own biological Son. This was fulfilled when God overshadowed Mary with His procreative power making her pregnant with Jesus Christ who became the only begotten Son of God.

The Fifth Purpose: "God created man in order to provide a many membered Bride for His Son." Jesus became a mortal Human so that He could shed His life-blood on the cross to purchase His Bride, a body of redeemed mankind. This purpose has been fulfilled, but the Holy Spirit is still working to complete the Bride.

The Sixth Purpose: God created man in order to bring forth the Church as the Body of Christ on earth to co-labor with Him as joint heirs in carrying out God's eternal purpose. This purpose is close to being finished. Just a few more million saints added to the Body to make it complete and brought to maturity and the ministry of Christ. They also are to demonstrate the kingdom of God in every nation until every nation on earth becomes a goat or sheep nation.

The seventh Purpose: "God created man to be a praise to His glory and worship Him in spirit and in truth".

The Eighth Purpose: God created man to fellowship with Him as a comparable and compatible fellow being.

Understanding these eight purposes will help us determine God's thinking and judgment on ministers who practice sin in their lives and answer the question, "How can these things be? We must keep in mind God's main purpose for creating man. The purposes for which God created man is greater and different than most Christians think. God's way of thinking about the human race is higher than man's as the heavens are higher than the earth. Too many Christians think of God as being a lonely old God in the universe with no one to fellowship, so He created man and He needs mankind so much that He welcomes anyone who will come and be with Him. Many see Jesus just as a big jolly Santa Clause, who loves everyone so much that He will let anyone in heaven who wants to enter. We will discover who God really is and His attitude toward man and sin and what He requires for man to enter into His Heaven.

Chapter 2
Origination of Sin

In God's eternal domain, there existed no such thing as Sin, rebellion or death. Almighty God has always been, but in eternity past He created the universe and several billions of living beings. In the endless universe of God's eternal creation, everything functioned in harmony and unity as God's Holy Spirit permeated and motivated all activity. The Bible mentions three of the eternal living beings, the Cherubim, Seraphim, and Angels. The Bible implies that the Seraphim (Is.6:2; Rev.4:8) were the major worshipers before the throne of God. They continuously cry out, "Holy, holy, holy is the Lord God Almighty". Their main ministry is to proclaim God's holiness and sovereignty over all things. The Cherubim acted as guards over certain areas, such as the one who was placed at the entrance of the Garden of Eden after Man was cast out. Others ruled over a Solar System or a galaxy like Lucifer, who was a covering Cherub whose headquarters was planet earth (Ez.28:14-16). All of the galaxies in the endless universe were the habitation of God and His eternal creation. Distance was no problem for they can travel from the throne of God to distant galaxies faster than a person in his house can go from one room to another.

The third group of eternal beings is called Angels. They are mentioned the most in Scripture. There are many types of angels; Archangels, war angels, ambassadorial angels, personal guardian angels and many others that are specialist within their own ranks. The Bible gives the names of two of the archangels; Michael is the General of all the warrior angels in heaven. God's name "The Lord of Hosts" means the God of the heavenly armies and is translated as such in most new translations.   The archangel Gabriel is the ambassadorial angel who reveals God's purposes and divine decrees by announcing them at God's appointed times.   All of these living beings gave praise, honor, glory, and loving allegiance to God as they fulfilled their created purpose. Everyone lived, worked and worshiped in an atmosphere of holy purity, peace, and joy.   There was nothing but a heavenly atmosphere with God and all of His creation. This heavenly condition continued for eternal ages until something completely contrary originated in one of God's major eternal beings.

THE ORIGINATOR OF SIN

Sin never existed in God's vast domain until a thought originated in Lucifer's heart, and he nurtured that thought until it became an attitude and finally an action that caused him to become the originator of SIN. The Prophet Isaiah and Ezekiel describe Lucifer, his ministry and what caused his downfall:

> *How you are fallen from heaven, O LUCIFER, son of the morning! How you are cut down to the ground. For you have said in your heart: 'I will ascend into heaven, I will exalt my throne above the stars of God; I will also sit on the mount of the congregation on the farthest sides of the north; I will ascend above the heights of the clouds, I will be like the Most High.' Yet you shall be brought down to Sheol, to the lowest depths of the Pit.''* Is.14:12-15 (Sheol and Pit are synonymous names of Hell).

Here we find the reason Lucifer was cast out of heaven. The beginning of Sin was not murder, adultery or lying but pride and self-exaltation. Lucifer set his will against and contrary to God's will. Five times he says, "I WILL..." exalt my position, be like the Most High, etc. He not only sought to overthrow God and sit on His throne, he also convinced one/third of the angels to join him is his rebellion. When Lucifer launched his attack toward heaven's throne room, God did not get off His throne to deal with Lucifer and his angels, but sent General Michael and his war angels to fight with them. Michael and his warrior angels easily won the battle and cast Lucifer and his angels back down on earth. All light was restrained from reaching earth. Lucifer and his angels lost all of God's light and presence and were bound in deep darkness. This caused beautiful earth that was Lucifer's headquarters to be become "without form and void". Earth was flooded with water until it covered the whole earth and then frozen into one great ball of ice. All the animals such as the great dinosaurs were destroyed by the fall of Lucifer. The earth remained in that state for possibly billions of years before God came to creatively restore the earth back to being a habitable place for His masterpiece creation that He would make from the dust of the earth in His own image and likeness.

Lucifer became known as the Devil, Satan, Dragon, and Serpent. Rev.20:2; 12:9   His angels degenerated into demons called evil principalities and powers and rulers of darkness and spiritual hosts of wickedness. Eph.6:12

> *And war broke out in heaven: Michael and his angels*
> *fought with the dragon; and the dragon and his angels*
> *fought, but they did not prevail, nor was a place found*
> *for them in heaven any longer. So the great dragon was*
> *cast out, that serpent of old, called the Devil and Satan,*
> *who deceives the whole world; he was cast to the earth,*
> *and his angels were cast out with him.* (Rev.12:7-9)

There are some people who you can give them everything, place in a high position in a close relationship with you and give them everything they need to be successful, yet they still want more and will even try to take your leadership position. Those kinds of people have the same spirit as Lucifer. Please pay close attention to God's description of Lucifer in Ezekiel's prophecy to the king of Tyre:

> *Thus says the Lord God. You were the seal of*
> *perfection, full of wisdom and perfect in beauty. You*
> *were in Eden, the garden of God; every precious stone*

was your covering: The sardius, topaz, and diamond, beryl, onyx, and jasper, sapphire, turquoise and emerald with gold. The workmanship of your timbrels and pipes was prepared for you on the day you were created. You were the ANOINTED CHERUB WHO COVERS; I established you; you were on the holy mountain of God; you walked back and forth in the midst of fiery stones. You were perfect in your ways from the day you were created, till iniquity was found in you. You became filled with violence within, and you SINNED; therefore I cast you as a profane thing out of the mountain of God; and I destroyed you O covering Cherub, from the midst of the fiery stones. Your heart was lifted up because of your beauty; you corrupted your wisdom for the sake of your splendor; I cast you to the ground (earth).

Lucifer had access to the very throne of God. He seems to have been the director of the music of heaven that penetrated the whole universe. He was God's special creation of perfection and beauty. He was adorned with precious gems in gold settings which glistened with dazzling brilliance. That is probably one reason he was called "Son of the Morning." He was a step above most of the other eternal majestic beings, not only in appearance but also God said that he was the model of perfection and full of wisdom. How could such a magnificent being so richly endowed by heaven do that which would cause him to lose it all including eternal separation from God and His heavenly glories? God declared that Lucifer was perfect in all his ways from the day he was created until iniquity was found within him. He had one-third of the angels under his charge, but he became dissatisfied with that position and begins to feel that he deserved more. Pride that had never been in God's creation came into being in Lucifer's heart. He wanted to be number one in the universe like God. He deceived himself into believing that he could overthrow God and sit on His throne and receive the worship that all creation gave the Almighty Eternal God. The created wanted to overthrow his Creator.

God knew that such a person or anyone who agreed with him could not be allowed to stay in heaven for it would disrupt the harmony and holiness of heaven. There can only be one true God and Lucifer was not a god and definitely not Eternal Almighty God. That is the reason there will be no human beings, regardless of their religious experience on earth allowed in heaven, who have the spirit and attitude of Lucifer. If a majestic perfect created being with such a mighty ministry can be cast out of heaven then that opens the possibility that any human being regardless of Christian experience, who has a spirit and attitude of Lucifer can be kept out of heaven. All Lucifer did was set his will against God's will and try to put himself in a higher calling and position than was God's will for him to fulfill. He became the personification of ambitious, selfish pride, self-exaltation, self-promotion and the belief that he could become God. He is the father of modern day humanism. Also, a professing Christian, who is ruled by their carnal self-life and lives according to the dictates of the lower flesh nature, are exemplifying the selfish pride of Satan. Jesus declared that unless a Christian took up his cross of SELF denial he could not be His disciple. We will discuss later the pros and cons of this problem of ministers and Christian leaders in determining, how can these things be and what is God's final judgment on the matter.

WHAT IS SIN?

The first mention of sin is when God told Lucifer, "You sinned." So what is God's idea of sin? At that time, there were not all of the evil activities such as murder, lying, immorality and numerous evil activities that take place in the human race today. The evil spirit world did not exist until Lucifer, and his angelic being followers were cast out of heaven and began to degenerate into all the evil demons they are today. There seems to be no answer to where and how demons originated other than Satan and his angels. There are demons representing every unrighteous sin found among the human race. We have to assume that just as sin originated in the heart of Lucifer and transformed him into an evil being, in the same way all the great and small fallen angels transformed into the multitude of unrighteous behavior that they motivate humans to manifest. That is how the world of Satan, fallen angels and demons came into being.

HOW DID SIN ENTER THE HUMAN RACE?

Everyone who reads this book will probably know about the story of the creation of Adam and Eve, who became the first human beings. Mankind came into being by the desire and decree of God. After God had taken six days to create everything on the earth and in the atmosphere around the earth, He formed the body of man with His own two hands from the dust of the earth. God's own image and likeness were God's blueprint and pattern for the formation of man. After finishing the intricate body of man, God breathed an eternal spirit into the body of man causing him to become a living being. God then took a rib from man's side and made a woman. The man and woman were put into a beautiful garden that God had prepared for them. Every fruit tree imaginable was in the garden. The beauty of flowers and plants with all the colors of the rainbow were everywhere in their gigantic park. God placed two special fruit trees in the very middle of the garden; the tree of the knowledge of good and evil and the tree of life. Eating the fruit of the tree of life would keep their bodies living indefinitely but if they ate of the tree of the knowledge of good and evil then death would begin to work in their bodies until they ceased to function. Eve was seduced by the serpent to eat the fruit of the forbidden tree. She gave some to Adam, and he ate of that which God had commanded them not to eat. They disobeyed the commandment of God causing them to SIN. Their disobedience to the revealed will of God activated sin into the human race. This activated the decree of God that death would reign in the human race. Notice what the Scriptures say about the sin of the one man, Adam. "Therefore, through one man sin entered the world, and death through sin, and thus death spread to all men because all sinned." "By one man's disobedience all men were made sinners." "Through one man's offense judgment came to all men, resulting in condemnation." "By one man's offense death reigned" in the entire human race." "The wages of sin is death." Rom.5:12-19; 6:23.

Man was the only eternal being God made in His own image and likeness. There was also another way man was made different than the seraphim, cherubim, and angels. The other three eternal beings were made as one entity with their whole person being eternal. Man was made with a physical body that could be separated from his eternal spirit being. God designed it that way so if man sinned by eating of the tree of the knowledge of good and evil he would be redeemable.

There are two kinds of "death"; spiritual and physical. Spiritual death is man separated from God. Natural death is when man's spirit is separated from his physical body, he stops breathing and dies. Adam and Eve experienced spiritual death when they were cast out of the Garden of Eden and thereby were separated from the presence of the Lord. Adam experienced physical death when his body died 930 years later. Sin caused both spiritual and physical death in the human race. That is the main reason the Bible declares that God hates sin in all its forms and manifestations. Sin is death, and God is life. The two are not compatible. Sin cannot enter and dwell in God's heaven. Man who sins is a sinner. Sinners must have a way of being cleansed from their sins in order to be reconciled to God.

When man sinned and was removed from the Garden, which was permeated with the presence of God, he died spiritually. But a way was made for man to be cleansed from his sin. God killed a lamb and shed its blood and probably sprinkled the blood on Adam and Eve and declared to them, your sins are forgiven! He explained to them that if they sinned or their children sinned they could only be cleansed by the shedding of the blood of a spotless lamb. God then took the skin of the lamb and made them clothing to cover their nakedness. He did this to typify the day that Jesus would come to earth as the Lamb of God and shed His blood for the remission of man's sin. The lamb's skin represented the robe of righteousness that redeemed sinners would receive. That is the main reason that Abel's sacrifice of a lamb was accepted, but Cain's offering of the fruit of the cursed ground was not

accepted. "Without the shedding of blood there is no remission of sin."
Heb.9:22

THE DEFINITION OF SIN:

In Bakers Dictionary of Theology in their article on "Sin," they make this statement. "No single Hebrew word is able to exhibit the concept of sin fully. The most common word for sin is *hattat* signifying 'a failing, a missing, sin.'" They go on to list other Hebrew words often used for Sin with the equivalent word in English. I will only list the English word and phrases: Wickedness, iniquity, perversion, guilt, transgression, rebellion, wrongness, vanity, negligence, lying, deceit, evil, breach of trust, injustice, and to disobey.

One of the main words for sin in the New Testament is *harmartia* which means a missing of the mark. Other Greek words that describe sin in English are: unrighteousness, lawlessness, impiety, transgression, a fall-indicating disruption of the right relationship with God, depravity, lust, and disobedience.

From 1964 till 1969 for five years I was a teacher in a residential Bible College. I taught classes covering all of the Old Testament and a few books in the New Testament. I taught the book of Romans for three different years. The first eight Chapters in Romans cover the subject of sin. I challenged the students to develop a definition of sin. It became a very confusing and complicated task to develop one statement that covers all that is sin. You can see from all the words used in the O.T. and N.T what a challenge it would be. We finally came up with a statement that covers all of the ramifications of sin. ***"Sin is man's thoughts and actions that are contrary to God's Word, Will and Way."*** In other words, anything that is said and done that is not according to God's nature, character and the biblical standards for righteousness is sin. All unrighteousness is sin. Whatsoever is not the way, the truth and the life of Christ Jesus are sin.

The Bible describes different kinds of sin. Sins of the flesh, sins of the heart and mind, sins of the spirit, sins of omission and sins of commission, sins that God hates more than some others, sins against God and sin against man, a sin unto death and the worst of all a sin called the unpardonable sin.

THE ROOT OF ALL HUMAN SINNING

Picture a tree with three trunks coming from one taproot beneath the ground and the three trunks with many limbs and branches growing up and out in all directions. The branches and leaves of the tree would represent all the sins of the human race. The three trunks from which all the branches and leaves grow from would be the Lust of the Flesh, Lust of the Eyes and the Pride of Life. The one big taproot that is the root to all the sinning above the ground is SELF. The ground around the taproot that gives it nourishment is the evil spirit world of Satan and the attraction of the dark things of the world.

The Three Basic Sources of Temptation:

> *"Do not love the world or the things in the world. If anyone loves the world the love of the Father is not in him. For all that is in the world---the lust of the flesh, the lust of the eyes and the pride of life---is not of the Father but is of the world."* 1John 2:15, 16.

These three avenues of sin cover the sins of the body, soul and spirit. These three have been the main tools Satan uses to tempt mankind. He used them on Eve in the garden, Jesus in the wilderness and every person since the creation of man. Every sin that is activated in the human race comes from the lust of the flesh, lust of the eyes or the pride of life.

LUST OF THE FLESH: "Body"

This produces all of the sins of immorality, sexual sins and perversion, carnality, most of the scriptures talking about being in the flesh which means living according to the dictates of the lower carnal nature. Romans 8 and Galatians 5 covers some of the sins that are committed when one lives according to the inclinations and motivations of the flesh:

> *"Those who live according to the flesh set their minds on the things of the flesh, but those who live according*

to the Spirit the things of the Spirit. For to be carnally minded is death, but to be spiritually minded is life and peace, because the carnal mind is enmity against God; for it is not subject to the law of God, nor indeed can be, so then those who are in the flesh cannot please God. Therefore, brethren, we are debtors—not to the flesh to live according to the flesh, for if you live according to the flesh you will die; but if through the Spirit you put to death the deeds of the body you shall live." Rom. 8:5-8.12,13.

"Now the works of the flesh are evident, which are; adultery, fornication, uncleanness, lewdness, idolatry, sorcery, hatred, contentions, jealousies, outbursts of wrath, selfish ambitions, dissensions, heresies, envy, murders, drunkenness, revelries, and the like, of which I tell you beforehand, just as I also told you in times past, that those who practice such things will not inherit the kingdom of God. For the flesh lusts against the Spirit and the Spirit against the flesh and these are contrary to one another, so you are not to do what your flesh tells you to. If we live in the Spirit let us also walk in the Spirit. For those who are Christ's have crucified the flesh with its passions and desires. For he who sows to his flesh will of the flesh reap corruption, but he who sows to the Spirit will of the Spirit reap everlasting life." Gal. 5:16-25; 6:8.

We will use four biblical characters to illustrate how Satan tempts mankind by the three sources: Lust of the Flesh, Lust of Eyes and Pride of Life.

Lust of the Flesh Examples:

EVE: The fruit on the tree of knowledge of good and evil was different. Curiosity led Eve to the tree, but the sense of taste stirred her imagination and tantalized her taste buds, for she felt it would be "good for food." Gen.3:6. The lust of the flesh caused her to take the first step toward sinning.

LOT: The lust of the flesh motivated Lot to choose the watered pasture lands and orchards of the territory around Sodom and Gomorrah for the area was like the garden God had planted for Adam and Eve. Lot's flesh lusted for the stability and comfort of the city over being constantly on the move like Abraham. It was his first step in ending up at the place of destruction.

DAVID: David's flesh motivated him to stay home and not go to war with his army. Idleness became the devil's workshop as he casually strolled on his balcony which overlooked the roofs of many homes close by. The sexual passions of David's flesh were set on fire when he watched Bathsheba taking a bath. It was the beginning of the end result of him committing adultery with Bathsheba.

JESUS: After fasting for forty days Jesus became ravenously hungry. The devil first tempted Jesus with the lust of the flesh, by telling Him to use His Son of God power to satisfy Himself by turning stone into bread.

LUST OF THE EYES: "Soul"

The Soul is the body of the mind, will, and emotions of man. The soul is between the body and the spirit of man. Christians with the Spirit of Christ within are continually receiving thoughts and impressions from the spirit to have righteous thoughts, attitudes and actions and at the same time being bombarded from the body (flesh) to think worldly and carnal thoughts that produce the works of the flesh. The Soul receives its worldly thoughts and emotional reactions from the five senses of the body---hearing, seeing, smell, feeling, and tasting. The eyes are the main ones that receive the sights in the world that inspire carnal thoughts. Such as looking at pornography activates thoughts and visions of fornication and sexual immorality. It also attracts demons of lust and gives them a legal right to oppress the viewer and if the practice of watching pornography continues for a while it opens the door for the demon of lust to enter the person and dwell in his flesh inciting impure thoughts and unholy passionate desires that can become stronger than the person's will to resist. When a Christian reaches that stage, they need someone to cast the demon out of them. I know some denominations do not believe that a Christian can have a demon dwelling in their flesh. My first experience with casting out demons was when I was age 19. A fellow student and I came out of Bible College together and started traveling and doing evangelistic ministry. We conducted a seven-week revival in a church in Toppenish, Washington. He would preach one night, and I would preach the next. Keith could play the piano, sing, preach and prophesy. In the fifth week of the revival after Keith had finished preaching and praying for the people, he seemed to become very depressed. Only five of us were still in the church. My future mother-in-law started talking to him and trying to encourage him. She came over to where I was flirting with her daughter who later became my wife and ask me to pray for Keith. I really didn't want to, but to satisfy her I went over and nonchalantly laid my hands on his head and started praying. But she began to pray in tongues very powerfully. I had my eyes closed praying, and suddenly I felt Keith trying to rise up and I opened my eyes. His eyes were rolled back in his head, and he spoke with a deep guttural voice saying, I'm going to kill you! Over the next three hours, we cast five major demons out of him. They talked back to us through his voice. They told us how and when they came into him and also argued with us and resisted leaving, but after three hours of battling by the Spirit of God in the name of Jesus all five were cast out. My first experience with demonology was casting demons out of my co-evangelist. After the seven-week revival was over, and Keith moved on to evangelistic work I remained as pastor of the church. For the first six months it seemed like every week some Christian would come for prayer, and as we would start praying for them demons would start manifesting and we would cast them out. Ten years later when I was teaching at a Bible College in San Antonio, Texas there was a six month period that students would come over for prayer and as we began praying demons would begin manifesting and we would have to cast them out. All of those ministered to were born again, tongues talking Christians. During the Charismatic movement, Derek Prince's main ministry was delivering Christians from demons. It is not my purpose to make a case on demonology in this book for that would require a whole book. Many books have been written on the subject concerning whether Christians can have demon activity in their lives.

We must realize that even without demons being involved mankind has the capability of producing the works of the flesh. They are works of the flesh and not just the works of evil spirits. The lust of the eyes is one of the three trunks of the tree that produces many sins in the lives of mankind.

Lust of the Eyes Examples:

EVE: The fruit of the tree of the knowledge of good and evil must have been uniquely attracting for Eve saw that, "it was pleasant to the eyes." As she continued to look at the fruit it stirred a desire in her to pick and hold the fruit until finally she was motivated to take a bite of it and then convinced Adam to eat. A look became a lust that produced disobedience to God's command.

LOT: "Lot lifted his eyes and saw all the well-watered plains of Jordan." He was led by the lust of the eyes and not by the spirit of God or proper submission to Abraham. Decisions made by the seeing of the eyes and not by unselfish reasoning in wisdom will always end in the loss of family, position and possessions.

DAVID: When David allowed his eyes to remain looking at Bathsheba's naked body his look of admiration turned into lust of the eyes. Lust is sensual desire to take and possess with the attitude that I must have that regardless of what I have to do to get it. It motivated David to do what he knew was wrong and moved him one step closer to committing two major sins. Lust has ways of deadening common sense and causing individuals to make dumb decisions and commit unrighteous acts.

JESUS: The devil sought to tempt Jesus with the lust of the eyes. "The devil took Jesus up on an exceedingly high mountain, and showed Him all the kingdoms of the world and their glory. And Satan said to Jesus, All these things I will give You if You will fall down and worship me." Then Jesus set the pattern of how we are to overcome the temptations of the devil---by the word of God. Jesus said to him, "Away with you, Satan! For it is written, 'You shall worship the Lord your God, and Him only you shall serve.' Then the devil left Jesus, and behold, angels came and ministered to Him." Jesus overcame each of the three temptations with Scripture.

THE PRIDE OF LIFE: "Spirit"

The first sin committed was pride which originated in the spirit of Lucifer and also originates in the spirit of man. The pride of life will cause man to do things that are contrary to God's way of life. Jesus revealed and lived the way, truth and life of God. The pride of life operates out of the "Self" realm of man: Self-righteousness, self-exaltation, self-promotion, selfishness, life being lived from the selfish carnal self-life, self-importance, haughtiness and selfish ambition and many other ungodly characteristics that pride produces.

People who are controlled by the Pride of Life are stuck in chapter seven of Romans. Chapters 6, 7, & 8 are the three "S" chapters---Sin, Self & Spirit. God does not emphasize His truths by capitalization, bolding or underlining but by repeating the same thought and words throughout a chapter. Chapter six the "Sin & Death" chapter in 25 verses speaks of Sin 17 times and Death 16 times and concludes with---the wages of Sin is Death but the gift of God is eternal life in Christ Jesus our Lord. Chapter Seven, the "Self" chapter repeats more than 50 times the personal pronouns of "me, my, myself & I" in 25 verses and less than five Godhead references. Chapter eight the "Spirit" chapter in 39 verses makes over 75 references to the Godhead and has only two mankind personal pronouns. A person must go through chapter six in becoming dead to sin and then through chapter seven becoming dead to the self-life. He can then enter into chapter eight and live his life in the Spirit with victory over sin and the flesh. He goes from sin-consciousness and then self-consciousness to God-consciousness. Then we can say with Apostle Paul, 'There is therefore now no condemnation to those who are in Christ Jesus, who do not walk according to the flesh, but according to the Spirit. For the law of the Spirit of life in Christ Jesus has made me free from the law of sin and death." Rom.8:1,2

Pride of Life Examples:

EVE: She believed the lie of the serpent, "You will not surely die. For God knows that in the day you eat of it your eyes will be opened, and you will be like God knowing good and evil." So when "Eve saw that the tree was good for food, that it was pleasant to the eyes, and a tree desirable to make one wise, she took of its fruit and ate. She also gave to her husband with her and he ate." Satan caused the pride of life to activate within Eve when she believed his lie, that she would be "like God" her Creator. Lucifer's self-ambition to be "like God" originated the spirit of the "pride of life" within him. When Eve was convinced that the fruit of the tree would make her wise, the pride of life was activated within her causing her to commit the act of the first sin of mankind. Eve and Adam committed the first sin of commission by breaking God's commandment---You shall NOT EAT of the tree of the knowledge of good and evil. The judgment for their sin was removal from their ministry in the Garden of Eden, separation from God and death began working in their bodies.

LOT: Lot's pride caused him to separate from Abraham, choose Sodom for his headquarters, willing to put up with their evil ways in order to be successful and have the best of the good land. It cost the loss of his wife, his wealth and all of his family except two daughters. His sin passed on to his daughters who got him drunk, and each had a son by their father. His descendants were the Ammonites and Moabites who became enemies of Israel and God.

DAVID: After David had yielded to the lust of the flesh and the lust of the eyes the pride of life took over his motivations and decisive actions. Bathsheba was a married woman, and David had now committed the sin of adultery with her. His pride told him he was king, and he had a right to anything he wanted. He also had a right to do whatever was necessary to obtain what he passionately desired. Bathsheba's husband was a warrior in David's army. David told General Joab to place Uriah in a dangerous position, withdraw from him allowing the enemy to kill him. Pride and lust caused David to commit two major sins of Commission---you shall not commit adultery, and you shall not murder. God's judgment was that the baby died, and David had continual problems with his Children.

JESUS: The devil tried to get Jesus to yield to the pride of life by throwing Himself of the pinnacle of the Temple and have the angels lower Him safely to the ground and everyone would be amazed and declare Him to be the Son of God. Force God to fulfill His written word that says the angels will bear you up, but Jesus said, "Yes that is God's written Word, but it is also written in God's Word, 'you shall not tempt the Lord your God.'" Saints and ministers who do not have a thorough knowledge of God's Word are more liable to be manipulated by the devil to make wrong decision and take the wrong actions.

SINS OF OMISSION AND COMMISSION

Sins of Commission are thoughts and actions that break the commandments of God, such as the Ten Commandments. It is doing that which we should not do; the "Thou shall not"…commit adultery, murder, lie, and etc. It is doing anything that the word of God says is wrong, unrighteous, contrary to God's nature and character. Remember the Bible, the Word of God is God in written form. God and His Word are one. The only way we know what is right and wrong is by the written Word of God. Man's thoughts, opinions, convictions and ideas of what is right and wrong are not the standard by which we should live. God will not judge mankind based on what they thought was right and wrong no more than just any religion will get a person into heaven. God has a standard by which all mankind shall be judged. Jesus Christ is God's way, truth, life and standard by which all shall be judged. Jesus was the Word made flesh, and now that Word has been put in written form and called the Bible. Other than personal testimonies and real people illustrations, the Bible will be our final authority for determining "How can these things be"?

EXAMPLES OF SINS OF COMMISSION:
David committing adultery with Bathsheba, Israel worshipping idols and continually doing what God had commanded them not to do,

Achan taking things for himself at Jericho after God had commanded Israel, not to do that. Anyone who breaks any of God's commandments or fails to follow God's directive words is guilty of committing a sin of commission.

SINS OF OMISSION:

Most Christians are guilty of the sin of omission more than any other. It is the sin of not doing what we know that we are supposed to do. It is the sin of negligence, procrastination, disobedience and stubbornly doing things our way instead of God's way. Remember the definition of sin is doing things contrary to God's word, will, and way. Usually, the sin of omission is not fulfilling the Rhema word of God to us personally, and the sin of commission is failing to obey and live the Logos written word of God.

EXAMPLES OF SINS OF OMISSION:

Saul is one of the best examples of a person committing the sin of omission. Samuel prophesied to Saul at his inauguration as king of Israel, at the end of the page long prophecy there was a paragraph about a time that would come when Saul would face a crisis. When that situation arrived Saul was to go to Gilgal and wait seven days and Samuel would come and offer sacrifices to God, tell him what he should do, make sacrifices to God and bring about a miracle of deliverance. Two years later the crisis arrived. Saul had 2,000 men under his command in Michmash and Jonathan his son had one thousand men under his command. Jonathan attacked a garrison of the Philistines that was stationed in Israel. This upset the Philistines, so they brought their whole army of 30,000 chariots, 6000 horsemen, and more than 500,000 foot soldiers. Saul figured this must be the crisis that the prophecy was talking about so he went to Gilgal and waited until the seventh day. During this wait, many of his soldiers became fearful, left him and hid in caves and thick forest. It was late the seventh day, and Samuel had not arrived yet, so Saul figured something had to be done. He forced himself to offer burnt offerings for God to work a miracle for him. Samuel arrived just as he was offering the sacrifices. Saul was from the tribe of Benjamin, only the tribe of Levi and the priest were allowed to make offerings of animals to the Lord. Samuel rebuked Saul and then he offered his own proper sacrifice as a priest-prophet of the Lord. Then Samuel prophesied this word to Saul, which shows the seriousness of the sin of omission. "You have done foolishly. You have not kept the commandment of the Lord your God, which He commanded you. For now the LORD would have established your kingdom over Israel forever. But now your kingdom shall not continue. The LORD has sought for Himself a man after His own heart, and the LORD has commanded him to be commander over His people, because you have not kept what the Lord commanded you."

Saul's omission sin was committed because of impatience, presumptive thinking, motivated by pressure from the fearful situation, and loss of confidence in the prophecy and promise of the prophet. He took things into his own hands and did it his way instead of the way God had told him. This happened in the second year of Saul's 40-year reign. God basically said, because you did this I am going to let you finish your kingdom reign over Israel, but I am canceling your children continuing your kingship rule. A few years later Saul committed another sin of omission. God told him through Prophet Samuel that He had promised Himself that He would punish the Amalekites for ambushing the Israelite when they were traveling through the wilderness about three hundred years earlier. He instructed Saul to take his army and kill everything that breathed in Amalek, every human being, and all the animals. Saul went and killed everyone except the king and also brought back the best of the cattle. When the Lord saw what Saul had done, He contacted Samuel and said to him, "I greatly regret that I have set up Saul as king, for he has turned back from following Me." Samuel then went to meet Saul, and Saul said to him, "Blessed are you of the LORD! I have performed the commandment of the LORD." But Samuel said, "What then is this bleating of the sheep in my ears and the lowing of the oxen which I hear?" And Saul said, they have brought them from the Amalekites; for the people spared the best of the sheep and the oxen, to sacrifice to the Lord your God; and the rest we have utterly destroyed. Then Samuel said to Saul, be quiet! I will tell you what the Lord said to me last night, and Saul said to him, speak on. So Samuel said, when you were little in your own eyes, were you not head of the tribes of Israel? And did not the Lord anoint you king over Israel? Now the Lord sent you on a mission and said, go, and utterly destroy the sinners, the Amalekites, and fight against them until they are consumed. Why then did you not obey the voice of the Lord? You did evil in the sight of the Lord. And Saul said to Samuel, but I have obeyed the voice of the Lord, and gone on the mission on which the Lord sent me, and brought back Agag king of Amalek; I have utterly destroyed the Amalekites, but the people took of the plunder, sheep and oxen, the best of the things which should have been utterly destroyed, to sacrifice to the Lord your God in Gilgal. So Samuel said: has the Lord as great delight in burnt offerings and sacrifices, as in obeying the voice of the Lord? Behold, to obey is better than sacrifice, and to heed than the fat of rams, for rebellion is as the sin of witchcraft, and stubbornness is as iniquity and idolatry. Because you have rejected the word of the Lord, He also has rejected you from being king. Then Saul said to Samuel, "I have sinned, for I have transgressed the commandment of the LORD and your words because I feared the people and obeyed their voice."

Saul was guilty of several sins. He had the problem of blame-shifting and self-excusing. He refused to take responsibility for his actions; he tried to self-excuse himself and justify his actions as revealed by the following statements; the people took the animals, I brought the king to prove I was in Amalek and destroyed the Amalekites and etc. He built a monument to himself and Samuel said "When you were little in your own eyes" which showed he had developed egotistical pride. Samuel told Saul that he had rejected the word of the Lord and was guilty of rebellion and stubbornness. He then explained that in God's judgment stubbornness is the same as iniquity and idolatry, and rebellion is as the sin of witchcraft. Saul's self-justifying attitude and sins of omission opened the door for the sin of pride to control his life. All of his sins caused God to withdraw His Spirit from Saul and send an evil distressing spirit to trouble him. "The Spirit of the Lord departed from Saul, and a distressing spirit (evil spirit-kjv) from the Lord troubled (terrified) him." They found a man to play the harp with the anointing upon him to drive the spirit away from Saul. That young man was David. Every time the evil distressing spirit would come to torment Saul David's anointed playing on the harp would cause the spirit to leave.

Even though, the Spirit of the Lord had departed from Saul he continued as king of Israel for another 25 years, won wars, expanded Israel and built some great works. During my 60 years of ministry, I have known pastors who committed several sins, lost the anointing but continued to pastor for many more years with the church growing and prospering. Sins of omission can sometimes be as serious as the sins of commission based on the spirit and character of the person. As a contrast king, David committed two sins of commission, murder and adultery which by the Mosaic Law required the death penalty. However, David did not lose his kingship heritage and the spirit of the Lord did not depart from him. Why, because he truly repented, did not justify his actions but took full responsibility for his sins. (Read David's long prayer of repentance in Psalm 51) He never committed those sins again.

A SIN UNTO DEATH

There is sin that causes physical and spiritual death, and there is sin that does not lead to death. Notice in the following scriptures that John is addressing Christians and talking about a fellow brother in Christ sinning:

> *"If anyone sees his brother sinning a sin which does not lead to death, he will ask, He will give him life for those who commit sin not leading to death. There is sin leading to death. I do not say that you should pray about that. All unrighteousness is sin, and there is sin not leading to death."* (1John 5:16,17KJV)

I could find no commentary where the theologian authors had a definite answer to what this "sin leading to death" really is. Some say he is referring to Jesus' teaching about the sin of "Blasphemy of the Holy Spirit". Others thought it might be a sin like Ananias and Sapphira committed that caused God to strike them dead. Acts 5:1-11. All agree that John is definitely saying that there is a certain sin or sins that will cause death to the individual Christian, but they do not know whether it is physical death or spiritual death or possibly both. Evidently, there are some sins more offensive to God and receive a greater degree of punishment. Some acts of disobedience, rebellion, and ungodly actions are accumulative and takes a person beyond the place for redemption. "For it is impossible for those who were once enlightened, and have tasted the heavenly gift, (gift of eternal life) and have become partakers of the Holy Spirit (Spirit baptized) and have tasted the good word of God and the powers of the ages to come, if they fall away, to renew them again to repentance, since they crucify again for themselves the Son of God, and put Him to an open shame." "Now the just shall live by faith, but if anyone draws back My soul shall have no pleasure in him." Heb.6:4-6; 10:38.

THE UNFORGIVEABLE SIN OF UNFORGIVENESS

There is a sin that cannot be forgiven unless a person takes certain actions. In the Lord's Prayer that Jesus taught His disciples He included this statement; "Forgive us our trespasses as we forgive those who trespass against us." Jesus is saying that God will only forgive us to the degree that we forgive others, for at the end of the Lord's Prayer in Mt.6:9-13 He makes this declaration in verse 14 & 15. "For if you forgive men their trespasses, your heavenly Father will also forgive you. But if you do not forgive men their trespasses, neither will your Father forgive your trespasses." This is stated by Jesus Himself that God the Father cannot and will not forgive the sin of unforgiveness. The Message translates these verses as follows "In prayer there is a connection between what God does and what you do. You can't get forgiveness from God, for instance, without also forgiving others. If you refuse to do your part, you cut yourself off from God's part."

Apostle Peter asked Jesus a question, "Lord, how often shall my brother sin against me, and I forgive him? Up to seven times?" Jesus said to him, I do not say to you, up to seven times, but up to seventy times seven." Jesus then gave a parable to illustrate His statement. A master forgave a man who owed him millions because he pleaded with him to do so. The Master did forgive his debt and freed him. The man went out and found someone who owed him a few hundred. The man could not pay and pleaded with the man that had been forgiven to forgive him the debt, but he would not and even had him thrown in jail until he paid the debt. When the Master heard what the man had done, he called him back in and said to him, "You wicked servant! I forgave you all that debt because you begged me. Should you not also have had compassion on your fellow servant, just as I had pity on you?" And his master was angry, and delivered him to the torturers till he should pay all that was due to him. Then Jesus spoke the divine principle that He was making known to His disciples by this illustration. "So My heavenly Father' also will do to you if each of you, from his HEART, does not forgive his brother his trespasses.

Probably this one sin causes more problems for Christians than any other. When a Christian does not forgive from their heart, it causes a root of bitterness to develop within their spirit and it begins to defile their soul and body. In counseling with thousands of Christians over the years, I discovered that most Christians do not grant Biblical forgiveness to those who have hurt and offended them. We are to forgive others even as Christ Jesus forgave us, "Forgive one another, even as God in Christ forgave you", "Forgiving one another, even as Christ forgave you, so you also must do." Eph.4:32; Col.3:13.

Deep hurts and offenses usually require about a year to be able to forgive from your heart. We grant verbal forgiveness because we know the Bible tells us we have to. But most time we still hold resentment and judgments against the person in our heart. If we respond to God's dealings with us, we then grant forgiveness from our soul and then finally we pull upon enough grace to forgive from out heart. Just verbal and soul forgiveness will not suffice. When we finally forgive from the heart it as though it happened to another person, we release all anger, resentment and judgments against the person and when we meet them we can look them in the eye and say God bless you and mean it from our heart. It does not make what they did to us right but it does make us right with God and clears things where God can fully forgive us and restore us back to a place of trust and fellowship with God.

BLASPHEMY AGAINST THE HOLY SPIRIT—THE UPARDONABLE SIN

"Therefore I say to you, every sin and blasphemy will be forgiven men; but the blasphemy against the Holy Spirit will not be forgiven men. Anyone who speaks a word against the Son of Man, it will be forgiven him; but whoever speaks against the Holy Spirit, it will not be forgiven him, either in this age or the age to come." *Mt.12:24-32. "Assuredly, I say to you, all sins will be forgiven the sons of men, and whatever blasphemies they may utter, but he who blasphemes against the Holy Spirit never has forgiveness, but is subject to eternal condemnation" because they said, "He has an unclean spirit."* Mk.3:22-30; Lu.11:15-20; 12:10

The Jewish religious preachers called Pharisees had just accused Jesus of casting devils out of the people by Beelzebub, a name for Satan, the prince of all evil spirits. Jesus identifies the accusations of the Pharisees of attributing the works of God performed by Jesus through the Holy Spirit as blasphemy. Jesus declared such accusation is a major sin in God's determination. Jesus declared that blaspheme against the Son of Man would be a forgivable sin, but blaspheme against the Holy Spirit would be an eternal sin that could never be forgiven. From all the categories of sin, this is one sin that no one wants to be found guilty. From the context in which Jesus made these statements, an application in our day could be Christian ministers who do not believe in the supernatural and accuse ministers who believe in and demonstrate the power of the Holy Spirit to cast out demons, work miracles of healings and speak in tongues by the Holy Spirit as being done by the power of the devil.

SINS=LOSS OF FULFILLING DESTINY VS. SINS=LOSS OF HEAVEN

The Bible reveals that there is sin that God's people can commit that cancels all or part of their prophetic destiny. There is sin that God's people can commit that if continued and not repented of can cause their name to be erased from the Book of Life.

We will examine the lives of two Bible characters who committed sins that hindered the fulfillment of their full calling. Saul, the young Benjaminite who became the first king of Israel, is a good example. When Saul committed his first sin of omission by not fulfilling his personal prophecy concerning waiting till Prophet Samuel came to offer the sacrifices, he cut off his full destiny. Samuel prophesied to Saul that he had acted foolishly and had not fulfilled the prophetic instructions that were given to him. He told him that if he had fully obeyed the word of the Lord that, "The Lord would have established your kingdom over Israel forever. But now your kingdom shall not continue... because you have not kept what the Lord commanded you." 1Sam.13:13,14. Samuel was conveying to Saul that if he had diligently obeyed the directive word of the Lord, thereby fulfilling God's will by doing everything the way God said to do it, then his kingship over Israel would have continued indefinitely with his descendants. Samuel had to change his prophecy based upon the actions of Saul. Remember the basic definition of sin is doing things contrary to God's instructive Word, Will, and Way. God called Saul's sin of omission as being foolish, evil, rejecting God, and God even said, "Saul has turned back from following Me, and I regret that I ever made him king of Israel." (ISam.15:11)

Partial Obedience Counted as Disobedience

Evidently, with God partial obedience is counted as disobedience to Him. Saul's sin of omission, not doing all He was told to do limited his ministry just to his lifetime otherwise it could have continued for generations of his children. God's word "now" your kingdom shall not continue was implemented 38 years later when Saul and his eldest son Jonathan were killed on the battle field. In Saul's second sin of omission (1Sam.15:28) God said through Prophet Samuel "Today" the Lord has torn the kingdom of Israel from you and given it to one better than you, (David). God's prophetic terminology is different than men. If God said to us that "today" something is going to happen, we would think within the next 24 hours. God's "now" is not necessarily immediately, and His "today" is not the day it was spoken. Jesus said, "behold I am coming soon." His "soon" has stretched out to almost 2000 years. Isaiah prophesied in his day, "Unto us a Child is born, unto us a Son is given." But it was some 700 years later that Jesus being born as the Son of God fulfilled that prophecy. When a prophecy is spoken it is being decreed by God that it is going to happen, but if no date or time is given then you cannot assume that it is going to happen when human reasoning has decided it should. I have learned from my 60 years of working in prophetic ministry that God thinks and talks different than we do when he is speaking to us personally or through His prophets. That it is one reason I wrote the trilogy of books on the Prophet and Prophecy. There is one whole Chapter on Prophetic Terminology & Timing and one on God's Word, Will & Way. As Isaiah declared, God's thoughts are not like our thoughts and His ways are higher than ours as heaven is higher and different than earth. (Is.55:8,9). To properly fulfill Gods prophetic instructions to us and avoid committing a sin of omission, we must gain a greater understanding of God's way of thinking and His prophetic terminology. God is the one that told Samuel to anoint Saul as the first king of Israel. Saul rejected doing things God's way so God rejected Saul and his ministry continuing after his death.

MOSES SIN OF OMISSION

The great man Moses is another example. He produced so much of God's Word, Will and Ways concerning how man should relate to God and to one another: The 10 Commandments, the laws of right and wrong in human affairs, the Feasts, the Tabernacle, and working the miracles that delivered God's people out of Egyptian slavery and took them through the wilderness by supernaturally supplying water from the Rock and Manna from heaven. While upon the mountain 40 days with God he received a video playback of the creation which enabled him to write the history of the creation of the heavens and earth and everything on it. Moses wrote the first five books of the Bible which are called the Pentateuch. Moses is esteemed as one of the greatest men in history by Jews, Christians, and Muslims.

Nevertheless, Moses was human like the rest of us. He had his strong points and his weaknesses. He committed a sin of omission that almost cost him his life before he ever launched into his ministry. He committed another sin of omission close to the end of his ministry that caused God to cancel part of His prophetic purpose and destiny.

Most Christians have read the story of Moses in the Bible, or they have watched the movie called the "The Ten Commandments" and Moses who was played by Charlton Heston. Moses killed the Egyptian and had to leave Egypt. He went across the desert to the land of Midian. He married Zipporah, the oldest of seven daughters of Jethro, a priest in Midian. He was 40 years of age when he left, and he stayed for 40 years and had two sons, Gershom and Eliezer. At the end of the 40 years, God spoke to Moses from a non-consuming burning bush. God revealed to Moses his call and destiny for him to fulfill. Moses up to that point had not had a revelation of God or even His name. Moses asked God what is your name that I am to tell the Children of Israel has sent me to deliver you out of Egypt? The Eternal Creator God said to Moses "I AM WHO I AM" and He said, "Thus you shall say to the children of Israel, 'I AM has sent me to you.' Also tell them, 'The LORD God of your fathers, the God of Abraham, the God of Isaac, and the God of Jacob has sent me to you.' This is My name forever, and this is my memorial to all generations." Ex.3:14,15.

Even with the supernatural burning bush and God speaking to Moses and revealing His name He was not able to convince Moses. He then worked two miracles to show Moses how powerful He was--- Turned Moses' rod into a snake and then back to a rod again, and then caused Moses' hand to become covered with leprosy and then restored it back to normal. Moses still made excuses why he could not go back to Egypt and deliver Israel and besides he stuttered so how could he talk with authority to Israel and to Pharaoh. God became frustrated with Moses and the scripture states that "the anger of the LORD was kindled against Moses." Then God told him that He knew that Moses brother Aaron was a good talker so He would speak to Moses and Moses would speak to Aaron what to say and then he would speak to Pharaoh. Moses would be like God, and Aaron would be His prophet spokesmen.

Finally, Moses was willing to go. He went back to his family, packed, and loaded up his wagon with all he wanted to take including his wife, Zipporah and their two sons. They left early in the morning, traveled all day and then stopped to spend the night at an encampment. Moses had the boys feed the animals; Zipporah began to prepare the evening meal, and Moses laid down to rest as he had been driving all day. After a while, she heard strange noises coming from the tent where Moses had gone to take a nap. She looked in on Moses and saw he was thrashing around and moaning like he was being choked. She yelled at Moses, What is wrong with you, what is happening? Moses couldn't talk, so Zipporah cried out to God, What's happening to my husband? God, do something my husband is dying! God said to her, I AM doing something I am in the process of killing him. ("The LORD met Moses at the inn and sought to kill him" Ex.4:24) Zipporah said, Lord why are you killing my husband? The Lord illuminated her mind and revealed to her that Moses had neglected in fulfilling the Abrahamic covenant of circumcision. If you will circumcise the boys, I will let loose of him and not kill him. I'm sure Zipporah thought, these young men are grown and in their 30s. This is going to be

— 47 —

embarrassing and very awkward to do. She may have thought, God you mean I have to do that which my neglecting and procrastinating husband should have done when they were 8 days old maybe I should move over there and help you kill him. However, she relented and took a knife and circumcised the boys and threw the bloody foreskins at Moses. When Zipporah took that action, God released His death grip on Moses. Ex.4:25,26. Aaron and Moses went on to Egypt to confront Pharaoh. Zipporah and the boys went back to Midian to wait and see if Moses would bring the Israelites out of Egypt. If so, she would join back with him at that time. Ex.18:1-6.

God had to deal with Moses concerning his sin of omitting circumcising his sons before He could allow Moses to fulfill his prophesied ministry of delivering God's people out of Egypt and taking them to the promised land of Canaan. The boys were in their mid-thirties, and God had not brought the sin to the attention of Moses. God meets Moses at the burning bush and gives him revelation of Himself and prophesies his calling and ministry to him, but does not bring up Moses sin of omission. God waits until He gets Moses willing to go, and he and his family are on their way to fulfilling their commission from God. Then God meets him at the inn and starts killing him. He does not appear to Moses and tell him, I am going to kill you if you do not circumcise your sons immediately. He just begins to kill him. His wife had to get the revelation of the cause of his dying condition and take the action needed to remove his sin of omission and reverse the death sentence. Evidently, if Zipporah had not come to his rescue and acted upon her revelation and circumcised the boys God would have killed Moses and raised up someone else to be the deliverer of His people. Regardless of what might have happened the fact is that Moses almost lost his life and failed to ever fulfill his calling because of one sin of omission. Thank God for wives who can hear from heaven, intercede for their husbands enabling them to fulfill their calling and destiny. My wife shall receive a great reward in heaven for she has done that for her husband several times. Praise God she did not leave me like Zipporah did Moses but has stayed with me through all our troubles and trials as we continue into our 60 years of marriage.

Moses committed another sin of omission which cancelled the last two of the prophetic promises that God had spoken to him. God started off the prophecy with I am the LORD and ended it with I am the LORD. God's seven "I will's" to Moses: I am the LORD. 1. I will bring you out from under the burdens of the Egyptians. 2. I will rescue you from their bondage. 3. I will redeem you with an outstretched arm and with great judgments. 4. I will take you as my people. 5. I will be your God. 6. I will bring you into the land. 7. I will give it to you for a heritage. I am the LORD. Ex.6:6-8.

The Israelites complained 10 different times during their two-year journey from Egypt to Canaan. Several times God was so angry with them that He was going to kill the older generation, but each time Moses interceded for the people and reasoned with God and talked him out of killing them. They complained and blamed Moses for all their problems until Moses became very disgusted with them. They came to a crisis of not finding water to drink for the congregation. They complained to Moses. Moses and Aaron went to the tabernacle and cried out to God. The Lord spoke to Moses the following: Take the rod; you and your brother Aaron gather the congregation together. Speak to the rock before their eyes, and it will yield its water; thus you shall bring water for them out of the rock and give drink to the congregation and their animals. And Moses took the rod from before the Lord as God commanded him. And Moses and Aaron gathered the assembly together before the rock, and he said to them; "Hear now, you rebels! Must we bring water for you out of this rock? Then Moses lifted his hand and struck the rock twice with the rod, and water came out abundantly, and the congregation and their animals drank." Then the LORD spoke to Moses and Aaron, "Because you did not believe me, to hallow Me in the eyes of the children of Israel, therefore you shall not bring this assembly into the land which I have given them." Nu.20:1-12

The sin of not doing God's will the exact way God told him to do it became a sin of omission. It cancelled his last two prophetic promises of going into the land and receiving an inheritance in the Land of Canaan. Why was the sin of Moses which seemingly was such a small mistake so serious with God, and why did it require such a serious penalty? The main reason was because everything God was doing with the Children of Israel was going to be recorded and used later for examples to His blood-bought Church. The book of Hebrews reveals that most everything in the Old Testament was for types, shadows and illustrations of what Christ came to purchase with His own blood, The Church. Acts 20:28.   Apostle Paul used the experiences of Israel in the Wilderness to give instruction to Christians concerning what to be aware of, what not to do, and that every sin incurs a penalty and can affect ones ministry for now and destiny for eternity. God is longsuffering, forgiving and merciful, but He cannot ignore the sins of rebellion, disobedience and selfish acts of His people. Every sowing has a reaping, and every cause has an effect. Paul revealed that the rock that Moses struck was a type of Christ who gives us the living waters of eternal life, if we will only drink. Jesus, the Rock of Ages, was crucified once for all mankind. He was struck once; for Moses to strike the rock twice ruined the typology. It upset God greatly, for Moses did it contrary to God's word, will, and way, which made it a sin of omission. That sin canceled God's prophetic promise of him entering his inheritance in the promised Canaan Land, which he had gone through so much to receive and enjoy. The Apostle Paul wanted the Christians to understand that all that happened to Israel was not recorded just for their historical record, it was all written for our learning and admonition upon whom the ends of the ages have come.

> Now all of these things happened to the Children of Israel as examples, and they were written for our admonition, upon whom the ends of the ages have come." "Moreover, brethren I do not want you to be unaware that all our fathers were under the cloud, and passed through the sea, all ate the same spiritual food, and all drank the same spiritual drink. For they drank of that spiritual Rock that followed them, and that Rock was Christ. But with many of them God was not well pleased, for their bodies were scattered in the wilderness. Now these things became our examples, to

the intent that we should not lust after evil things as they lusted. And do not become idolaters as were some of them. As it is written, 'The people sat down to eat and drink and rose up to play.' Neither let us commit sexual immorality as some of them did, and in one day 23,000 fell dead: nor let us tempt Christ, as some of them also tempted, and were destroyed by serpents; nor complain, as some of them also complained, and were destroyed by the destroyer. Therefore, let him who thinks he stands take heed lest he fall. (1 Cor.10;11,1-12).

God's sevenfold prophetic promise spoken to Moses was for all that came out of Egypt with Moses. The number of the males 20 years and older who came out of Egypt were 603,550. Only two out of that number fulfilled all seven prophetic promises---Joshua and Caleb. The rest of them committed the sin of omission by refusing to do what was God's revealed word and will---go in and possess the Land of Canaan. It was the sin of unbelief. They would not believe that God's word to them was true and workable. Moses had sent a leader from each of the 12 tribes to spy out the land. They searched out the Land for 40 days and came back with fruit from the land and reported that it was a land flowing with luscious green pastures, fruit trees and vine producing fruit. They even brought back one cluster of grapes which took two men to carry between them on a pole. There were multitudes of animals including milk cows. It truly was just like God said; land flowing with milk and honey. Ten of the spies reported that all that God had said about the Land was true, but they gave a negative report. "Nevertheless, the people who dwell in the land are strong; the cities are fortified and very large; moreover we saw the descendants of Anak, king of the giants there." They reported that all of the seven "ite" tribes that Moses described were there, and God was right, they are greater and mightier than we are. Duet.9:1,2. Joshua and Caleb interrupted them and said yes, yes all that they say is true but God told us all of that while we were on our journey to this place. He also said not to be dismayed about that because He would be the great equalizer by fighting for us. Caleb then spoke to all the leaders, "Let us go up at once and take possession, for we are well able to overcome all the inhabitants and make it the Land of Israel!" But the ten doubtful leaders spoke up and emphatically declared that "We are not able to go in and possess for they are seasoned mighty warriors and some are men of great stature, giants that made us look and feel like grasshoppers in our own sight and, and so we were in their sight." The Israelis believed the bad report of the ten, they complained and wept self-pity tears and screamed at Moses, "Why has the Lord brought us to this land to fall by the sword, that our wives and children become victims? Would it not be better for us to return to Egypt? Let us select a leader besides Moses and return to Egypt." Moses and Aaron fell on their faces and started praying. Joshua and Caleb stood up and shouted to the people, "The land we passed through to spy out is an exceedingly good land. If the LORD delights in us, then He will bring us into the land and give it to us, a land which flows with milk and honey. Only do not rebel against the LORD, nor fear the people of the land, for they are our bread; their protection has departed from them, and the LORD is with us. Do not fear them." The Israelites would not be inspired to believe. Instead they took up stones to stone them, but the glory of the Lord surrounded Joshua, Caleb, Moses, and Aaron. Then God spoke out of the glory cloud; "How long will these people reject Me? And how long will they not believe Me, with all the signs which I have performed among them? I will strike them with pestilence and disinherit them, and I will make of you a nation greater and mightier than they!" Moses interceded for the people with a 5-fold appeal to God. God basically said that he would not kill them right now but was sentencing them to wander in the wilderness for 40 years until all those who were 20 and older died. Joshua and Caleb would be the only two to live and enter and conquer Canaan land with the younger generation. The time of God's rejection of that generation would be based upon the number of days they spied out the land, a year for each day. Then God said, "I the LORD have spoken this. I will surely do so to all this evil generation who are gathered together against Me. In this wilderness they shall be consumed, and there they shall die for their infidelity."

God killed the 10 spies who gave the bad report that caused the congregation to complain against God and discouraged them from fighting to take their promised land. Some might ask, why would God reject Israel and decree their death in the wilderness? Here is God's reason: "Because all these men who have seen My glory and the signs which I did in Egypt and in the wilderness, and have put Me to the test these ten times, and have not heeded my voice, they shall certainly not see the land which I swore to their fathers, nor shall any of those who rejected Me see it."

The LORD then gave the reason He was going to keep Joshua and Caleb alive during the 40 years wandering and then have them go in and possess the Promised Land. They saw the giants; in fact, Anak the head of all the giants was in the area that Caleb spied out, and later he fought and destroyed them. He was 40 years old when he spied out his portion of Canaan. He entered the land with Joshua and the younger generation when he was 80. After five years of fighting as a leader in the Israeli army, they came to his inheritance. He reminded Joshua that Moses had promised this area as his inheritance because he had wholly followed the Lord. Caleb declared to Joshua, "Give me my mountain for though I am age 85, I am just as strong for going to war as I was at 40." Joshua 14:6-15. God declared His reason for giving Caleb special privileges, "Because Caleb has a different spirit in him, and he wholly followed Me fully. I will bring him into the land where he went, and his descendants shall inherit it." The new 21st Century 3rd Reformation Joshua generation saints will have the "different spirit" of Caleb, his warrior attitude and ability, and "wholly follow the LORD fully." They will come to the 3rd level of the overcomer. First, they overcame by the blood of the Lamb. Secondly, they overcome by the word of their testimony. Third level, they overcome by loving not their lives unto death (to self, to wholly live and manifest the life of Christ.) They will be fearless believing the odds are no problem when God Almighty is fighting for them against their enemies.

GOD'S PROPHETIC DECREE TO HIMSELF!

After pardoning the people according to the plea-bargaining of Moses, God Almighty made a prophetic promise to Himself; AS TRULY AS I LIVE, ALL THE EARTH SHALL BE FILLED WITH THE GLORY OF THE LORD!" Nu.14:21. God inspired the prophet Habakkuk to prophesy how it was going to happen and to what extent; "The earth will be filled with the knowledge of the glory of the LORD, as the waters cover the sea." Hab.2:14.

THE PROPHETIC DECREE OF JESUS CHRIST!

Jesus made a prophetic decree. **"I Will Build My Church!"** Jesus purchased His Church with His own blood, authorized it by His resurrection from the dead, birthed it by His Holy Spirit and then commissioned His Church to be His Body on earth to fulfill all His will. Jesus did not just say, I will birth My Church but, I will BUILD My Church. His Church was glorious for the first 300 years, but false teachers and religious leaders began to formalize and deaden most New Testament truth. By 500AD, the Church entered its 1000 year Dark Age. The Prophet Isaiah declared that God was upset with His ministers because none of them were actively believing for restoration or saying "Restore!" Is.42:22. Prophet Joel prophesied that God would restore all that was lost. Joel 2:25. Apostle Peter prophetically declared that Jesus is coming again, but He cannot return, "UNTIL the RESTORATION of ALL THINGS which God has spoken by the mouth of all His holy prophets since the world began." Acts 3:21.

In 1500, the Holy Spirit activated the 2nd Reformation to bring about the full restoration of the Church. There have been nine major restoration movements over the last 500 years that has brought the present truth Church to New Testament truth and manifestations as demonstrated in the book of Acts, which reveals the acts of the Church. The experiences of the Children of Israel during their journey from Egypt to entering Canaan, portrays the nine restoration movements from the Protestant Movement in 1500 to the Prophetic-Apostolic

Movement in the last two decades of the 20th Century and the Saints Movement in 2007. The Protestant Movement brought the Church out of its Egyptian bondage to religious dead works, and the Prophetic-Apostolic Movement crossed the Church over its Jordan River into its Canaan Land. In 2008, The Holy Spirit launched the 3rd & Final Reformation, which activated the Church into its military campaign of possessing its Canaan Land---Rev.11:15. The purpose and ministry of the 3rd and Final Church Reformation is to fulfill God's final prophetic scriptures for the Body of Christ to fulfill concerning earth, mankind, and all creation.

THE BODY OF JESUS FULFILLED---THE BODY OF CHRIST FULFILLING

The personal body of Jesus was God's instrument to fulfill prophetic purposes that God had determined from the foundation of the world. That body went through 30 years of preparation from birth to 30 years of age and then God anointed Jesus with the Holy Spirit and Power to demonstrate that He was the true Messiah and the manifest Son of God. The last purposes that Jesus fulfilled were; being crucified, resurrecting from the grave, sending the Holy Spirit to birth the Church and endow each saint with their own spirit-language. When Jesus ascended, He took His ministry to the Church and divided it into five ministry gifts---apostle, prophet, evangelist, pastor, and teacher---and gave them to certain of His disciples. He said to the Father, "I have finished the work which you gave me to do. And now, O Father, glorify Me together with Yourself, with the glory which I had with You before the world was." Jn.17:4,5. Jesus was saying Father I have fulfilled every prophetic purpose I was to accomplish by taking on a human body on earth. Father said, Yes, You have, now come and sit at my right hand until your Church makes all enemies your footstool. "The man Jesus, after He had offered one sacrifice (of Himself) for sins forever, sat down at the right hand of God, since that time He is waiting for His enemies to be made His footstool" Heb.10:13

Who is Jesus waiting on to make His enemies His footstool? Jesus is waiting in Heaven for His corporate Body on earth, The Body of Christ, to fulfill all things and make all enemies His footstool; Just as Father God waited for His body, The Body of Jesus, to fulfill all things and take the keys of death and hell away from His enemy the devil. Jesus came from heaven to earth and could not return to heaven until He had fulfilled all things; just as He has now gone from earth to heaven and cannot return to earth until His Church fulfills all things. Jesus in His resurrected body is seated at the right hand of God but by His Holy Spirit, He has made his home and headquarters in His Church. Eph.2:19-22 reveals that the Church members are being fitted together to grow into one gigantic holy temple in the Lord and are being built together for A DWELLING PLACE OF GOD in the Spirit here on earth. The Church is now heir to God and joint-heir and co-laborer With Christ in fulfilling all things. Until Christ comes back to earth in His resurrected body, everything that He is to accomplish on earth will be done with and through His Body of Christ, the Church. That is the reason the Church has to be restored to fullness of truth, power and the maturity of Christ. That is the reason Apostle Paul declared that the fivefold ministers of Christ must minister to the Church "UNTIL we all come to the unity of the faith, and of the knowledge of the Son of God, to a perfect man, to the measure of the stature of the fullness of Christ."

Israel was brought out of Egypt, not just to be freed from slavery to Pharaoh but to go in and make the kingdoms of Canaan the kingdom nation of Israel. The Church was brought out of its Egypt of the Dark Age, not just to be free from the slavery to dead religious works but to become a victorious Church to make the kingdoms of this world the kingdom of Jesus and His Church. The prophetic-apostolic movement crossed the Church over its Jordan River and now the 3rd Reformation has engaged the Church in the battle to make the kingdoms of this world the kingdoms of Jesus and His Church. The challenge before the Church is the same as the Challenge Joshua and the Israelis had in taking Canaan. It will be the same for the Church as it was for Israel and the spies that spied out the land of Canaan. For every two ministers that will be saying that we are well able to demonstrate the kingdom of God and fulfill all things yet to be fulfilled, there will be ten ministers saying like the ten spies said, that we are not able to be and do all that God says in His word the Church is to do in these last days. I definitely want to be a part of the Joshua-Caleb type ministers. Those who discourage God's people from being the victorious Church and overcoming all things will be in trouble with God like the 10 spies who gave a bad report.

Moses is to be commended for interceding for God's people when they sinned and angered God several times. Believe it or not God thoroughly knows man and His decisions are always best even when He is very angry. If he would have allowed God to kill off those rebels as He wanted to do; God said He would have risen up an obedient nation greater and mightier than those for Moses, then he could have taken them into Canaan and possessed it. However, Moses insisted on keeping those that came out of Egypt though they were a stiff-necked, rebellious and complaining people. They finally provoked Moses to the place that he struck the rock twice causing him to commit the sin of omission which cancelled his prophetic destiny and kept him from entering Canaan. When they came to Canaan and the people Moses saved from God's wrath refused to go in God had to kill them anyhow by sentencing them to wander in the wilderness until they all died.

There is another example showing it would have been better for God's first prophetic word to have been fulfilled. King Hezekiah was a righteous ruler and a great reformer. But when Hezekiah was 39 years old and had reigned for 14 years he became very sick. The Lord sent Isaiah the prophet to him with this word, "Set your house in order, for you shall die; and not live." Immediately Hezekiah began to pray, weeping bitterly, plea bargaining with God to let him live longer. God spoke to Isaiah, and told him to return back to Hezekiah and that He was extending his life for 15 more years. I taught the historical books for three years in Bible College. We discovered that there were ten major atrocities that happened during those 15 years. The worse was that Manasseh was born during that time and became king at 12 years old when his 54-year-old father, Hezekiah died. Manasseh was the wickedest king ever to reign in Jerusalem. He did evil practices even worse than the Amorites did before Israel came into Canaan. He even put a carved image of the goddess Asherah in the holy temple of the Lord. His sins caused God to make the final decision to send Judah into Babylonian captivity. Hezekiah may have enjoyed those extra 15 years of life, but what happened in those few extra years caused Judah to go into bondage, the temple destroyed, most of Jerusalem tore down and God's people to enter centuries of suffering and becoming foreigners in a foreign land.

Chapter 3
Determining True & False Ministers

WHO ARE TRUE & WHO ARE FALSE MINISTERS?

The Bible speaks of ministers within the Church that are true ministers of Jesus Christ and it also speaks of ministers that are not true representations of Jesus Christ. They are called "False" pastors, teachers, apostles and prophets, and the scriptures reveal that there will even be false Christ's. It also speaks of false Christians, false witnesses and false disciples of Christ Jesus. We want to discover from the Scriptures that which determines whether a person is true or false.

Definition of FALSE: Deceptive, contrary to what is true or correct; erroneous, untrue, or incorrect; uttering or declaring what is untrue; being deceitful, treacherous, or faithless; not genuine; counterfeit or artificial; employed to deceive or mislead. Also "spurious" which means that the person is not legitimate, for they are not speaking or ministering from the true source. They could be outwardly saying and doing the right things, but it is coming from a wrong spirit and motivation.

Definition of TRUE: From a Biblical and Christian perspective Jesus is the Way, the TRUTH, and the Life. Jesus was the Word made flesh. God's will, way, and Word manifest through the body of Jesus Christ. Therefore, that which is according to the context and content of the Bible is TRUE, and that which is contrary to God's Word is FALSE. A TRUE person is one who is rigidly righteous, honest, loyal, free from deceit, truthful; being consistent with the actual state of things; transparent, pure and true through and through without any hidden agenda, wrong motivation or manipulation. A true person is one not living a double life for he is not one type of person in the pulpit and another type of person in his private personal life.

THE CRUCIAL SCRIPTURE

The main scripture that makes this such a serious situation is what Jesus declared in the gospel of Matthew 7:21-23-NKJ. I usually use the New King James version as my standard scripture reference and then use other translations to expand and enhance the meaning and clarity of the scripture:

> *"Not everyone who says to Me, 'Lord, Lord' shall enter the kingdom of heaven, but he who does the will of My Father in heaven. Many will say to Me in that day, "Lord, Lord, have we not prophesied in Your name, cast out demons in Your name, and done many wonders in Your name?" And then I will declare to them," I never knew you; depart from Me, you who practice lawlessness!"*

This scripture is emphasizing that there are going to be some ministers who Preach but do not Practice; Hear but do not Heed, Proclaim but do not Produce, Minister but do not Mature, they Agree but do not Appropriate. They preach Holiness but do not live Holy. They are more interested in their image in ministry than entering the ministry of being conformed to the image of God's Son, Jesus Christ. Jesus Christ and Apostle James both said that it is not the HEARERS of the Word that are justified before God but the DOERS of the Word. It is not the preachers of the Word that are righteous before God, but the Preachers who appropriate the Word and practice its righteous principles. Jesus declared that It is not the ones who say Lord, Lord, that shall enter the kingdom of heaven, but he who DOES THE WILL OF MY FATHER!

Jesus's New Covenant Teaching:

Please note what verses 13-20 say just before Jesus makes the statements in verses 21-23 of Chapter Seven. I am giving it to you in a modern English version (The Message) which probably sounds more like it did when Jesus spoke it in the common language of the people, using illustrations that were everyday things that the people could relate to and understand.:

> *Don't look for shortcuts to God,. The market is flooded with surefire, easy-going formulas for a successful life that can be practiced in your spare time. Don't fall for that stuff, even though crowds of people do. The way to life---to God!- Is vigorous and requires total attention. Be wary of false preachers who smile a lot, dripping with practiced sincerity. Chances are they are out to rip you off some way or other. Don't be impressed with charisma; look for character. Who preachers ARE is the main thing, not what they say. A genuine leader will never exploit your emotions or your pocketbook. These diseased trees with their bad apples are going to be chopped down and burned.* (Mt.7:13-20)

> *"Knowing the correct password - saying, "Master, Master," for instance - isn't going to get you anywhere with me. What is required is serious obedience - DOING what my father wills. I can see it now - at the final judgment thousands strutting up to me and saying, "Master, we preached the message, we bashed the demons, our God-sponsored projects had everyone talking." And do you know what I am going to say? "You missed the boat. All you did was use me to make yourselves important. You don't impress me one bit. You are out of here."* Mt.7:21-23.

This long teaching session of Jesus began in chapter five of Matthew and continued till the end of Chapter Seven. It says the multitudes followed Jesus, but He went upon a high hill, and His disciples followed, sitting down and listening to Jesus teach. He started off by teaching them the Beatitudes; then Jesus declared to them that they are the salt of the earth and the light of the world; they are to let their light shine. Jesus declared that He didn't come to destroy the law, but to fulfill it, by preparing a new way of Grace and Truth. He then taught that there would be different levels and rewards for those who make it to heaven. Those who taught the truth and practiced it would be greater, and those who taught the truth but did not practice fully would be least in the kingdom of heaven. Jesus revealed that Grace and Truth would be a much higher standard of living than the Law. For under the Law as long as one outwardly did everything required they got by, but Jesus said, "your righteousness must exceed the righteousness of the Scribes and Pharisees, if not, you will by no means enter the kingdom of heaven". Under the law it said, you shall not murder, but Jesus revealed that under His new covenant order, If a person is angry and unforgiving toward a brother in the Lord he is in danger of the judgment and if he calls his brother a fool he is in danger of hell fire. Jesus declared that if you do not forgive others who trespass against you, then your heavenly Father cannot and will not forgive your trespasses. He concludes chapter five with this challenging charge, "Therefore you shall be perfect, just as your Father in heaven is perfect."

The Higher Law of Grace and Truth:

Jesus taught that under the law, as long as you did not commit the act of adultery you were not guilty, but under grace if a man looked at a woman and lustfully imagined committing adultery with her, he was guilty of the sin of adultery and under condemnation. In chapter six Jesus taught them not to do good works to get the praise of man or to look righteous in the eyes of others. The law judged the act, but Jesus said that He judges the heart motive as well as the outward act. The motive of the heart plus the act equals the "works" (M+A=W) by which all men will be evaluated for rewards in heaven or levels of punishment in hell.

ETERNAL DESTINY DETERMINED BY A BOOK

The determining factor concerning whether a person will spend eternity with Christ Jesus in heaven or with the devil in the lake of fire is just one thing; whether their name is found written in the Book of Life. "Anyone not found written in the Book of Life was cast into the lake of fire." Rev.20:15. Rewards in heaven or degrees of punishment in hell are determined by what is written in the multitude of heavenly record books which contains every thought and act of every human being who has ever lived on planet earth. "And books were opened and the dead were judged according to their works, by the things which were written In the books." The one Book of Life determines who is allowed entry into heaven. What is written in the books determines rewards in heaven or levels of punishment in hell. Rev.20:12-15; Lu.12:41-48.

Jesus the Model and Only Way to Enter Heaven:

Jesus then teaches them what we call today, "The Lord's Prayer." Jesus begins chapter seven teaching them not to be judgmentally critical of others. For most of the time when one person criticizes another person for having a splinter (problem) in their eye, they have a Log-problem in their own eye.

Jesus then gave them the golden rule, "Do unto others as you would have others to do unto you." He then told them to enter the narrow gate (which is no wider than Jesus Himself for Jesus is the way, the door and the only gate into Heaven), for broad is the gateway that leads to destruction and multitudes go that way. But narrow is the gate and difficult is the way that leads to life, and there are few who find it.

Next Jesus talks about hypocrites and false preachers. They look and act like sheep on the outside but on the inside they are "ravenous wolves". They are to be judged not by their seemingly great ministry, gifts, and works but by the fruit of their character and hidden life. They are trees which produce no righteous fruit, so they are destined to be cut down and burned. Therefore by their fruit you shall know them.

The Main Scripture for Discussion and Decision:

And that brings us back to our key verses in Matthew 7:21-23. Some Protestant theologians who are strong Calvinists suggest that this passage is speaking of a person who is not a born-again Spirit baptized Christian but a pretender. Their doctrine does not allow for anyone who has at one time been born again to ever lose their right to heaven. They say once you become a son of God you can never lose that position or be disowned.

The Bible does teach us that God's grace can keep us from falling and present us spotless before God; That nothing in this world or hell can keep us from serving and loving the Lord Jesus Christ, for where sin abounds grace does much more abound. If we commit sin after we are saved, we do have an advocate to forgive us of our sin and cleanse us from all unrighteousness, our Lord Jesus Christ

But nowhere does the Bible say that if a born-again Christian quits attending church and begins to live an ungodly life by lying, committing adultery, drunkenness, foul language like the ungodly use, criticizing the church and blaming God for his problems, and dies in a drunken state without a repentant heart or asking forgiveness, nowhere does it state or even indicate that person would be allowed entrance into heaven.

The answer that the extreme grace theologians give concerning whether a Christian who dies in that state of being would miss heaven is simply that they were never saved to start with. They also say that God would always bring a true child of God back to repentance before they died, for once a son you will always be a son regardless of the sins you commit and God would never allow anyone that was a once born again son of God to ever go to hell. They interpret the scripture in 1 John 3:9 as saying that a person who has been born of God cannot sin, that is, that any unrighteous acts he commits is not counted as sin, because he has been born of God.

Can a Christian Commit Sinful Acts?

We need to consider: when a Christian commits a sin of adultery, drunkenness or murder does it make it a lesser sin than when a non-Christian commits the same acts? Is a sinful act less sinful for a

Christian than for a non-Christian? The reality is that sin is sin regardless of who commits it. Sin will defile saint and sinner alike. God is not a respecter of persons. He does not say to one person, telling a lie is a sin for you, but to another person it is not a sin for you to tell a lie. Whether an act is sinful, is not determined by who commits the act or whether they believe it is sin to do a certain thing, it is strictly determined by what God says about it in His Word. If a person was killed instantly in a car accident and suddenly was standing before Christ Jesus at the gate into heaven and Jesus should ask, why should I allow you into heaven when you were committing the sin of fornication before you died? They might say to God, "I didn't think it was wrong to live in sexual relationships with someone without being legally married to them. It was common practice in my society, and I didn't hear any preachers preach that it was a sin. I was born again, baptized in water, joined the church and attended the local church now and then." Jesus will have to ask this person if they had read in His Word that all the "sexually immoral," which includes all adulterers, fornicators, homosexuals, lesbians and any others committing perverted acts of sex, "shall have their part in the lake which burns with fire and brimstone, which is the second death." Rev. 21:8. All sins must be forgiven by Jesus and cleansed by His blood for a person to be righteous enough to enter heaven.

There is a very controversial scripture that says in the NKJV; "Whoever has been born of God does not sin, for His seed remains in him. The promise was made to Abraham's one 'Seed', which is Christ, the incorruptible seed." (Gal.3:16; 1 Pet.1:23) The seed that remains within is Christ, and He does not and cannot sin. "And you know that Jesus was manifested to take away our sins, and in him there is no sin. And whoever abides in Christ does not sin" Jn. 3:5,6. The Amplified Bible gives the best clarity, sense and true meaning as is revealed from the Greek language.:

> *Everyone who has this hope [resting] on Jesus Christ cleanses (purifies) himself, just as He is pure (chaste, undefiled, and guiltless). Everyone who commits (practices) sin is guilty of lawlessness; for (that is what)*

sin is, lawlessness, (the breaking, violation of God's law by transgression, our neglect–being unrestrained and unregulated by God's commands and His will). You know that God appeared in visible form and became man (Jesus) to take away [upon Himself] sins, and in Him there is no sin [essentially and forever]. No one who abides in Christ [who lives and remains in communion with and in obedience to Him–deliberately, knowingly, and habitually] commits (practices) sin. No one who [habitually] sins has either seen or known God [recognized, perceived, or understood Him, or has had an experiential acquaintance with Him. Boys (lads), let no one deceive and lead you astray. He who practices righteousness [who is upright, conforming to the divine will, in purpose, thought, and action, living a consistently conscientious life] is righteous, even as He is righteous. But he who commits sin [who practices evildoing] is of the devil [takes his character from the evil one], for the devil has sinned (violated the divine law) from the beginning. The reason the Son of God was made manifest (visible) was to undo (destroy, loosen, and dissolve) the works the devil [has done]. No one born (begotten) of God [deliberately, knowingly, and habitually] practices sin, for God's nature abides in him [His principle of life, the divine sperm, remains permanently within him]; and he cannot practice sinning because he is born (begotten) of God. By this it is made clear who take their nature from God and are His children and who take their nature from the devil and are his children: no one who does not practice righteousness [who does not conform to God's will in purpose, thought, and action] is of God, neither is anyone who does not love his brother (his fellow believer in Christ). (1 Jn. 3:3-10AMP)..

If a person is committing sins, it reveals that they are not "abiding" in Christ and not being motivated by Him for He has no motivation to sin. James 1:13-15 declares, "Let no one say when he is tempted, I am tempted by God'; for God cannot be tempted by evil, nor does He Himself tempt anyone. But each one is tempted when he is drawn away by his own desires and enticed. Then, when lustful desire has conceived, it gives birth to sin; and sin, when it is full-grown, brings forth death."

Before we can justly deal with Mt.7:21-23, we must answer the following question: Can a person who has had all his sins washed away by the blood of Jesus and become a new creation commit sin? Can a new creation who has been created by the hand of God willfully commit sin? The man Adam was a new creation of God, yet he sinned and was cast out of his inheritance in the Garden of Eden. The Spirit of God or Christ in us cannot and will not sin. But the human spirit which has been cleansed by the blood of Jesus can commit a sinful act in thought and deed. The Bible declares that Lucifer sinned though God created him pure and perfect. Lucifer, "You were the seal of perfection, full of wisdom and perfect in beauty. You were perfect in your ways from the day you were created, till iniquity was found in you." Jesus declared "He who perseveres and endures to the end will be saved [from spiritual disease and death in the world to come]." "Thus shall he who conquers (is victorious) be clad in white garments, and I will not erase or blot out his name from the Book of Life" Mt. 10:22; Rev.3:5 AMP.

Jesus is saying that those who quit along the way and stop living the Christian life will not be saved. If a Christian does not overcome sin and the works of the flesh but starts living like the wicked, they take the chance of their names being erased from the Book of life, and only those whose names are still written in the Book of Life will be allowed entry into heaven. Moses declared to the Israelis that they had committed a great sin, when Aaron made the golden calf and told the people, this is your god, O Israel, which brought you out of the Land of Egypt. God's wrath burned hot against them, and He was ready to consume them. Moses made a desperate appeal asking God not to kill them; and said to God that if you won't forgive them, then blot my name out of Your book which You have written (my name within). And the LORD said to Moses, "Whoever has SINNED against Me, I will BLOT HIM out of My Book (of Life)." Ex.32:30-33. This conveys the following: God the Father, that so loved the world that He gave His only begotten Son to redeem sinners, also says that anyone whom He has written in His Book, if they have unforgiven sins against God when they stand before Him; that person's name would be blotted out of His Book. Jesus the Son of God, that died on the Cross to redeem sinners; revealed that if anyone did not overcome, which means they quit living a righteous life, He would BLOT (erase, remove, take out) their name out of the Book of Life.

Jesus declared to the Church Members in Laodicea that those who were neither hot nor cold, but lukewarm, He would vomit out of His mouth. *"He who overcomes will be clothed in white garments, and I will not blot out his name from the Book of Life; but I will confess his name before My Father and before His angels." "I know your works that you are neither cold nor hot. I could wish that you were cold or hot. So then, because you are lukewarm, and neither cold nor hot, I will vomit you out of My mouth."* Rev.3:5,16. To blot something out of a book, it has to first be written in the book. To vomit something out means it has to have been first taken in. A person has to be IN Christ in order for Christ to vomit him OUT. A pilot cannot be ejected out of a plane unless he has first been established in the plane. A Christian cannot be ejected OUT of Christ unless he has first been established IN Christ. All of Christ's promises to the churches concerning heaven and great rewards were only to those who would be overcomers and have an ear to hear what the Spirit is saying to the churches. Rev.2:1-3:22.

Can A Person's Name Be Removed from the Book of Life?

There is a record book in heaven called the Book of Life. Paul refers to it in Phil.4:3 when he exhorted them to *"help those women who labor with me....whose names are in the Book of Life."* The only way a person can have their name written in the Book of Life is to receive Jesus Christ as their personal Savior by confessing their sins to Jesus and allowing Him to cleanse them from all sin by His blood.

They must be born again by the Spirit of God and become a new creation in Christ Jesus. Jesus said, *"He that believes and is baptized will be saved, but he who does not believe will be condemned."* And *"Most assuredly, I say to you, unless one is born of water and the Spirit, he cannot enter the kingdom of God."*

Jesus testified in the last few verses of the last chapter in the Bible that some people would do certain things that would cause Him to take away their part (name) out of the Book of Life. The Bible teaches that for any major thing to be accepted as truth it has to be proven by two or three witnesses. That means you need more than one scripture to prove the validity of any major doctrine of the Bible. The Book of Life is a major truth in the Word of God. Whether a person's name can be removed, blotted out, erased or taken out of the Book of Life is a major issue in dealing with our Key Scripture.

HEAVEN'S BOOK OF LIFE

Rev.20:14,15 *"And Death and Hades were cast into the lake of fire. This is the second death. And anyone not found written in the BOOK OF LIFE was cast into the lake of fire."*

Rev.13:8 *"All who dwell on the earth will worship the (evil beast) whose names have NOT been written in the BOOK OF LIFE of the Lamb slain from the foundation of the world."*

Rev. 17:8 *"...All who dwell on the earth will marvel, whose names are NOT written in the BOOK OF LIFE."*

Rev.21:27 *"Only those whose names are written in the BOOK OF LIFE are allowed to enter the heavenly city, New Jerusalem."*

Rev.3:5 *"He who overcomes shall be clothed in white garments, and I will not BLOT OUT his name from the BOOK OF LIFE. But I will confess his name before My Father and before His angels."*

Rev.22:19 *"If anyone takes away from the words of the book of this prophecy, God will take away his part from the BOOK OF LIFE, from the holy city, and from the things written in this book."*

Ex.32:33 *"And the Lord said to Moses, 'Whoever has SINNED against Me, I will BLOT HIM OUT of My BOOK OF LIFE.'"*

Ps.69:28 AMP *"Let them be blotted out of the book of the living and the BOOK OF LIFE and not be enrolled among the [uncompromisingly] righteous (those upright and in right standing with God).*

The main truths we receive from these scriptures are that there definitely is a Book of Life in Heaven. When a person accepts Christ Jesus as their personal savior, their name is written in the Book of Life. The Word of God declares that there are certain conditions whereby a person's name will be removed from the Book of Life. Different translations use the words blotted out, removed, erased, his part taken away from the Book of Life, etc. The clear truth is that some people's names that have been placed in the Book of Life can be removed and will be removed by Almighty God.

Our Key Scripture Exegeted:

Notice what they declare to Jesus, "Lord, Lord, have we not prophesied in Your name, cast out demons in Your name and done many wonders in Your name?" This would not be non-Christians or modernistic ministers who do not believe in a born-again experience or the supernatural. The name of Jesus is not a magical name that anyone can use to cast out devils. All the power of heaven is invested in the name of Jesus, but one has to be a believer in Jesus Christ in order to use the name of Jesus to cast out demons.

Non-Believers Can't Do It!

There was a Jewish Priest who had seven sons. They tried to cast out demons by the name of Jesus like apostle Paul was doing. But the evil spirit/demon said to them, "Jesus I know, and Paul I know, but who are you?" Instead of coming out of the man the evil spirit arose within the man's body and beat the men ripping all their clothes off, causing them to run out of the house and into the street as fast as they could wounded and naked. When this happened, it caused the fear of God to sweep through the area producing great respect for the name of Jesus. It made them realize that Jesus Christ, who Paul was preaching, was not the name of one of their many idols, but He was truly the Son of God. The inhabitants of the city took their idols and magical books to the town square, piled them together and burned them. It caused the Word of the Lord to grow mightily and prevail throughout the whole area. Acts 19:11-20.

From this incident mentioned in the book of Acts, we can see that the devil only has to flee when the name of Jesus is being spoken against him by a born again baptized Christian. When a person is saved and baptized in water, they take on the name of Jesus Christ. That is the reason the followers of Jesus were first called "Christians" in Antioch, for it means those who belong to Christ. Apostle Peter preached the first gospel message after the Church was birthed on the day of Pentecost. When Peter preached the gospel of Christ to the thousands of Jews who were gathered at the birthing of the Church, they asked Peter what they needed to do to get right with God, and receive what those there in the upper room were manifesting with great joy and excitement!" Peter responded and declared God's Way of salvation which set the New Testament standard for a person to be reconciled to God whether Jew or Gentile. "Repent, and let every one of you be baptized in the name of Jesus Christ for the remission of sins, and you shall receive the gift of the Holy Spirit." Acts 2:38. When a person believes in Jesus and is baptized in water in His name, they are authorized from heaven with the power of attorney to use the name of Jesus- in prayer and in casting out demons, "Whatever you ask in My NAME, that I will do that the Father may be glorified in the Son. If you ask anything in MY NAME, I will do it." John 14:13,14. It is also in the NAME of JESUS that believers are authorized to cast out demons, speak in tongues and heal the sick. "He who believes and is baptized shall be saved; but he who does not believe will be condemned. And these signs will follow those who believe: In MY NAME they shall cast out demons...speak in tongues...lay hands on the sick and they shall recover." Mark 16:16-18. Notice the emphasis is not only the name, but IN the name, not WITH the name of Jesus Christ. The name "Jesus" is not a mystical magic wand with which you can touch a person and immediately have the demons flee. A person has to be IN

Christ to cast out demons IN the name of Jesus; in other words, they must be a born-again Christian.

Based on this scriptural understanding and divine principle, we can see that for a person to get answers to prayer and cast out demons, they have had to at one time been born again and baptized in water. Those whom Jesus spoke those words to had to be ministers who manifested the supernatural in their ministry by prophesying, casting out demons and doing many wonderful works in the name of the Lord Jesus. The qualifications for eternal relationship with Jesus Christ are the same qualifications for all Christians and ministers; even though Historical Protestant, Evangelical and Holiness preachers do not minister in prophesying, casting out demons and working signs and wonders, yet everyone will be judged and then rewarded or sentenced by the same divine standards.

Quote from Matthew Henry's Commentary: "A man may be a preacher, may have gifts for the ministry, and an external call to it, and perhaps some success in it, and yet be a wicked man; may help others to heaven, and yet come short himself. This should be an awakening word to all Christians. If a preacher, that cast out devils, and wrought miracles, be discounted by Christ for working iniquity; what will become of us if we are found as such? And if we are as such, we shall certainly be found as such! At God's bar, a profession of religion will not bear out any man in the practice and indulgence of sin; therefore let everyone that names the name of Christ depart from all iniquity." Apostle Peter declared "For the time has come for judgment to begin at the house of God; and if it begins with us first, what will be the end of those who do not obey the gospel of God. Now if the righteous one is scarcely saved, where shall the ungodly and the sinner appear?"

Apostle Paul declared, "I discipline my body and bring it into subjection, lest, when I have preached to others, I myself should be disqualified." The Greek word for disqualified is also translated; become a castaway, rejected and a reprobate. Paul never expressed anywhere in his 14 books, which he authored in the New Testament, that he was assured that heaven was guaranteed to him regardless of what sins he committed after he was born again and even became a preacher.

Sufficient Grace For Living Righteously and Victoriously:

However, Apostle Paul was very emphatic about the grace of God giving us power to live victorious over everything, and that while we are living by God's grace nothing can separate us from the love of God. Jesus promised that He would remain faithful in His covenant with us, but if we break covenant we cut off our relationship with Him. Jesus promised to never leave us nor forsake us, but if we leave Jesus and forsake His way of life then He cannot allow us and our way of life into heaven. On His part He is committed to us to the end, even to the gates of hell; but we must stay committed to Jesus Christ to the end for Him to be able to give us the prize of entry into heaven. It is not the one who begins the race, but the one who finishes that receives the prize.

Christians Given Power To Cast Out Demons.

Judas was called and ordained by Jesus to be His chosen apostle the same as Peter, James, John and the other chosen ones. Judas received the same commission to preach the kingdom of God, heal the sick and cast out demons. Matthew 10:1-8 reveals that Jesus chose twelve of the disciples that had been following Him to be His twelve apostles. He gave all twelve (which includes Judas) the power over unclean spirits, to cast them out, and to heal all kinds of sickness and all kinds of disease. Then Jesus commissioned them to go out on a missions trip and preach saying, "The kingdom of heaven is at hand, heal the sick, cleanse the lepers, raise the dead and cast out devils. Freely you have received, freely give". Mt.10:5-8.

Sometime later, Jesus commissioned 70 others to go on a mission trip and do the same things He told the Apostles to do, plus heal the sick and say to them, the kingdom of God has come near to you. Jesus declared, "If I cast out demons by the Spirit of God, surely the kingdom of God has come upon you." They returned with joyful excitement, saying, "Lord, even the demons are subject to us in Your name." Then Jesus said to them, "I saw Satan fall like lightning from heaven. Behold I give you the authority to trample on serpents and scorpions, and over all the power of the enemy, and nothing by any means shall hurt you. Nevertheless do not rejoice in this, that the spirits are subject to you, but rather rejoice because your names are written in heaven." Jesus was saying that it is good to get excited that you can cast out demons, but you should rejoice more that your names are written in heaven (in the Lamb's Book of Life). Why? Because a Christian can make it into heaven even though they never exercise their God-given authority to cast out demons, but they cannot make it into heaven if their name is not found written in the Book of Life!

Judas Chosen and Ordained an Apostle

Judas was a chosen and ordained preacher-apostle of Jesus Christ, yet he fell away, betrayed Jesus and then went out and committed suicide by hanging himself. There is no doubt that Judas went straight to hell and is there for eternity. After the Apostles watched Jesus ascend to heaven, they obeyed the last command that Jesus gave them; go back to Jerusalem and wait there until I send you the promise of the Father, which would birth the Church and give each one the Holy Spirit's gift of their own spirit language. While they were waiting, Peter received the revelation that they needed to fill the position that Judas had with them. They decided that Jesus chose twelve, and they should keep it at twelve. Peter stated, "*Judas was numbered with us and obtained a part in this ministry*." They prayed for Jesus to help them choose the right person, "*to take part in this ministry and apostleship from which Judas by transgression fell, that he might go to his own place*". Acts 2:15-25. Peter acknowledges that Judas was an apostle with an apostolic ministry with them, but he fell by transgression and went to his own place—hell. Transgression is synonymous with iniquity and lawlessness.

> *"I Never KNEW you; depart from Me, you who practice lawlessness."*

The two main things that disqualified them from entering heaven were that though they preached the word of God and had a miraculous ministry, they still had the spirit of iniquity and practiced lawlessness. Iniquity and lawlessness are doing those things that are contrary to God's righteousness. Unrighteousness is doing those things that God says is not right to do. Lawlessness is a spirit and attitude that causes a person to do things contrary to God's Word, Will and Way. Iniquity/lawlessness is a spirit and attitude originating from a Christian's stubborn self-will and rebellion which causes him to commit lawless acts. Prophet Samuel declared that to God, *"Rebellion is as the sin of witchcraft, and stubbornness is as iniquity and idolatry"* I Sam. 15:23. A Christian can commit the sin of witchcraft, idolatry and iniquity by simply rebelling against God's word and stubbornly living and doing things their own way. These are all serious sins in God's sight; enough for Jesus to have to say, depart from Me, you who practice iniquity and lawlessness.

The second thing that disqualified them from having entry into heaven was Jesus's declaration that, *"I never knew you"*. To gain God's use and meaning for a word we have to go to the book of beginnings, Genesis. *"Now Adam KNEW Eve his wife, and she conceived and bore Cain." "And Adam KNEW his wife again and she bore a son and named him Seth."* Gen.4:1,25. And in the New Testament it says that the angel revealed to Joseph in a dream that Mary was pregnant by the Holy Spirit, so it was alright for him to marry her. *"And Joseph KNEW her not till she brought forth her firstborn, and called His name JESUS."* Mt.1:18-25. Each of these scriptures reveals that "KNEW" conveyed the reality of an intimate relationship. In marriage, it speaks of sexual intercourse between a husband and wife that causes a woman to become pregnant. That is the main application of the statement in Gen.2:24 & Mt.19:5 that says a man shall be JOINED to his wife, and they shall become one flesh. 1Cor.6:17 says, *"He who is joined to the Lord is one spirit with Him."* Man and wife joined together become one flesh. God and Man joined together become one spirit. A woman can leave her husband, separating from him, and they no longer are one flesh, united as one. Christians can leave their husband-Jesus separating from Him, and they are no longer one in spirit with Christ Jesus.

REDEMPTION VS. RELATIONSHIP

What was Jesus conveying when He said, I never knew you? He is saying, You received My blood for the forgiveness of your sins and was baptized in My name which gave you My power of attorney to manifest My miraculous ministry, but you never became one with Me. You never allowed your spirit to become one with My Spirit. You never allowed your spirit to become like My spirit of holiness, righteousness, submission and obedience to all of God's ways. You allowed Me to cleanse you of your sins making you righteous before God. You accepted Me as your Savior, but you never allowed Me to become Lord of your life in all of your ways. You kept on doing those things that I hate, and I cannot allow into My heaven. (Jesus loves righteousness but HATES all iniquity and lawlessness-Heb.1:9) I wrote your name in the Book of Life when I redeemed you, but your continual sinning in your personal life has caused Me to have to blot your name out of the Book of Life. I have the Book of Life open before Me, and I do not see your name there, so depart from me you worker of iniquity with the spirit of lawlessness. If I let you into heaven, your pride, selfishness, stubbornness to do things your way and lack of submissions to my authority would disrupt the purity and heavenly relationship that all the holy angels and saints have with one another and God. I cast Lucifer out for his pride, selfishness and rebellion to My authority and heavenly way of Life, so I cannot allow you in with you having Lucifer's same spirit, attitude and way of thinking and being in your personal life. I created Lucifer pure and he was perfect in all of his ways; he led My great orchestra and choir that permeated the universe and heaven with music and singing that blessed Me and all of my creation. He did mighty works and brought glory and praise to My name until the prideful spirit of self-ambition originated in his heart motivating and deceiving him into believing he could overthrow Me and rule as God of the Universe. I had to cast him out of my heavenly domain and the one-third of the angels that were in agreement with him. Preacher, I created you and redeemed you from all your past sins and made you a new creation in Me. You were purified by My blood, and I called you to be a minister for Me. You preached great and blessed many people and brought glory to My name. But you allowed the lust of the flesh and the pride of life to corrupt your soul. Oh, you continued to use the faith and gifts that I had given you to bless my people, but you forsook your call to be personally related to Me in an intimate way. I never knew you in an intimate way. You gave Me your sins, but you would not give Me your life to be lived according to My nature and character. I have to say to you as I did Lucifer, Depart from Me you worker of iniquity.

WHY DOES GOD WORK WITH PREACHERS WHO ARE UNRIGHTEOUS IN THEIR PERSONAL LIFE?

This is real confusion to church members and the people of the world. Why does God work with ministers who are living a double life? The minister may be preaching and ministering as a pastor of thousands or a traveling minister preaching to great crowds with mighty miracles taking place in his ministry, and yet be committing major sins in his personal life. In my 60 years of ministry, I have known of ministers from all ministerial areas of Christendom who seemed to be very successful in the eyes of man but discovery was made that they were guilty of major sins. In the late 1950s and early 60s there were hundreds of evangelists that arose throughout the world. By the mid-1970s, you could count on your two hands the ones that remained. Men such as Billy Graham, Oral Roberts, T.L. Osborne and a few others were still maintaining their ministry in integrity and righteousness. Most of the rest were going off morally, doctrinally, in their business dealings or ministering with the pride, self-ambition and self-promotion of Lucifer himself.

People ask, why would God confirm these ministries by working miracles, souls being saved or great financial prosperity? The fact is that God is not confirming their ministries at all, but a divine principle is at work here. Mark 16:20 gives the principle that helps us understand how these things can be. It says that after Jesus had spoken to the Apostles about preaching the gospel with accompanying miracles of casting out devils and healing the sick, He was received up into heaven and sat down at the right hand of God. And the disciples went out and preached everywhere, the Lord working with them and CONFIRMING THE WORD through the accompanying signs.

God Confirms His Word:

God does not work miracles, save souls, or prosper a person to confirm the person or their ministry. God does work miracles to convince people that He loves them and wants to save them, heal them and bless them. Consider this; I could take a bad street person, clean him, put him in a suit and have him get up in a meeting and quote John 3:16 and some young man whose mother has been praying for him for years hears that scripture, becomes convicted and gets saved. Was God confirming the bad street person or was He confirming His Word? God is not involved or interested in confirming man's pride, ego or desire for fame and success. Father God does promise to honor and promote those who humble themselves and live their lives to honor and obey God and do all things according to His Word, Will and Way. God confirms His Word with souls being saved and miracles of healing because the preacher preached God's truth of salvation and miracles, and someone received and believed the truth of God's Word and the truth set them free from sin and sickness.

Gifts Given Sovereignly by Grace---But Operated by Faith

I have been teaching on manifesting the supernatural for most of my six decades of ministry. In the late 1980s I wrote a teaching manual on "Manifesting Spiritual Gifts". We refer to it as the MSG Seminars where we teach, activate and train people how to manifest spiritual gifts. The reason I share this is because the principles that are revealed in this teaching gives insight concerning how ministers can minister the supernatural while being ungodly in areas of their personal life. Since we started MSG Seminars in the early 1980s myself and the 3000 ministers under my Bishop oversight have taught, activated and trained over a quarter of a million saints and ministers on every continent of the world in manifesting their spiritual gifts.

The manifestation of the supernatural spiritual ministry is part of the restoration of the prophetic and apostolic ministry. I Cor. 3:6 Reveals that New Testament ministers are more than preachers and teachers of the Word, they are also ministers of the Holy Spirit and the life of Christ. New Testament ministers called and commissioned by Jesus Christ are given the power and authority to minister the supernatural manifestations of the Spirit of God the same as they are authorized and empowered to preach the Word of God.

Principles That Need to be Understood:

In teaching on the manifestation of the gifts of the Holy Spirit, there are several important truths that need to be understood which also helps to understand the subject we are dealing with. First, all divine gifts are given by Almighty God to those who will believe and receive them. The only qualifications are to believe and receive. For example, the gift of eternal life is given to those who believe in their heart on the Lord Jesus Christ and confess their sins to Jesus for His forgiveness and receive Him as their Savior and Lord of their life. A person is saved by God's grace through their faith in the Lord Jesus apart from any religious works or merits of the individual. Gifts are given not earned. Wages are earned by our works. That's the reason the Bible says, *"The wages of sin is death, but the gift of God is eternal life."* Rom.6:23.

Gifts are given by the graciousness and loving desire of the giver. Jesus Christ is the Giver of eternal life. God so loved the world that He gave His only begotten Son as a gift to whosoever would receive Jesus as their savior could have the gift of eternal life. He that has the Son of God dwelling in him has the gift of eternal life. The divine principle of God is that His gifts are given not based on the worthiness of the receiver, but just because God wants to give the gift. The only requirement to manifest the gift is to believe, receive and exercise the faith to minister the gift for personal edification or to bless others.

Gifts of God Are Freely Given---Not Earned:

The same principle holds true for the gift of the Holy Spirit. The Holy Spirit's gift of the spirit language is given to Christians simply because they believe and receive. They can manifest the gift anytime they want to by active faith. Gifts are sovereignly given by the will of God, but they are received and manifest by the faith of the believer. The gift of the Holy Spirit is given to a Christian not based on their doctrinal accuracy, faultless character, morality, maturity or proper human relationships. It is simply given because their past sins have been forgiven, they have heard and believed the truth that the Holy Spirit's gift of the spirit language is for them, they received by faith and started speaking in tongues. The Holy Spirit's gift of the spirit language is given to a believer's redeemed spirit. It gives believers the ability to pray from their spirit by faith just like they pray from learned ability in their natural native language. Paul declared, "*If I pray in an unknown tongue, my spirit prays but my understanding is unfruitful. I will pray with the spirit and I will pray with my understanding.*" Notice that Paul explained that it wasn't the Holy Spirit doing the praying, but His own spirit which has been gifted by the Holy Spirit with that ability.

Christ/the Holy Spirit is within us and can inspire and direct our spirit what to pray. But our spirit can pray in its gifted spirit language without it being sovereignly directed by the Holy Spirit. Most of the time when we pray in tongues it is our spirit praying to God, praising God and interceding in behalf of our outward natural man. Apostle Paul, the greatest authority on speaking in tongues with our spirit language, declared that "*when I pray in tongues MY spirit prays.*" However, when we are motivated and directed by the Holy Spirit in intercession and warfare it is the Holy Spirit flowing with our spirit in the spirit language to accomplish God's purposes.

Inner Spirit Man - Outward Natural Man 2Cor.4:16:

Our inner spirit being knows and perceives so much more than our natural mind and body knows and perceives. It is like the reality that our brain is capable of much more than we use it for. Scientist figure that we only use about 10% of our brain power. The average tongues-talking-Christian uses less than 10% of the purposes and power of their spirit language. That is one of the reasons I wrote the book *"70 Reasons For Speaking In Tongues"*. It gives 15 Biblical proof reasons, 30 personal benefits and blessing reasons and 25 powerful spiritual ministry reasons for praying with our spirit language. I teach and minister these truths to help Christians to increase their percentage of benefits appropriated from 10% to 30, 60, to possibly 90% of God's purposes for gifting believers with their own spirit language.

OUR ETERNAL SPIRIT BEING AND OUR NATURAL MORTAL BODY

Our inner spirit being man has all the facilities and members of the outward natural man. The Bible speaks of the spiritual mind which means our spirit being has a spiritual brain. Our inner spirit being has all the members and parts that the physical body has. When a Christian dies physically, their spirit being leaves their body, and the angels take them to heaven. They are real people in a real world. They can talk to the others in heaven, hug them, sit down and eat together, etc. God made man different than angels. Angels are only spirit beings with spirit material bodies. God first made man a body from the dust of the earth and then breathed a part of His eternal spirit into man's body and man became a living spirit-soul being living in a natural body. God made the body of man that way so that if he sinned and became mortal his spirit could be redeemed and given everlasting life even though his body would die and be separated from his eternal spirit being. God gave man a spirit that cannot cease to be; it is an eternal spirit. Every human being who has breathed the breath of life becomes an eternal spirit being that will continue to exist after the body dies, either in the eternal place of heaven or hell. The hellish place called the Lake of Fire is described as the second death for all humans who end up there. The first death is spiritual death which means they are separated from God and dead in their trespasses and sins. They are spiritually dead though they are alive and functioning in their mortal body. Death for humans is a transition and state of being. The physical body ceases to function and deteriorates but the human spirit-body transitions to another place and continues to live on eternally. If they are never born again and exchange their state of eternal death for the gift of eternal life, they are cast into the lake of fire which is the second death, the eternal state of those who miss heaven. Those who are only born once die twice, but those who are born twice only die once. If a person is only born naturally and never born again then they will die naturally and then enter the second death which is the lake of fire. But a person who is born naturally and then born again by the Spirit of God will only die once; a natural death, and then enter eternal life.

Man A Three-Part Being:

It is essential that we understand the makeup of man. Man is a three-fold being, spirit, soul, and body. Paul prayed for the Thessalonian Christians that their whole BODY, SOUL, and SPIRIT would be preserved blamelessly until the coming of the Lord. Our spirit is our inner eternal being. Our soul consists of our mind, emotions and will, and it is the body of the spirit. The body is our natural flesh and bone being which houses our soul-spirit being. We can say, I have been redeemed in my spirit, I am being redeemed in my soul/self-life, and I shall be redeemed in my body. My spirit has been redeemed from sin by the blood of Jesus, my soul self-life is redeemed and being sanctified by the Spirit of God and my body will be redeemed to immortality at the second coming of the Lord Jesus.

All Divine Gifts Received and Ministered the Same:

The principles for receiving and manifesting the gift of eternal life, and the gift of the Holy Spirit are the same principles for receiving and manifesting the GIFTS of the Holy Spirit. The gifts of the Spirit are also called the manifestations of the Spirit. All Christians who have been born of the Spirit and baptized with the Spirit have been given the ability to manifest one or more of the nine gifts of the Spirit. The manifestation of the Spirit is given to every Christian. 1 Cor.12:7.

The manifestation of the Spirit is given to each one for the profit of all: for to one is given the word of wisdom through the Spirit; to another the word of knowledge through the same Spirit, to another faith by the same

Spirit, to another gifts of healings by the same Spirit, to another the working of miracles, to another prophecy, to another discerning of spirits, to another different kinds of tongues, to another the interpretation of tongues. But one and the same Spirit works all these things, distributing to each one individually as He wills. (1 Cor.12:7-11.)

Please note that these manifestations of the Spirit are GIVEN! They are not earned or appropriated by the works of man, but they are given by the Holy Spirit. They are not loaned to the believer but are given by the sovereign will of the Holy Spirit. The word "Given" reveals that the gifts are imparted into the spirit of a Christian, and they become a part of his spiritual abilities. It is the same as when the Holy Spirit gives the believer the ability to pray in a spirit language. When a gift is given it abides within 24/7; twenty-four hours a day and seven-days a week. Whether it is the Eternal Life gift, the Holy Spirit's spirit-language gift, or one or more of the nine gifts of the Holy Spirit. Gifts are given by God's grace, but they are manifested and ministered to others by the faith of the believer. *"Having then gifts differing according to the grace that is given to us, let us use them: if prophecy, let us prophesy in proportion to our faith."* Rom.12:6 Prophecy is also mentioned as one of the nine manifestations/gifts of the Spirit. If prophecy can be activated by faith then all the other gifts can be activated the same way. We have proven over the last 30 years of activating over 250,000 saints and ministers in prophetic ministry, which includes all the gifts and supernatural manifestation of the Spirit that gifts are activated and manifest by the faith of the minister or saint. That is the reason Paul exhorted Timothy to *"stir up the gift of God which is in you."* He then said to him to be bold and confident in doing this *"for God has not given us a spirit of fear, but of power, and of love, and of a sound mind."* 2Tim. 1:6, 7.

Commanded to Desire, Stir Up & Manifest Gifts

Peter exhorted the Christians to not be ignorant of spiritual gift but to *"earnestly desire spiritual gifts,"* *"You stir up (activate) your* gift," and *"use their God-given gifts to minister to others."* "As each one has received a gift, minister it to one another, as good stewards of the manifold grace of God." 1Peter 4:10. There are no scriptures that tell us to pray that God will move with His supernatural gifts and bless people. But it does tell us that God has given gifts to us and we are to stir them up and manifest and minister them to others by the knowledge that we have them and the faith that we have been given the ability to manifest them by the Holy Spirit's empowerment.

Ministers Can Manifest Miraculous Without Being Sinless:

Jesus does say several times that He has given the saints power to cast out demons, heal the sick and manifest God's miraculous power. I have known ministers over the years who had received the gift of faith and the working of miracles. They could preach the word concerning faith, healings and miracles. They would pray for people, and blind eyes would be opened, cripples would walk and numerous other miracles. However, at the same time they were in an adulterous affair. I knew another minister who started using whiskey to help him relax and go to sleep after a tense tiring service. He then started using it to relax him some before preaching. He soon became an alcoholic. He would drink a pint of whiskey before preaching. By the time he was up preaching he had become staggering drunk. Thousands of people out in front of him in his tent meeting thought he was swaying and staggering under the mighty anointing of God. They would get excited and shout as he proclaimed God's miracle working power. Hundreds would get saved, be healed of sicknesses and diseases and miracles of blind eyes opened and cripples healed. How can these things work? Because the drunken minister preached the truth of God's Word concerning salvation and His will and power to heal and perform miracles. The gifts were operating in his life, and some of the people believed the preached word and received from the God that they believed in for His blessings. He was a Pentecostal brother and knew that drunkenness was a sin, and repented daily for his drunkenness. He died an early death caused by his drinking. The wage of that sin was physical death. Because he never justified his drinking nor self-excused himself, but was continually repentant, He no doubt made it to heaven but lost much of his reward. I have discovered over the years from counseling with ministers and from personal experience that as long as a person is repentant and sorry for their sins, God will keep working with them for years until they are delivered from their bondage to sin. And His Fatherly love will keep the sin hidden from public exposure. However, I noticed that if the minister became proud and began to justify his sin and feel that he had a special right to sexual immorality, drunkenness, or other sins because of his high position in the Church world; God would deal with him for a period of time but if the minister became resistant to conviction from God and hardened his heart by self-deception then God would shout from the house tops what was being done in secret.

Very important things to know and remember; Do not assume that everything you are doing in your personal life is right with God because you are financially prospering, pastoring a growing church, having signs, wonders and miracles in your ministry or being a very successful Christian business person. None of those things are guarantees or proof that you are not sinning in your personal life. The word of God is the only standard by which your right standing with God can be accurately determined. Gifts and ministries are operations of God's love and mercy to His people. God will use those who will believe, receive and dare to minister the supernatural regardless of their imperfections or sins of omission or commission.

For the perfectionist and holiness oriented saints, I exhort you to not allow your imperfections and personally committed sins of omission or commission to keep you from being used of God to manifest the gifts of God. Continually seek forgiveness, deliverance and to overcome every un-Christ-like thought and action, dying to the self-life and continually being conformed to the likeness of Christ Jesus. Continually fulfill Apostle Paul's admonition to the Corinthian Christians; *"Let us cleanse ourselves from all filthiness of the flesh and spirit, perfecting holiness in the fear of God."* 1 Cor.7:1; Heb.12:1. But do not let Satan, who is the continual accuser of God's people, keep you from ministering in your calling and gifts for Christ's sake and His Church. This must be avoided while you are in the process of overcoming all things and being conformed to the likeness and character of Christ Jesus.

Godly Character Vs. Charisma Manifestations:

Apostle Paul covered the subject of receiving and manifesting divine gifts in Chapters 12, 13, and 14 of 1 Corinthians. In Chapter 13 he made the contrast between charisma and character. He emphasized that what made him a pure man of God was not his great knowledge and manifestations of miraculous ministry and doing good works but how much of Christ's character and nature he possessed and manifested. He uses the Greek word *agape* which is translated as Charity or Love. The core being and nature of God is Love for the Word declares that God is Love. Paul gives the characteristics of love in verses four through eight of First Corinthians thirteen. Whatever God the Father is Jesus is, so we can rightly say that love is the character and nature of Christ Jesus. When Paul is saying that doing all these things without love, *"I am nothing and it profits me nothing,"* he is saying that without Christlike character doing all these things profits me nothing. Charisma without Character profits nothing. Gaining heaven would be profitable for an individual but doing all these works is no guarantee that an individual will gain access to Heaven if they do not at the same time have Christlike Character and are doing all these things to the glory and honor of God and not for selfish motives. Divine *agape* love is not like human love that is thought of as a romantic feeling and sentimental emotion toward someone. God's love originates from His Spirit and nature not from His emotions, and it is the same with us. The reality and proof of having love is determined more by what we do than what we feel. Apostle John declared we know we love God and have His love abiding in us when we keep His commandments and relate to others with the attributes of God's love. Now let us read these scriptures and think *"Christlike character"* every time the word *"love"* is used.

I am Nothing & It Profits Me Nothing:

Though I speak with the tongues of men and of angels,
but have not love-Christlike character, I have become as

sounding brass or a clanging cymbal. And though I have the gift of prophecy, and understand all mysteries and all knowledge, and though I have all faith, so that I could move mountains, but have not love-Christlike Character, I am nothing. And though I bestow all my goods to feed the poor, and though I give my body to be burned, but have not love-Christlike character, it profits me nothing.

Could Apostle Paul be suggesting when he says, "I am nothing, and it profits me nothing" that it includes being denied entrance into Heaven? We are not saved by works but by grace, but after being saved if we do not put on the new man of Christ's nature and character, but continue to live our own life and not His, then we are nothing and profitless. Could that be cause for Jesus to say, "I never knew you in an intimate relationship, therefore, depart from me you worker of iniquity."? If doing all these great works without having the love-character of Christ gives no profit to the person having and manifesting all these things: If the person does make it into heaven, then it is definitely saying that those who manifest charisma without Christ's character will not receive any rewards in heaven for their ministry on earth. Since no one knows for sure the full extent of what Paul meant by *"It profits me nothing"* then I would strongly recommend that we make *"being conformed to the image and likeness of Christ"* our number one goal and ministry. We can see from Paul's revelation and knowledge of the Church and God's purpose for man why he made this his priority and greatest ministry. Therefore, since we have this ministry (of being transformed into Christ's image from glory to glory) we do not lose heart. For we know that all things work together for good to those who love God and are called according to His purpose...which is for each child of God to be conformed to the image of God's Son, Jesus Christ, that He might be the firstborn of a family of mankind transformed into Christlikeness. 2Cor.3:18-4:1,11; Rom.8:28,29

BALANCED, PROGRESSIVE & PRODUCTIVE

Paul summarizes Chapters 12 & 13 of 1 Corinthians in the first verse of Chapter 14, *"Pursue love-Christlike character, and desire to manifest the supernatural gifts of the Holy Spirit, but especially that you may prophesy."* This is the balanced approach for Christians who want to be and do all God wants them to be and do. God desires that we possess and manifest both the fruit of the Spirit and the gifts of the Spirit. The fruit of the Spirit and the gifts of the Spirit are received and manifest by the same Spirit. They are both supernatural graces of Jesus Christ. However, they have a different operation; gifts are given, but fruit is grown. Fruit of the Spirit is for character and the gifts of the Spirit for ministry to others. The ideal would be divine gifts being manifest by Christians who have the character and godliness of Christ. But the reality is that God has to use imperfect vessels to manifest His gifts. When teaching on this subject, I tell Christians that God will use them because they are the best He has, and is that good news or bad news for God.

There is another key scripture that reveals why unrighteous preachers and saints can manifest their calling and ministry even though they are not godly in all their ways. *"The gifts and callings of God are without repentance."Rom.11:29.* Notice what other translations say about the gifts and callings of God: they are irrevocable...no change or purpose can annul God's gifts and call...God does not withdraw His gift and His call. The gifts of salvation, spirit language, and the gifts of the Spirit are given to individuals, and they are not recalled for the life of the person regardless of their way of life. At the judgment seat of Christ, all gifts from God will be taken away if they were not used or they were abused and overridden by unrighteousness of the individual. But during this life the supernatural gifts can be manifest by a preacher or saint by faith regardless of their lifestyle. That is not the ideal, but it is the real. That is another reason why some preachers can have great spiritual manifestation and ministry, but be lacking godly Christlike character.

Chapter 4
The Ten "M"s

MATURING AND MAINTAINING MINISTRY
AND FOR DISCERNING TRUE AND FALSE MINISTERS

During the 1980s and 90s, I was pioneering the Prophetic Movement and training men and women called to be prophets, prophetic ministers, and prophetic saints. I developed the 10 "M"s" as truth-tools for training and making those I was teaching and training true and mature ministers. They are 10 words that begin with the letter "M" in English and Spanish. They are foundation stones and building blocks necessary for building the ministry that can house God's glory and stand the test of time in being a true minister with a God-anointed and approved ministry. (I was using the NIV considerably at that time and most of the scripture references in this chapter are from the NIV.)

The personal character of any minister is the foundation of his or her ministry. If ministers build a building of ministry greater than their foundation of righteous character then the weight of the ministry building will cause the foundation of character to crack, sometime to the extent that the whole building crashes to the ground. In recent years we have seen all too clearly that even those Christians whose ministries may have all the so-called signs of "success," such as financial prosperity, international fame and popularity, and even signs following, are doomed to a humiliating collapse if they fail to build their works on a solid base of personal purity and maturity, which is continually being conformed to the image of Christ.

In discerning true and false ministers, it helps tremendously to examine the "Ten M's for maintaining and maturing ministry." These are ten areas of our personal lives and ministry that need examination and correction if we are to prove ourselves to be true ministers of God. We have studied in Chapter two all the various sins of omission and commission, sins that will cancel all or part of minister's prophetic destiny and ministry, sins that lead to spiritual death and sins that can blot ones name out of the Book of Life. Anyone of the 10 M's out of order can start a chain reaction and open the door for sin to enter. If sin is entertained then it invites demonic oppression. If the person does not repent of their sin and cease practicing it, they open themselves to self-deception and pride causing self-willed hardness of heart which leads to spiritual death. Therefore, it is very important that we study the 10 M's and allow them to examine our life and ministry thoroughly. Any "M" out of order can be adjusted by submitting to God, resisting the devil, being renewed in our minds and transformed by the Spirit of God.

1.)   MANHOOD (OR WOMANHOOD).

God created humankind in His own image (Gen. 1:26,27). All the sinning of man is done in his thoughts and by acts of the body. The body of man is neither good nor bad in and of itself. When God finished making the body of man, it had no thinking, motivation or action. God then breathed into man an eternal spirit which made him a living soul being with thinking, emotions and a free will. Man became a spirit-soul-body being, a three-in-one being like God Himself; made in God's own image and likeness. Therefore, the body of man is important to God. Every thought and action of the body comes from and is motivated by spirit---man's spirit, God's Spirit or Satan's spirit. Man has the power to accept or reject any thought or motivation regardless from where it originates. Man is not a mechanical robot, but a living human being made from the pattern and DNA of his Creator with the potential to mature into Christ's character and capabilities.

In the New Testament Apostle Paul reveals that Christ wants to live in the body of man and make it the temple of God. The body is to be holy the same as the spirit and soul of man. The newly created man was to be the very expression and demonstration of God on the earth.

No man ever fully did that until the Man Christ Jesus came and fully demonstrated God in and with His body. "For in Christ, there is all of God in a human body." Col.2:9LB. Apostle Paul challenges the Corinthian Christians with this question, "Haven't you yet learned that your body is the home of the Holy Spirit God gave you and that He lives within you? Your own body does not belong to you. For God has bought you at a great price. So use every part of your body to give glory back to God, because He owns it." 1 Cor.6:19,20LB.

I present these truths concerning the body because of the false teaching coming from some ministers; that is, it makes no difference what you do in your body, because God is only concerned with the spirit of man; that your can serve God with your mind and spirit even though the body is committing immoral acts. To be God's true man or woman, you must be holy in your spirit, your soul, and in your BODY. It was man's body that was made in God's image and man's spirit came from the breath of God. God rightfully owns the human race by the fact that He created man and woman. However, if mankind uses what God purposed for good and to be a praise to His glory, for evil and corrupts their whole being with sin then God disowns them, and the only way they can get restored to God is by being redeemed. Jesus owns the body, soul and spirit of His saints because He redeemed them with His own precious blood. To be a true man or woman of God on earth we must live our lives according to the life of Christ and glorify God with our spirit and body knowing that we are not our own but belong wholly to Jesus Christ who redeemed us and lives in us. Gal.2:20.

God also created the body of man for another purpose other than man to have a body to live in on earth. I believe that when the Eternal created Adam, He made him with the kind of body that Father God wanted His Son to have and live in for eternity. He gave Adam and Eve power to reproduce after their own kind, and He planned that four thousand years down the road, a woman descendant of theirs would be overshadowed by the Holy Spirit to conceive Jesus, who was God in the flesh. Jesus was born with a mortal human body that portrayed and demonstrated His heavenly Father to the world. The Son of God's mortal body died on the cross and shed its life's blood for the redemption of humankind. That human body was placed in a grave, but God resurrected and immortalized the body of Jesus. That same body was taken to heaven and seated at the right hand of the Father. That human body is now the eternal body of God the Son forevermore. Christ thus became a God-Man--humanity's perfect God and God's perfect man.

FOUNDATION BEFORE THE BUILDING---MAN BEFORE MINISTRY

With Jesus in mind as the pattern, God had to make Adam and Eve first in His own image and likeness before they could perform their "ministry" in the Garden of Eden. The same is true of us: God wants to make us like Jesus before we can minister fully as Jesus did. God must make the man or woman before He manifests through them a mighty ministry. Father God had Jesus go through 30 years of becoming God's Man before He became God's minister and the manifest Son of God.

I remember one night in 1956 when I was preaching in Bellingham, Washington, I was telling the congregation that we must be like God. I meant, of course, that we are to be godly, to be holy, having the moral character of God. But in that moment as I spoke, I heard the Holy Spirit say, "If you put it that way, the people will despair; they'll think of God the Father, and they know they can't be like God who is everywhere present, all-powerful and all-knowing. Instead, tell them to be like Jesus, the perfect man who was the perfect expression of God."

The Church Race.

We aren't destined to become God, as New Age teaching would have it. But we are predestined to be conformed to the image of Christ Jesus (Rom. 8:29). God created the man Adam to be the father of the whole human race. Abraham was called to be the father of the Hebrew race. But Jesus came to be the spiritual father of a new race of humankind called the "Church race" which makes Jew and Gentile one people of God.

This race of people on earth, have eternal life in their spirits while their physical bodies are still mortal. At the end of the Church age, all the members of this Church race will have their bodies transformed into eternally immortal bodies. Such a transformation will not change them into any other creature other than human beings, but they will be human beings as God originally and ultimately intended for them to be.

The resurrection-translation of the saints will make their bodies as eternal as their spirits are now. The same Spirit that raised Jesus from the dead will make their physical bodies as immortal as His. Though the Church race of humankind is destined to be spiritual citizens of heaven, yet they will have immortal flesh-and-bone bodies, like the one Jesus now has seated at the right hand of God (Phil. 3:21).

God made humanity in the Garden of Eden the way He wanted the race to be throughout eternity: with a spirit, soul, and body conformed to God's own image and likeness. God never intended for humankind to evolve into angels, cherubim, seraphim or God Himself. We as saints will never become angels or God, but we will be like the perfect man, Christ Jesus.

Why should we ever want to be anything else? The human being is the highest being God ever created on earth or anywhere in the universe. Blood-washed, redeemed humankind is destined to be joint heirs with Jesus Christ of all that God has and become the Bride of Christ. (Rom. 8:17). There is no higher calling in the universe than to be a new-creation member of the eternal Church race.

Jesus exhorted His followers, not to rejoice in the spiritual power and apostolic ministry He had given them, but to be glad that they were God's people with their names written in the Lamb's Book of Life (Luke 10:20). Paul received this truth and demonstrated it by not boasting in his position as an apostle or in his power to cast out demons and heal the sick. Instead, he boasted in the greater calling and ministry of being changed "from glory to glory" until he reached Christ's image and likeness (2 Cor. 3:18; 4:1)).

Our highest calling and most important goal is not to be the greatest apostle, prophet or prophetic person, but rather to be Christ's type of man or woman that God wants us to be both now and forever. Humankind was made the way it's supposed to be in order to fulfill God's will and work throughout eternity. Redeemed human beings have the highest calling and greatest destiny of any of God's creation.

Make Christlike Character Your Aim.

For us to be godly--that is, like God--means for us to be like Jesus, who is our perfect pattern as believers and as ministers. That means saints must be fully human as well as Godly. Jesus was pure man and God at the same time on earth. A few Charismatic and Prophetic saints become what I call "spooky-spiritual." They become mythical and mysterious and so out-of-this-world-minded that they are not living in Christ's divine reality on earth. Christians must become God's type of man or woman, who knows how to walk in a natural way on the earth while walking in a supernatural way in the Spirit. Our flesh and bone bodies are not sinful for when cleansed by the blood of Jesus and sanctified by the Holy Spirit they become the instrument of God to fulfill His will and do His work on earth.

Man Ministering with the Love-Character of Christ Jesus:

Paul told the church at Corinth: "Follow after charity, and desire spiritual gifts" (1 Cor. 14:1). I believe that the best definition of charity is mature, Christlike character. One way to paraphrase this verse would be: "Follow after Christlike character while you desire to minister spiritual gifts at the same time." Even as we pursue a goal of ministry through spiritual gifts and activities, we must remember that the overarching goal is character.

Another translation says, "Make love your aim." Apostle John declares that God is Love. That makes the life of Jesus the personification of love, for He was the complete demonstration of who God is. We must make Christ's character our primary aim, our ultimate goal as we minister. When Paul was telling the Romans about God's ultimate intention for us, he didn't talk about our position, our message, or our ministry. He spoke instead of our character: "For whom he did foreknow, he also did predestinate to be conformed to the image of His Son, that he might be the firstborn among many brethren"

(Rom. 8:29). Our transformation into Christ's image is what God is primarily after, so whatever happens to us, it is working together for our good toward that goal (Rom. 8:28).

In the ultimate purpose of God, then, there are no "good" times or "bad" times for those who love God and are called according to His purpose. The "bad" time you are going through just now may well be the best time for your eternal gain, because it may be doing the most to move you toward the goal of becoming God's true man or woman, like Jesus was and is God's true man. The tough times for the "outer man"—your temporal physical, emotional, financial, and social being--may well be strengthening your "inner man"---your spiritual eternal being (2 Cor. 4:16).

After all, if we are honest, we must admit that we tend to grow the least when everything is going smoothly. Our years of preparation for mature manhood and womanhood are more important than our years of ministry. For without proper personal preparation, our mighty ministry performances will become perverted and cannot permanently endure. Remember Father God is looking forward to a family of men and women who are like He envisioned, planned and created man and woman to be. He loves people more than He loves performances, mankind more than mighty ministry.

Over the years, I now see, my enemies have taught me more than my friends. Through them, I have learned much wisdom, forgiveness, patience, longsuffering, and understanding of human nature which has made me more God's kind of man, a man of God. That's the reason I take the attitude when people draw a small circle and exclude me, I just draw a bigger circle and include them. For Jesus said love your enemies, pray for them who persecute you and bless those who curse you. Why should I do that? Because, they are helping fulfill my divine destiny goal of being dead to self and conformed to the life of Christ. From an ultimate standpoint, Christians don't have problems; we only have predestinated purposes ordained by God to conform us to the image of Christ. All things do work together for our good to fulfill God's greatest purpose for our lives—being conformed to the likeness of Jesus Christ. Rom.8:28,29.

Since the scripture declares that Jesus Himself was made perfect through suffering (Heb. 2:10), how can we expect it to be otherwise for us? And if Jesus spent thirty years preparing for three and a half years of ministry, we too should not be surprised if God spends a large portion of our lives building our manhood or womanhood before launching us into our ultimate ministry. To maintain our ministry and mature in it, then, we must make sure we allow God the time and process He requires to make us into the man or woman that He knows will be needed for us to be and do what He has called us to.

JUDGING MINISTERS!

In judging true and false ministers, the quality of manhood or womanhood must be judged. We must evaluate ministers apart from their ministry, position, title, or gifting. In such an evaluation, we should ask ourselves, is he or she the kind of person I would want for my best friend, neighbor, or co-laborer in God's kingdom throughout eternity?

I have known mighty, miracle-working ministers who had built great spiritual works--yet in their personal manhood or womanhood they had so many un-Christlike attributes that I wouldn't want them as a personal friend. I wouldn't even want to spend my vacation with them, much less eternity.

REMEMBER: We may not manifest our present ministry throughout eternity, but we will be the type of person we are in eternity. I can find no scriptural text that declares we will receive a transformation of character at death or at the return of the Lord. The resurrection-translation of the saints at the end of the age is designed to change only one thing: Our physical bodies will be transformed from mortal to immortal (Phil 3:21; 1 Cor. 15.51; 1 Thess. 4:17).

On the other hand, Christlike character comes about through a different transformation--the "renewing of our minds" (Rom. 12:2), the continual change into His image from glory to glory (2 Cor. 3:18). With this truth in mind, John declared:

Beloved, now we are children of God, and it has not appeared as yet what we shall be. We know that, when He appears, we shall be like Him because we shall see Him just as He is. And everyone who has this hope fixed on Him purifies himself, just as He is pure (1 John 3:2,3 NASB, emphasis added).

These are some of the reasons God has more concern about His ministers' being real, Christlike men and women than about their being mighty ministers. God's judgment of whether a minister is true or false will be determined by probably 90% on the life of the person and 10% on the performance of the minister.

2.)   MINISTRY.

In the "M" of Manhood we majored on the person more than the ministry, now we want to examine the ministry of the man. The area to which we must give attention if we are to mature in ministry is the fruits of that ministry. Jesus pointed to this area when He warned His disciples about false ministers who would come to them as ferocious wolves in sheep's clothing. Jude said this about these ministers: "They are spots in your love feasts, while they feast with you without fear, serving only themselves." They are clouds without water, carried about by the winds; late autumn fruit trees without fruit, twice dead, pulled up by the roots; raging waves of the sea, foaming up their own shame; wandering stars for whom is reserved the blackness of darkness forever," He said of true ministers that "by their fruit you will recognize them" (Matt. 7:15-20).

How long does the positive effect of our ministry last? Is it all froth, or is there abiding fruit? After all the excitement, shouting, singing, and manifestations are over, what remains that is of value? Apostle Paul declared that some ministry is more noise than life giving ministry, like sounding brass or clanging cymbals. He said that even though the minister understood all mysteries, could prophesy and had faith to work miracles; yet he did not have the love-character of Christ Jesus, he was nothing and there was no profit in what he did. ICor.13:1-3.)

Does our ministry manifest the anointing of God--that is, the divine enablement of grace to accomplish God's intended results? Or is there more talk than true power? The apostle Paul insisted: "My message and my preaching were not with wise and persuasive words, but with a demonstration of the Spirit's power, so that your faith might not rest on man's wisdom, but on God's power....The kingdom of God is not a matter of talk but of power" (1 Cor. 2:4,5; 4:20). We have no excuse for not demonstrating the supernatural dimension of spiritual gifts in our ministry, since the word if God emphatically declares, "The Manifestation of the Spirit IS GIVEN to EACH ONE for the profit of all." (1 Cor.12:7)

Is our preaching or prophesying productive? Is the word we speak positive, pure, and proven? Have we been accurate, and has our ministry produced the fruit of the Spirit in those to whom we've ministered?

Though we are no longer under the Mosaic Law, we should keep in mind the seriousness in God's eyes of ministering in His name. He told the ancient Israelites: "But a prophet who presumes to speak in my name anything I have not commanded him to say...must be put to death" (Deut.18:20). IN New Testament Church, that would mean his ministry should be rejected and hopefully removed from ministry if he has a record of prophesying inaccurate words or a teacher teaching unscriptural things.

How do we know whether our words have been truly of God? In the same biblical passage, God told the people how to judge: "If what a prophet proclaims in the name of the Lord does not take place or come true, that is a message the Lord has not spoken. That prophet has spoken presumptuously" (vv. 21,22, NIV). Ministry is judged differently than the minister. The preacher is judged by the things we discussed under Manhood. The ministry, whether it is prophesying, preaching or teaching is judged by its biblical accuracy in context and content; whether the ministry is presented in God's love and wisdom and whether it is presented with anointing, revelation and life giving impartation. Some ministers speak only from head knowledge without any heart and anointing in their ministry.

In addition, we should consider whether our preaching or prophesying has caused people to stumble or has discredited the ministry in any way. Paul was able to declare: "We have put no stumbling block in anyone's path so that our ministry may not be discredited" (2 Cor. 6:3). He went on to report how he and those who ministered with him had endured hardship, opposition, hard work, slander, and deprivation, yet through it all they had given no one genuine cause to condemn their work.

This is not to say, of course, that our ministry should never stir controversy or criticism; even Jesus and Paul had those problems in abundance. But it is to say that we should suffer for the sake of truth and righteousness in our ministry, not for the sake of unnecessary stumbling blocks we have erected by causing undue offense (1 Pet.. 4:15).

Function in Full Authority.

I want to encourage and challenge all Christian ministers to function in their full authority as New Testament ministers. The apostle Paul said that God "hath made us able ministers of the New Testament; not of the letter, but of the Spirit: for the letter kills, but the Spirit gives life" (2 Cor. 3:6). He was emphasizing the great truth that born-again, Spirit-filled ministers can minister the Holy Spirit gifts and graces as easily as they preach the Logos Word of God.

All that the Holy Spirit has been commissioned to be and do for the Church, the New Testament minister can minister to God's people. The revelation of this truth gave me the faith to minister spiritual things with the same authority and anointing I have in preaching the Word. Those ministers who understand this truth and are ministering the Spirit the same way they minister the letter of the Word, are those I would call "prophetic-apostolic ministers."

All New Testament ministers need to become able ministers in the Holy Spirit to prove that they truly manifest the kind of ministry God intends for them. In light of this application of Paul's words, all Christian ministers should have the manifestations of the Spirit in their ministry, and all saints should manifest prophetic ministry.

This is one reason Paul commanded the Corinthian Christians to "desire spiritual gifts" (1 Cor. 14:1) and "covet to prophesy" (v. 39), for we "may all prophesy (manifest prophetic ministry) one by one" (v. 31). If a minister only ministers the truths from the written Word of God he is only fulfilling half of God's purpose for fivefold ministers ministering to the saints. Church ministers should minister the Logos and the Rhema Word of God to those to whom they minister. A New Testament minister should minister by the enablement of the Holy Spirit and minister the gifts of the Spirit that have been given to every saint and especially to five-fold ministers. ICor.12:7-11. Let's all manifest true ministry that pleases our Father God, by obeying the admonition of Apostle Paul to make full proof of our ministry by properly ministering both the Word and the Spirit of God.

3.)   MESSAGE.

The Bible says we should be "speaking the truth in love" (Eph. 4:15). Paul tells us here that the message of a mature minister should first of all be life-giving present truth. It should present the word of God in a way that is thoroughly scriptural, doctrinally sound, and well-balanced in the light of the full testimony of the Bible.

Second, Paul says, the message should be spoken in love. To understand what he means by "spoken in love" we have to include Paul's description of what love is in 1 Corinthians 13:4-8. Not just the content but also the spirit of the message should be right. For it is possible to be doctrinally right, but spiritually wrong. Truth is truth regardless of how it is presented, but the person presenting the truth can do it with a spirit and attitude that is contrary to the spirit and nature of Jesus Christ.

Our preaching, teaching, and prophesying can be scriptural, theologically sound, and well-balanced, yet still be delivered with a tone, a motivation, and a spirit that is out of order because it is not according to divine love. The Pharisees had some right doctrine, but their spirit, their attitude, and their relationship with God were all wrong. They were full of pride, narrow-mindedness, and self-righteousness. Also, if a minister has hidden sin in his life those who are discerning will sense it and have a hard time receiving the minister's message. My daughter is a very discerning concerning people, and sometimes she would say, I don't like that man. I discovered that when she felt that way about a person there were some of his M's out of order in his life. She is a people person and usually likes people, so I instructed her not to say I don't like that person but say to me, Dad there is something not right about that person. Every time my wife or daughter has not felt right about a person it has proven in time that they were right. I remember one particular minister that wanted to be ordained with our ministerial network. His application looked great, and he had a national ministry, but every time my wife and daughter were around him they had red warning lights go off inside of their spirit. We never did ordain him with us, and later it was discovered that he was having sexual affairs with different women as he traveled in ministry. His message was biblically sound, but his spirit and personal life were out of order.

Of course, the converse is true as well. We can have the right spirit, attitude, and motivation--we can be quite loving and humble-- and yet have wrong doctrine. So we cannot judge the doctrinal correctness of a minister on how much we like him or her personally. Doctrine is judged strictly on the Bible.

At the same time, biblical orthodoxy and supernatural power don't always go together. I have met many teachers and other ministers who are doctrinally correct, yet they manifest a little divine anointing or power. On the other hand, we cannot judge a person's message to be doctrinally sound simply because he or she is able to perform signs and wonders. This reminder will become increasingly important in these last days as the devil manifests his supernatural power more and more through counterfeits of God's works.

Yet another truth we must keep in mind in the area of the message is that God blesses His Word, and He confirms it. When the disciples went out to fulfill the Great Commission after Jesus had ascended into heaven, the Scriptures tell us: "Then the disciples went out and preached everywhere, and the Lord worked with them and confirmed His word by the signs that accompanied it" (Mark 16:20).

The Bible does not say here "God confirmed their great statements of faith lest they look like fools, lest they be embarrassed, and their fleshly ego be deflated." No--God does not confirm us; He confirms His word.

We must not say, "I quoted Scripture; I took a stand. Now, God, your reputation is at stake; you've got to back me up!" If we do, the Lord will answer, "Who says? I made myself of no reputation during my ministry on earth, for I was only concerned with doing the will of My Father. Phil.2:7. My concern is not for My reputation or yours, but that you preach My truth in love." Jesus didn't try to become popular or famous; He never asked, "Would you make sure that this miracle gets in the newspaper?"

God confirms His Word; not our flesh, our desires, or our presumptive boasting. He is not concerned to preserve our fleshly pride. He is concerned that we have a good report, that we portray the gospel correctly, that we fulfill His will. But He is not concerned with our popularity. Once we realize that truth, we can release ourselves from a great deal of pressure. Jesus will promote those who promote Him and His cause, but we are not to promote ourselves.

Have you ever wondered why some ministers who preach the Word of God but live lives of sin have nevertheless had results? We've all read or heard about preachers or evangelists who were exposed as adulterers or alcoholics, and yet even while they sinned habitually, people were saved, healed and delivered through their preaching of God's word.

Why, we ask, does God seem to give approval to their behavior this way? Why does He confirm the lives of such people? The answer, of course, is that He does not confirm them; He confirms His word that they preach. An atheist could stand up in a packed stadium and read and proclaim Bible truths, and some people would probably give their hearts to the Lord as a result. That's because God's Word has power in itself, and God confirms His Word. The gospel itself, not the one who preaches it, is "the power of God unto salvation" (Rom. 1:16).

We should not be surprised, then, that on judgment day the Lord will be able to say that He never knew some who in His name prophesied, cast out demons and performed miracles (Matt. 7:23). He will say, "Yes, you proclaimed my name, you used my gifting, and I confirmed my word. But your life was not in line with my character; I can't take you."

All ministers and church members need to study continually the word of God to show themselves approved to God (2 Tim. 2:15). Our message must be not only biblically balanced in the fundamentals of the Christian faith, but also "established in the present truth" (2 Pet. 1:12). For us to minister and mature in our "M" of message, we must retain the basic while continuing to incorporate all presently restored biblical truths into our message.

4.) MATURITY.

The Bible wisely warns us not to place new Christians in places of leadership, but to wait until they have had a chance to be proven and to mature (1 Tim. 3:6). Even so, maturity does not come automatically with time.

The traits of maturity in the Christian life are listed by Paul when he recites for the Galatians the fruit of the Spirit: love, joy, peace, patience, kindness, goodness, faithfulness, gentleness, and self-control (Gal. 5:22,23). In addition, we can add to this list the fruit of godly wisdom, which James says is pure, peaceable, considerate, submissive, full of mercy and good fruit, impartial and sincere (James 3:17). But sadly enough, all too many ministers have failed to allow the dealings of God and hard experience to cultivate in them a divine maturity.

The truly mature person manifests the characteristics of God's agape love Apostle Paul described to the Corinthians: patient, kind, not envious, not boasting, not proud, not rude, not self-seeking, not easily angered; not keeping a record of wrongs; not delighting in evil but rejoicing with the truth; always protecting, trusting, hoping, persevering; never failing (1 Cor. 13:4-8).

Have you ever tried to handle a person with extensive burns? Their injury makes it almost impossible for them to be touched without feeling pain. They are like a bundle of raw nerves, sensitive to the slightest touch. If you reach out to touch them, they will withdraw from you.

I have known some ministers who are like that in their personality and their emotions. You have to be careful when you're around them because the slightest negative word or glance makes them feel injured. They tend to be unapproachable, untouchable, defensive, thin-skinned and easily offended.

Such people need to grow enough emotional "skin" to recover from their injuries and to be covered properly. So essentially their problem is immaturity, and it can only be resolved by emotional and spiritual growth. I counsel ministers like that to trade their dolphin hide in for an alligator skin and their chicken feathers for duck feathers so that these things will roll off of them like water off of a duck's back. Immaturity causes the most problems in human relationships. Most people do not expect ministers to be immature. One of the biggest manifestations of immaturity is selfishness. If the self-life is not crucified, it will open the door to many problems. That's why Jesus said that unless a person takes up his cross and denies himself he cannot be His disciple, and he certainly should not be a ministerial representative of Jesus Christ. There are over 30 scriptures on growing and maturing until we come to the maturity of Christ Himself. That is the reason mature fivefold ministers must minister to the saints until they become, "A mature man, unto the measure of the stature of the fullness of Christ Himself, growing up in all things in Christ who is head of all the members of the Body of Christ."

God Is Looking for Faithful Servants.

Faithfulness is also an important quality of maturity. It is the quality of endurance with persistence in pursuing God's purpose, being dependable and trustworthy with man and God. When the master in Jesus' parable, which typifies Jesus speaking to His servant-ministers, commended His servants, did he say, "Well done, great spiritual prophesier, miracle worker, prophet, apostle"? No! He said, "Well done, GOOD and FAITHFUL servant" (Matt. 25:21). "Good" equals Christlikeness for there is none good but God. "Faithfulness" equals consistency and continual growth in ministry. On the day of judgment, we will not be judged by how many books we wrote, how many people knew our name, how many countries we traveled in, how many people we ministered to, or whether or not we became a pastor or bishop. God will check in His books which contain the works of His Children to determine rewards and positions for eternity. All of those who were found to have been GOOD & FAITHFUL receive rewards to rule and reign with Christ, like the overcomers mentioned in the book or Revelation. The one who did not use what God had given him, which was a talent/gift of God, received the following statements from the Lord, "You wicked, lazy and unprofitable servant. Take the one talent from him and give it to the one who received five, used his talents profitably and now has ten."

The unfaithful servant hid his talent because he had the wrong concept of his master and he was afraid to use his talent. Jesus then established His divine principle, that everyone who faithfully uses all that God has given them will be given more; and he will have abundance. Additionally, everyone who has just a little but does not use even the little, will have it taken from him. Jesus then said, "Cast the unprofitable servant into the outer darkness. There will be weeping and gnashing of teeth." Mat.25:14-30.

I tell saints when I teach on the gifts of the Spirit, these three servants represent three different Christians; one received five gifts, one received two, and one received only one gift. The servants with five and two put theirs to use and doubled them. The one with one gift hid his and was afraid to use it. This is where I developed the saying, "Use them or lose them!" Then I usually say, "I do not know whether the place where the unprofitable servant was sent represents the bottom rung of the ladder to heaven, or the top rung of the ladder of hell. Personally, I do not want to find out by experiencing what that place is and where it is located! I am determined to be all God called me to be and use everything Jesus Christ has given me!" That's why Paul told Timothy to stir up the gift within him and use it, for God has not given us a spirit of fear, but love, power and a sound mind to minister the gifts God has given us. 2 Tim.1:6,7. The two profitable servants had maturity in their thinking, attitude and ministry. The unprofitable servant demonstrated immaturity in his understating of God which produced his immature attitude and actions.

Did you ever hear about the famous minister who stood before the Lord, and the Lord asked, "What did you accomplish for me?"

"Well, Lord," said the minister, "what do you think about those ten books I wrote?"

"I don't know," the Lord answered. "I never read them." (When I tell that story some friends will ask me if I thought Jesus read any of my books. I teasingly tell them, He doesn't have to read them He dictated them!)

God is not as impressed with all of our achievements as we tend to be. But He is impressed with our goodness and faithfulness.

"When I was a child," Paul writes, "I talked like a child, I thought like a child, I reasoned like a child. When I became a man, I put childish ways behind me." (1 Cor. 13:11). Can we say the same thing? Have we learned to put behind us the selfishness, possessiveness, and desire for attention that can only be labeled childishness and unfitting for a mature son or daughter of God?

Theological Maturity.

Meanwhile, emotional and social maturity are only part of the big picture. Have we also grown mature in our theology and in our understanding of Scripture? Or is our doctrine still simplistic, shallow, self-serving, or narrow-minded?

Are we still "infants, tossed back and forth by the waves, and blown here and there by every wind of teaching and by the cunning and craftiness of men in their deceitful scheming" (Eph. 4:14)? Hebrews says that we must go beyond feeding on the "milk" of elementary teachings to the teaching of righteousness that is "solid food" for the mature, "who by constant use have trained themselves to distinguish good from evil" (Heb. 5:12-14).

Loving Jesus Is the Key.

Who is a mature person? Mature people are those who have overcome their character flaws. They have been delivered from their iniquities, weed-seed attitudes and pitfalls as portrayed by several Bible characters. (Described fully in my book, "Prophets-Pitfalls to Avoid and Principles to Practice."

We will never reach our full potential unless we allow God to bring our manhood or womanhood to maturity. And the Bible makes it clear that maturity is accomplished mainly by loving Jesus Christ with our whole being and allowing Him to be the Lord of every area of our lives. Apostle John declared that the way we know we love God is by faithfully keeping His commandments and by having Christ's loving care for our brothers and sister in the Lord. (1Jn.4:7-5:3) Mature Christians with their 10 "M's" in order have a humble appreciation for their salvation in Christ Jesus. They maintain a respectful attitude with the reverential fear of God which enables them to faithfully life the life of Christ.

5.)   MARRIAGE.

Yet another critical area that deserves our attention as ministers is our marriage and family life. God's Word is clear: Our marriage is to reflect the kind of loving relationship we find between Christ and the Church (Eph. 5:22-33). Wives must respect and submit to their husbands even as husbands respect and live considerately with their wives (1 Peter 3:1,7). And husbands must love their wives with Christ's kind of love--not lording over them, but treating them as fellow-heirs of the grace of God. Otherwise, our prayers--and our ministry in general--will be hindered (1 Peter 3:7).

Our spouses should be our best friends. If we find that someone else is growing closer to us than our own spouse, then we are in danger of an "emotional adultery" that could lead to worse things.

Our home must be in biblical order. Our children must be well-disciplined and well-cared for (1 Tim. 3:2-5). But at the same time, we must not take our concern about our children's behavior to the kind of extreme that demands they provide perfect models all the time "for the sake of the ministry." This kind of unrealistic expectation can lead to our children resenting and rebelling against the local church, especially if they are also expected to make continual sacrifices "for the sake of the ministry." That is part of what Paul meant when he said: "Fathers, do not exasperate your children" (Eph. 6:4, NIV).

Ministry Must Not Compete With Family. Meanwhile, we must not allow the ministry to deny us adequate time and energy to build a healthy relationship with our children, as is all too often the case with ministers. If that happens, then we're likely to learn the truth of a common formula for family disaster: Rules without relationship lead to rebellion.

This takes us to the matter of priorities. The proper order of priorities in our lives is God first, wife and children second, and ministry third. To keep this order intact, many times we must simply draw a line and decide that on a particular occasion, when ministry to others threatens to encroach on our ministry to our family, we must choose in favor of our family.

This is true even in seemingly small matters. Take the telephone, for example. When we're in the middle of dinner, a serious conversation with our spouse, or some other important family time, if the phone rings do we automatically jump up to answer it? If we do, then we may be saying to our family that the phone--and the people we minister to on the other end of the line--are more important to us than they are. There may be times when we must choose to let the phone ring. Otherwise, we may end up spending more time fathering others than being a true husband and father to our wife and children.

I once counseled with a man whose marriage was in trouble and who came to me to say that he believed his wife was hindering his ministry. He wanted a divorce.

In his estimation, his wife didn't share his zeal and his burden for the ministry. He lamented long and loud the great needs of the Church, which he declared to be the beloved Bride of Christ. He emphasized the blessing he could be to the Church if he just didn't have the problem of his wife's being a weight of resistance, which was causing him to sin against God by not fulfilling his preaching ministry. He even felt the Holy Spirit had given him scripture to justify his plans to divorce his wife: "Lay aside every weight, and the sin which doth so easily beset us" (Heb. 12:1).

I told him clearly that I believed such a divorce would be contrary to God's will, and that his marriage needed to take priority over his ministry until it could be restored to a loving relationship. I urged him to go home and love his wife the way Christ loved the Church. But he didn't seem convinced by what I said, and he was apparently disappointed that I didn't agree with his reasoning.

A few months later I saw him again, and he told me that he was working out his relationship with his wife. When I asked him what had changed his mind, he told me that one day in prayer he had been crying out to the Lord, "God, your Bride is in such bad shape; she needs help! I have to be free from my wife so that I can take care of your Church!"

Then God surprised him with His reply. He said, "Do you really think I'm going to entrust my Bride to you when you can't even take care of your own bride?" As the apostle, Paul posed the question to Timothy (1 Tim. 3:5): If we can't care for our own household, how can we care for the household of God?

6.) METHODS.

Hypocrisy is one of the greatest saboteurs of ministry. The problem of ministers whose practice doesn't match their preaching goes back to biblical times, as attested by Paul's words to Titus: "They claim to know God, but by their actions they deny him" (Titus 1:16, NIV).

We could paraphrase this passage today to say: "They profess that they're charismatic, present-truth, prophetic people. They confess that they're Christians and children of God. They claim to be God's ministers. But they deny him by their non-Christian, ungodly methods."

In our ministry methods, we must be what I like to call "rigidly righteous." We must have no mercy on the works of the flesh; we must treat them as deceptive enemies who are out to destroy us by manipulating us to do things that will bring death to our relationship with God. If we do not crucify our worldly flesh, it will crucify our spiritual life.

In ministry, as in any other endeavor, the end does not justify the means. We cannot conclude, for example, that in order to impress people more deeply with God's power and grace, we can justify exaggeration in our personal testimony or in relating some miracles that took place in our ministry. Maintaining proper methods precludes what I jokingly call "speaking evang-elastic-ally"--that is, stretching the truth. We must walk in absolute integrity.

I have read newspaper accounts before in which an evangelist was quoted as saying that thousands attended a meeting, where hundreds came forward to the altar. Yet I was at those meetings myself, and I knew that the numbers were considerably lower. When I asked the evangelists why they didn't tell the truth, they explained: "If I give numbers that are greater, more people will get excited and turn out the next night, and more will be saved. So my little lie results in more people going to heaven."

I doubt that "more souls" was the only motivation for such deception; the evangelist probably also wanted to look more successful. But even if evangelism were his only motivation, the method would still be wrong. The end does not justify the means, and a lie cannot serve the truth.

Honesty in Finances.

We must also practice absolute honesty in our handling of finances and be ethical in all our ministry dealings with others, especially in fundraising. Some ministries, for example, manufacture "crises" or use guilt manipulation to squeeze donations out of Christians. But we must be above those sorts of questionable tactics.

I read every book I could find on financial prosperity, and I must say that the faith movement brought forth some important truths concerning biblical methods in this area. Oral Roberts's book on seed faith was a particular help to my wife in gaining the biblical concept that we must sow money to reap money. The spiritual law of sowing and reaping has certainly worked in our lives: We began applying it long ago, and by the late 1970s we were completely out of debt. Since then we have mostly stayed out of debt and have personally continued to prosper as we give abundantly.

Sadly enough, however, some ministers have used this truth to take large "prove me offerings" for themselves. The truth they taught was right, but the minister's motives and methods were wrong. In light of that practice, I'm concerned about unscrupulous, self-promoting ministers using the truth of the "prophet's reward" and "prophetic offerings" to manipulate people selfishly. I anticipate that some prophetic ministers with the wrong motive will promise Christians in return for big offerings to their own ministries a prophet's reward. The promise of a continuing financial supply plus the miracles money can't buy are only parts of the prophet's reward. The Bible plainly speaks of a person being specially rewarded for blessing a prophet in the name of a prophet. But when Jesus made this statement He never intended it to be used as a tool for ministers to manipulate people for their own selfish purposes (Mt. 10:41). It is not wrong to inspire and motivate people by using biblical events as long as our motive is right, not trying to manipulate people for our own personal gain. It is not wrong to bring out the biblical truth on giving and use biblical illustrations to encourage people to practice the truths that bring prosperity, no more than it would be wrong to use the scriptures in praying and give testimonies of answered prayer to encourage people to pray more. The same is true concerning worship, witnessing, altar calls and any activity that is scriptural.

In addition, keeping our word, paying our bills, maintaining accurate records, and treating our staff members with basic kindness all come under the requirements of proper methods. Paul speaks in Romans of those "who hold the truth in unrighteousness" (Rom. 1:18). Such people have the truth of God, but they are not right in their methods. According to Paul, "The wrath of God is revealed" against them. If we expect to be used by God in ministry with His pleasure, especially in these last days and the Third Reformation that we have entered into we must be thoroughly transformed to God's nature of "rigid righteousness."

For forty years, the Israelites wandered in the wilderness without being circumcised. But when they crossed over the Jordan

River to take Canaan, God required that they cut away the flesh and consecrate themselves through circumcision. (Joshua 5:1-8).

The Charismatic Movement brought many Christians out of bondage giving them liberty and joy in the Holy Spirit. Denominational Christians came out of the Egyptian bondage of dead religion, but like the Moses generation they kept journeying but wandered in the wilderness, still carrying the flesh of ungodliness and not yet entering into God's promise land. I believe that God was gracious during that time and did not call to account many ministers who were not rigidly righteous in their methods.

Nevertheless, I also am convinced that the Prophetic-Apostolic Movement took the present truth Church over Jordan and into its Canaan to conquer it. God is not allowing His overcoming advancing Joshua generation saints to remain uncircumcised. He will require of us that we cut away the flesh of ungodly methods and consecrate ourselves to Him in holiness. And He will call us to account if we don't like He did Achan.

7.) MANNERS.

When Paul wrote Titus, he included in his letter a list of qualifications for an overseer, as well as reminders about how all the people were to behave. These instructions help us see the kind of manners that should characterize God's ministers:

> *Since an overseer is entrusted with God's work, he must be blameless--not overbearing, nor quick-tempered, not given to drunkenness, not violent, not pursuing dishonest gain. Rather he must be hospitable, one who loves what is good, who is self-controlled, upright, holy and disciplined....Remind the people to be subject to rulers and authorities, to be obedient, to be ready to do whatever is good, to slander no one, to be peaceable and considerate, and to show true humility to all men.* (Titus 1:7,8; 3:1,2)

All Christians, but especially Christian ministers, should be different from the world in their manners. Love must be the rule for their relations to others--and love is not just a feeling. Love is a principle we practice, a way of life. Love is gentle, polite, kind, and discreet; self-controlled, peaceable, considerate, and slow-tempered. In short, love is mannerly, and the manners of a Christian minister should show him or her to be a gentleman or a lady.

A Poor Example:

We once sent a team of several ministers overseas to bless a conference of ministers. All the prophets gave accurate prophetic words. The preaching of the ministers was sound, and many miracles accompanied their ministries. But the national coordinator requested that one of the visiting ministers in particular not come back to that nation.

Their complaint was not about his ministry, but his manners. He had been rude, demanding, selfish and disrespectful to most of those with whom he had come into contact, from waitresses in restaurants to the host coordinator. The host said he had to follow him making apologies for him. I and some of my leadership ministers counseled him when he returned. He would not acknowledge his bad manners and resented and refused our counsel. We released him from being an ordained minister with our Christian International Apostolic Network.

Even a seemingly little "M" like manners can close doors to people and their ministries. A prophet or any minister has no excuse for being rude, crude, ill-mannered or obnoxious. On the contrary, true ministers of God will portray proper, Christlike manners in their dealings and ministry with others.

Gentlemen Aren't "Sissies."

In the rural Oklahoma culture in which I was raised, the manners of a gentleman were not valued. Gentlemen were considered "sissies." I was taught as a boy to be rough and tough. So it took years of God working on me to teach me that His standard for Christian ministers was not a macho hardness, but rather a gentle kindness. I wonder how many other men might have the same kind of upbringing to have to overcome.

One requirement for ministers that is especially important here is that they "slander no one." Another translation says that we must "speak evil of no one." That means we must guard our tongues when talking about our relatives, our neighbors, our boss, our employees, our fellow ministers--even our enemies. Our speech, as Paul told the Colossians, should always be "full of grace, seasoned with salt" (Col. 4:6).

No Coarse Language.

Another type of speech that must be avoided is coarse language. Paul told the Ephesians: *"Do not let any unwholesome talk come out of your mouths, but only what is helpful for building others up"* (Eph. 4:29, NIV). Profanity, vulgarity, blasphemy, and other impure language simply have no place in the vocabulary of a minister of the gospel of Jesus Christ.

Jesus said, "*Out of the abundance of the heart the mouth speaks*" (Matt. 12:34). If we tend to use foul language under stress, then we need to get the foulness out of our heart. We must ask God to deliver us and to set a guard over our lips.

In whatever form, ill manners will tend to discredit our ministry. Are we on time for our appointments, or do we keep people waiting? Do we write thank you notes for gifts and other kindnesses, or do we forget to show gratitude? Do we wait our turn in conversation, or do we tend to interrupt others as they speak? Do we treat store clerks with respect, or are we impatient and demanding? Even in small matters, when we deal with others, we need to remember that we have no excuse for rudeness.

"Love is patient, love is kind. It does not envy, it does not boast, it is not proud. It is not rude, it is not self-seeking, it is not easily angered, it keeps no record of wrongs" (1 Cor. 13:4,5). Ministers of God are called to be ladies and gentlemen.

8.)   MONEY.

Money is neither good nor evil in itself. It is an inanimate object with neither virtue nor vice. Money is simply the medium of exchange for earthly things, just as faith is the medium of exchange for heavenly things. Money is merely earth's currency for purchasing human services and material items.

The Bible teaches that the love of money is the root of all evil (1 Tim. 6:10). But the Bible doesn't teach that it's wrong to be wealthy. Some of the richest people on earth in their day were some of God's chosen people, such as Abraham, David, Solomon, and Job.

It's God's will that His people prosper and be in good health, even as their soul prospers (3 John 2). God loves to give abundantly to His children, but they are not to have a love, which is an obsessive desire, for an abundance of earthly things. He promises that if we seek first His kingdom and His righteousness, then all the material things we need will be added to us (Matt. 6:33).

The Christian can have money, but money must not have the Christian. It's a matter of heart attitude, motive, and biblically ordered priorities. The love for the earthly power that wealth can give has been for many the instrument to indulge "the lust of the flesh, the lust of the eyes, and the pride of life," which the Apostle John calls the "world" and says, "If anyone loves the world, the love for the Father is not in him."(1 John 2:15,16). Money isn't sinful, but it can certainly provide the opportunity for sinful desires to be fulfilled, just as money can provide the means for the righteous to do great things for the kingdom of God.

The Love of Money.

The Bible confirms what we might conclude from some headlines in recent years: The love of money can get ministers in deep trouble. Paul wrote to Timothy:

People who want to get rich fall into temptation and a trap and into many foolish and harmful desires that plunge men into ruin and destruction. *"For the love of money is a root of all kinds of evil. Some people, eager for money, have wandered from the faith and pierced themselves with many griefs"* (1 Tim. 6:9,10).

Sadly enough, in recent times we often heard an extreme teaching that left the impression that the wealthier you were, the more material things you had, the greater proof it was that you were spiritual and had great faith. On the contrary, however, if material gain shows that a person is godly, then all the rich people of the world should be godly--and we know that is obviously not true.

I believe that if we trust and obey the Lord, He will supply all our needs and prosper us. But we can never assume that simply because we have cars and boats and houses and lands, those things are a sign of God's approval on our lives. Paul assures us that those who *"suppose that gain is godliness"* are mistaken. On the other hand, *"godliness with contentment is great gain"* (1 Tim. 6:5,6).

Consequently, we must realize that if we pray for wealth, we are praying for temptations, snares, and heartaches. The higher we go up the mountain of financial "success," the less the vegetation grows, the harder the wind blows, and the lonelier it is. I've seen very few ministers who became wealthy and yet were still able to maintain integrity in their other "M's."

For that reason, we should follow Paul's warning to *"flee from all this, and pursue righteousness, godliness, faith, love, endurance and gentleness"* (v. 11, NIV). To that we can add Jesus' own words: *"Watch out! Be on your guard against all kinds of greed; a man's life does not consist in the abundance of his possessions"* (Luke 12:15).

Practical Guidelines.

Christian ministers would do well to follow a few practical guidelines for their use of money. In particular, we should note that of all the "10 M's," money is probably the most sensitive area for the relationship between itinerant and local ministers. The giving and receiving of offerings and honorariums can lead to touchy issues. I have pastored locally and also traveled in ministry, so I can tell you from firsthand experience that both pastors and traveling ministers are sometimes abused, and their funds misused.

At CI, we have made it a policy always to do the best we can financially for a guest speaker, but we can't speak for everyone. Local ministries range widely in their attitudes toward honorariums: Some are quite generous, others are downright dishonest, and most give at an average level.

Guidelines for the Local Minister.

I would offer a few simple rules for the local minister, usually a pastor, who invites a guest speaker in to speak at a church meeting or conference. First, you should have an established minimum that you give anyone who comes to minister. At the present time in the United States, I would recommend that this minimum be between three hundred and one thousand dollars based on the maturity of the minister and how effective his ministry is to your saints.

In fifty years of extensive traveling ministry, I have received anywhere from $100 to $5,000 for one service, and from $1,000 to $10,000 for a week of meetings at one church. These were special honorariums given me personally as a guest minister.

Standard practice is for the local ministry to pay for all travel expenses round trip. If guest ministers are on a long itinerary, then general policy is to pay the travel expense to bring them from where they last ministered and to take them to the next place of ministry.

In my experience, most denominational churches don't take up a special offering to give exclusively to the guest minister, especially those with larger congregations (over 500 people). Instead, they usually have a set amount for Sunday meetings and midweek services. Non-denominational churches, on the other hand, tend to take up a special offering to give exclusively to the minister.

Factors Affecting the Honorarium.

A number of factors will determine whether the honorarium is a minimum offering, average or abundant: Did the local and translocal ministers allow God to get involved in the honorarium? Did the pastor initiate the invitation to the guest minister, or did the guest minister request opportunity to speak at the church? Is the guest minister seasoned, with years of proven ministry, or is he or she still young in the maturing process?

Perhaps most important, was the ministry to the church average, or did the guest minister give him or herself to extra hours of ministry in prophesying to individuals, praying for the sick, or being instrumental in causing many souls to be saved, bringing new families to the church, or raising money for the church? The minister who just teaches for an hour, fails to pray for anyone, and simply leaves to go eat and have fellowship should receive different consideration from one who preaches for an hour and then goes on to prophesy and minister to scores of people the gifts of the Spirit, either laying on hands individually or praying for large groups at a time.

Avoiding Discouragement.

It can be quite discouraging to be dedicated, anointed ministers who give themselves unselfishly to the saints for hours of heavy ministry when the pastor gives them a minimal offering. In that situation, much grace is required to keep a positive attitude and the joy of the Lord.

Let me share a vital truth and attitude that has kept my wife and me from becoming discouraged, resentful or bitter when offerings were not in proportion to ministry given or did not come close to meeting our basic needs. Itinerant ministers must take the attitude: "I'm working directly for God, and He writes my paycheck." We must always remember that God is our source, not the local pastor, the church, or anyone else.

No doubt God doesn't make money in heaven and then send it to us on earth. Money is made and distributed on earth by people. But God is the One who is faithful to lead people to give according to His promise to us.

When my wife and I took this attitude, we found that God will always find someone who is willing to respond to His direction to give above average. Their giving is then able to make up for those who did not have the heart and vision to give sufficiently to match our ministry and meet our needs.

Some Personal Examples.

To give an example or two: In our early days of ministry in 1959, I ministered every night for two weeks in a particular church.

My wife was in her ninth month of pregnancy with our son Tom, who is now 55.

Every night I preached and ministered prophetically to ten to twenty people. Though I was there fourteen days, the pastor never took up an offering for me until the last night. There were about a hundred and twenty-five people regularly attending, with many new people each night.

The pastor gave me the offering in an envelope just as I was leaving to take my wife to our home in Washington State to have her baby. When I opened the envelope, I found only eighty-five dollars in it. My heart sank.

The pastor could easily have received five times that much for me if the opportunity had been given to the people more often during the two weeks of ministry. But as it was, those eighty-five dollars was all we had to our name. And I needed several hundred dollars to put my wife in the hospital for delivery.

After grumbling and complaining awhile, we remembered that God was our employer, and He would write the paycheck. When people fail, God remains faithful.

When we arrived in Yakima Valley, Washington, where the baby was to be delivered, a minister invited me to speak for three nights. The honorarium he gave me was two hundred and forty-three dollars. Another minister had me speak only on Sunday morning, but gave me seventy-five dollars. In that one service, I received almost as much as I'd been given for two weeks of preaching, praying and prophesying in that other church. We were able to pay the total cost of $220.00 for both the hospital and our doctor who delivered the baby.

God keeps the record of our labor of love. When pastors and others don't do us right, God will cause others to provide for us with super-abundance. Over all these years, the economy has changed, and the figures have increased about ten times. But the principle of God's faithfulness has never changed.

Many years ago, for example, we ran into a problem when we discovered that a group that had invited me to minister did not believe in women ministers. My wife nearly always traveled with me in ministry as a co-speaker and prophetic minister; she and I came as a "package deal," and for years our hosts have willingly paid travel expenses for both of us. So I insisted that she be with me on this trip as well. But our hosts refused to pay for my wife's ticket, which was over six hundred dollars.

We paid for the ticket. Then, after four days of ministry at the gathering, I received only a thousand dollars. That meant the two of us only netted four hundred dollars for four days of preaching and prophesying to hundreds of people. It was the lowest offering I had received in over a decade.

Nevertheless, God is faithful. He had me speaking in a four-day conference the following week that not only paid my wife's ticket and covered all our expenses, but also gave us an offering of four thousand, five hundred dollars.

The traveling minister must realize that God works on the law of averages. He will find faithful people who will give sufficiently to meet all our needs according to His riches in glory (Phil. 4:19).

Some Unethical Practices.

In our early years of ministry, we also encountered some unethical practices on the part of a few local pastors. On several occasions, a pastor would use our name and ministry as the reason for taking an offering. At least several hundred dollars would be given by the people (we knew, because individuals would tell us later how much they had given)--yet as we were leaving, the pastor would give us a sealed envelope with less than a hundred dollars in it.

This practice is obviously dishonest. It's wrong for a pastor to urge his people to give, saying every penny of the offering will go to the guest minister, and then in reality give only a small portion of the offering to the guest.

The traveling ministry is one of the few professions in which you agree to render services without any idea of what the financial remuneration will be. You can see why some ministers, after being cheated a few times in this way, want to have a guarantee up front or perhaps even a contract signed before they will agree to minister. I have always refused to set a money amount requirement on my ministry. I know a few of the ministers with great ministries and international television ministry require a minimum of $25,000.00 dollars for a one day meeting. They say they need that much to pay for their airplane to fly them and their assistants to your place and back. They compare themselves to ex-presidents who receive 25-50,000 dollars honorarium for speaking at a conference, university graduation or some other type of gathering.

Unethical Itinerants:

In a similar way, pastors can tell you about visiting ministers who have demanded the right to take their own offering. Other itinerants have been known to beg and press for funds to support an overseas orphanage, and then never send any of the offerings to the institution as promised. Still others have used biblical principles of giving to prophetic ministry in order to manipulate people into giving thousands of dollars. In fact, I know of some churches that have been so stripped financially by meetings held by these kinds of itinerant ministers that it took several months to recover.

Obviously, unethical practices in the "M" of money are not limited to any one group. Both local and translocal ministers have been guilty of abuses.

Ministers of every type do well to remember that God considers our handling of money a serious business. He declares in the Bible that the way we acquire and dispense money will be a determining factor in whether God releases to us our true riches of spiritual ministry (Luke 16:11). If a person uses money selfishly and unethically, God says that person will not use spiritual gifts and anointing properly.

9.)   MORALITY.

It should go without saying that sexual immorality has no place in the life of a Christian minister or any child of God and that our firm standard must be sexual purity. But I would estimate that up to a third of the charismatic and Pentecostal ministers in our generation have fallen into some form of sexual immorality. I know of about fifty such pastors. If what we have seen on television is the tip of the iceberg, can you imagine what might be going on in secret?

Years ago when I was in Bible college, Stanley Frodsham, an early Pentecostal teacher, said that in the 1930s he was casting demons out of a man, and one particular demon claimed to be a prince of devils who had just received an assignment from hell. He insisted that he had been given authority to release a new horde of demons of adultery and deception within the Church. Judging from what I've seen in the last few decades, that devil may well have been giving an accurate account of his assignment.

Honor God With Your Body:

The Bible warns us against sexual impurity--all sexual activity outside the bond of marriage--in no uncertain terms:

Do you not know that the wicked will not inherit the kingdom of God? Do not be deceived: Neither the sexually immoral nor idolaters nor adulterers nor male prostitutes nor homosexual offenders...will inherit the kingdom of God....Flee from sexual immorality. All other sins a man commits are outside his body, but he who sins sexually sins against his own body. Do you not know that your body is a temple of the Holy Spirit, who is in you, whom you have received from God? You are not your own; you were bought at a price. Therefore, honor God with your body" (1 Cor. 6:9,10,18-20).

Of course, sexual immorality also includes illicit sexual fantasies, pornography, and sexually arousing films or television programs. These things lead us into temptation and wear down our resistance to it. Though we sometimes desire to be tempted and tantalized by the prospect of sin, God wants us to run the other direction. So with the words of the Lord's Prayer, we must say to God, "Lead us not into temptation" (Matt. 6:13).

Heart Attitudes:

In fact, according to Jesus' words, sexual impurity begins before the overt action of immorality. It grows in the hidden attitudes of our heart. "You have heard it said," the Lord noted, "Do not commit adultery.' But I tell you that anyone who looks at a woman lustfully has already committed adultery with her in his heart" (Matt. 5:27,28).

We may have a wrong desire to act immorally, but not have an opportunity to fulfill that desire. Yet the act of entertaining that wrong desire is itself sinful. I had one minister tell me that the way he overcame negative thoughts was quoting a particular scripture, "God forbid that I should glory (think, meditate) save in the cross of Jesus Christ." Jesus overcame the wrong thinking from the devil by quoting Scripture (Gal. 6:14; Matt. 4:1-11).

Once an immoral sexual act has in fact been committed, the resulting bond, I believe, is deeper than we realize. Paul says: "Do you not know that he who unites himself with a prostitute is one with her in body? For it is said, 'The two will become one flesh'" (1 Cor. 6:16). Considering that union, I think anyone who has had an illicit sexual relationship needs to be cut free from that bond and receive inner healing. In fact, I personally believe that if a man joins himself to a prostitute, he in some sense takes on all her sins and joins them to his own.

In light of these realities, we do well to heed Paul's words to the Ephesians: "Among you there must not be even a hint of sexual immorality, or of any kind of impurity" (Eph. 5:3). The tragic results of failure in this area are sure to shipwreck a ministry.

Male/Female Relationships in the Church:

Men and women of God must develop the attitude Paul exhorted Timothy to take toward the opposite sex. He said to treat "older women as mothers and younger women as sisters, with absolute purity" (1 Tim. 5:2 NIV). I believe this instruction would rule out full body embraces for greetings between Christian brothers and sisters in the Lord, as well as full, long kissing on the mouth. Men should give women at most the same kind of quick "hug and peck" they would give to a female relative.

No minister suddenly decides one day that he or she will commit adultery with a friend's spouse, a secretary, a counselee, or a worship leader. Most sexual sins start out as a seed thought or a seemingly innocent or kindly action. What starts out right can end up wrong if not properly guarded and directed.

In the parable of the sower, Jesus spoke of a man who had sown nothing but good seed in his field. Yet as it began to grow, the sower noticed that the field also contained weed seeds. When the man asked how that had come about, the answer was that an enemy had sown bad seed in the field during the night (Mt. 13:24-30).

Like that sower, we may sow only the seeds of a pure attitude and proper action. But our enemies, the devil, and our carnal nature, will sow weed seeds of the lust of the flesh, the lust of the eyes, and the pride of life. Then subtly one of these seeds will sprout right alongside the good seed, and suddenly a look, a touch, a complimentary word will activate a fleshly, sensual desire and suggestion.

While in seed form, the two kinds of attitude and behavior look almost identical. But once they sprout, people who are on guard against weed seeds will immediately notice a slight difference. They will be aware that the inward feelings and reactions of their heart and soul are just a little different.

At that point, the Holy Spirit will whisper with a warning: "Beware; the weed seed sown by the enemy has just sprouted." If the person is sensitive to the Holy Spirit and has a heart to be rigidly righteous, he or she will immediately pluck up the weed by not repeating that thought or action. The old saying that "an ounce of prevention is worth a pound of cure" is certainly true in these situations.

Two Applications:

I believe there are at least two applications to Jesus' comment that to lust after someone in your mind is to commit adultery in God's sight. First, Jesus was saying that if a man or woman deliberately meditates on adultery with mental images, to the extent of visualizing the action and sensing the fleshly feeling of a sexual relationship with a particular person, then even though the outward sin was not committed, yet the sin of immorality took place within the heart. It was committed through deliberate desire, daydreaming, visualization, imagination, and willful meditation.

The second application indicates that the beginning of a sin in its seed thought stage is just as serious as the full-grown plant of the act. For if the seed is not rejected, it will surely sprout. And if the seed sprouts and is allowed to grow, it will eventually come to harvest time when we reap the consequences of a sinful act.

It's not a sin to be tempted with a lustful thought. But it's wrong to meditate upon the sinful suggestion with desire and enjoyment. We can't keep dirty birds from flying by and catching our attention. But we don't have to let them light on our heads, build a nest, lay eggs, and hatch other vultures which love rotten, stinking flesh.

Every Thought in Captivity: Paul declares that we should bring every thought and imagination of the mind into captivity to the mind of Christ--that is, to holy, virtuous biblical principles, practices, and thoughts. One minister has said that when he finds his mind drifting into fleshly daydreaming, he shouts the scriptural text, "God forbid that I should glory (think, meditate) save in the cross (death to the flesh) of Jesus Christ!"

The only offensive weapon Christians have in the armor of God described by Paul (Eph. 6:13-17) is "the sword of the Spirit, which is the word of God." Jesus overcame every temptation of Satan during their encounter in the wilderness by quoting scripture. We too can find numerous scriptural texts to be used against every temptation and suggestion of Satan and the selfish flesh.

If any touch, look, or close working relationship creates sexually-inclined thoughts or feelings, then they must be crucified immediately. The scriptural admonition to "flee...youthful lusts" (2 Tim. 2:22) and to "abstain from all appearance of evil" (1 Thess. 5:22) must never be forgotten as we maintain and mature the "M" of morality. (For more on this subject, see "The Deception of Ministerial Mates" in the section "Pitfalls for Prophetic Ministers.")

10.) MOTIVE.

When I first went to Bible college, I had what I thought was a vision to be a missionary to India. But after I studied that country and learned how terrible the conditions were there, I lost my "vision." It turned out to be, not a true vision from God, but only a romantic idea of my teenage years.

Looking back now, I realize that if I'm honest, I must admit that my motives in wanting to be a missionary were not pure. I had not seen myself struggling in India with poverty, hunger, sickness, and other poor conditions. Instead, I had imagined myself standing on the platform, preaching, laying hands on the sick, raising the dead, bringing thousands to the Lord. I saw myself writing back home to my family about it all and having them say, "Look! Our boy has made it. Look at the miracles. Wow--he's somebody!"

I was motivated by what I thought was an opportunity for personal glory. How many other ministers, if they were honest, would admit that they have had to crucify that same motivation?

Jesus emphasized that the hidden motives of the heart must be recognized and purified. We won't be judged just for our actions, but for our deeds/works--which includes both our actions and our motives.

For example, Jesus said, "Be careful not to do your `acts of righteousness' before men, to be seen by them. If you do, you will have no reward from your Father in heaven" (Matt. 6:1). People look at our outward behavior, but God looks on the intentions of the heart (1 Sam. 16:7). Do we minister in order to serve, or in order to be seen? Are we "addicted...to the ministry of the saints" (1 Cor. 16:15KJV), or do we want to be recognized as great ministers? Are we motivated by a desire to fulfill God's will, or by some personal drive, such as a lust for power, fame, pleasure, or wealth?

In short, do we minister out of a heart full of God's love? If not, then the Scripture says that our ministry is nothing: "If I have the gift of prophecy and can fathom all mysteries and all knowledge, and if I have a faith that can move mountains, but have not love, I am nothing. If I give all, I possess to the poor and surrender my body to the flames, but have not love; I gain nothing."

BEWARE THE WEAK LINK

We should emphasize that few if any ministers could make a perfect "score" with regard to all ten "M's." We all have room for growth, improvement, and correction. That's why all the CIAN ministers are required to allow those to whom they minister a chance to complete a form evaluating their "10 M's." We realize that each of us has areas in which we need to grow and that others may see such areas more clearly than we can ourselves. Most people have blind spots concerning certain areas of their lives.

Nevertheless, we should never assume that just because most of these areas in our life might be in good shape, we can, therefore, neglect the others. It only takes one problem area to derail a ministry.

Out on the grounds of our ministry's campus, where new construction is taking place, we have a large bulldozer sitting idle. The motor still runs well and the body is in good shape, but the caterpillar treads on it are worn out, and we've been told that the rest of the machine is not worth the cost of replacing the treads. So the failure of a single part to work properly has stopped this powerful machine from being used.

The same is true of the "ten Ms." It only takes one part to break down for our entire ministry to come to a screeching halt. So we must be diligent to give our attention regularly to every one of these areas. And we should keep in mind that even an area we normally consider our greatest strength, if left unguarded, can easily become a double weakness.

As the old saying goes, a chain is only as strong as its weakest link. Imagine this picture: You're hanging over a cliff of tragic disaster in your ministry. The only thing holding you safe is a chain whose ten links are these ten "M's" in your own life. If any one of those links is in danger of breaking, just how safe are you?

Don't become so proud and confident of the links of the chain that are functioning well that you ignore the one link that needs strengthening. Decide today to begin making a regular inspection of each link--each one of the "ten Ms" in your life. Strengthening each one is the best way to maintain and mature a godly character that will provide your ministry with a solid and stable foundation for growth. Those who diligently keep these "10 M's" in biblical order will maintain and mature in their personal lives and prophetic ministry. They will remain true ministers and when they stand before the Lord Jesus Christ they will hear those all-important words of Jesus Christ, "Well done, good and faithful servant; you have been faithful over a few things, I will make you ruler over many things. Enter into the joy of your Lord." Mt. 25:21,23. And Jesus says to His overcomers: "I will give to eat from the tree of life, which is in the midst of the paradise of God." "Hold fast what you have until I come. He who overcomes and keeps my works until the end, to him I will give power over the nations—as I also received from My Father." "He who overcomes shall be clothed in white garments, and I will not blot out his name from the Book of Life; I will confess his name before My Father and before His angels." "To him who overcomes I will grant to sit with Me on My throne, as I also overcame and sat down with My Father on His throne." There is nothing more important in this life or eternity than to be an OVERCOMER! Live the Life, pay the Price, Be an Overcomer.

Chapter 5
The Prophet Balaam:
A True Prophesier but a False Prophet
A True Ministry but a False Minister

The prophet Balaam should be thoroughly studied by every minister and especially prophets. The story of Balaam proves that a person can have a true ministry but be a false minister. The following scriptures found in the Old Testament cover the story of Balaam. Reading them, one would think that Balaam was a true and mighty prophet of God. (Num. 22:1--24:25; 31:8-16; Deut. 23:5,6; Josh. 13:22, 24:9,10; Micah 6:5). The "God" that talked to Balaam is the same God (ELOHIYM) who created all things, talked to Abraham and is the God of the Bible. Balaam could give a true word of the Lord, yet he became a false prophet in his personal attitude and way of life. His example teaches us that judging the prophet and judging the prophetic word are two different matters. A person can have a true ministry but be a false person. Though we are using the example of a minister who is a prophet, these principles apply to all ordained ministers, Christian business leaders and all Christians.

MINISTERS JUDGED BY A HIGHER STANDARD

Apostle James declares that ministers who teach others and are representing Jesus as one of Christ's fivefold ministers will be judged by a higher standard than non-leadership Christians. God demands more and expects more of leaders than followers. God is not a respector of persons, but He does require a higher standard of those who have the higher ministerial responsibility of representing the ministry of Jesus Christ.

"*Not many [of you] should become teachers (self-constituted censors and reprovers of others), my brethren, for you know that we (teachers) will be judged by a higher standard and with greater severity [than other people; thus we assume the greater accountability and the more condemnation].*" James 3:1 AMP. "*When we teachers of religion, who should know better, do wrong, our punishment will be greater than it would be for others.*" LB.

Example of The Prophet Minister and His prophetic Ministry:

The prophetic ministry of the Prophet is judged in three areas. **First,** his prophetic message must conform to biblical truth. **Second**, objective, verifiable statements about the past and present can be checked against the facts. **Third**, predictions for the future are judged by whether they come to pass.

Judging A Minister:

We must judge whether a minister is true or false in a different way. True and false prophetic ministers are discerned by their character, the spirit of wisdom, the fruit of the Holy Spirit in their personal lives, and the fruit of their ministry that remains after the initial manifestations of miracles, prophecies and preaching.

As we read all the scriptural references to Balaam throughout the Bible, especially those references in the New Testament, we discover his iniquities and character flaws. To his credit, we must note that Balaam held to one important prophetic rule. He refused to prophesy anything except what God had given him to say. In fact, he even declared to King Balak of Moab that he could prophesy no differently even if he gave him half his kingdom. Yet Balaam was nevertheless ambitious for fame, fortune and prestige. The New Testament scriptures state that he was perverse which means he was stubborn and self-willed, and he loved the wages of unrighteousness. He was underhanded and manipulative. Probably the main reason Balaam would only prophesy exactly what God told him was he figured that big angel with the drawn sword had followed him and was listening to everything he said.

Some "Ms" in Order, Some Not:
Evidently, though Balaam had some of his "Ten M's" in order, he had enough of them out of order to cause him to be judged a false prophet by **Jesus** (Rev. 2:14), **Peter** (2 Pet. 2:15,16) and **Jude** (Jude 11) in the New Testament. Please note their description of the character of these false ministers and the effects and fruitlessness of their life and ministry.

"These men are spots in you love feasts, while they feast with you without fear, serving only themselves. They are clouds without water, carried about by the winds; late autumn trees without fruit, twice dead, pulled up by the roots; raging waves of the sea, foaming up their own shame; wandering stars for whom is reserved the blackness of darkness forever. Woe to them! *"For they have gone in the way of Cain, run greedily in the error of BALAAM for profit, and perished in the rebellion of Korah." Jude 1:11-13.*

Jesus said to the Church at Pergamos: "But I have a few things against you, because you have there those who hold the doctrine of BALAAM, who taught Balak to put a stumbling block before the children of Israel; to eat things sacrificed to idols and to commit sexual immorality."Rev.2:14

> *But these (false teachers) are like natural brute beasts made to be caught and destroyed, speak evil of things that they do not understand, and will utterly perish in their own corruption, and will receive the wages of unrighteousness, as those who count it a pleasure to carouse in the daytime. They are spots and blemishes, carousing in their own deceptions while they feast with you. They have eyes full of adultery and cannot cease from sin, enticing unstable souls. They have a heart trained in covetous practices, and are accursed children. They have forsaken the right way and gone astray, following the way of BALAAM the son of Beor, who loved the wages of unrighteousness; but he was*

rebuked for his iniquity; a dumb donkey speaking with a man's voice restrained the madness of the prophet. These are wells without water; clouds carried by a tempest, for whom is reserved the blackness of darkness forever. (2Pet.2:12-17)

Balaam's "M's" of message, ministry, manhood, and morality appear to have been in order, but his "M's" of motive, maturity, methods, and money were not. Though he was committed to speaking nothing but pure words from the Lord, yet he was self-determined and lusted enough for power and possession to persist in hoping that God would allow him to prophesy something that Balak would reward.

God told Balaam when he first inquired about going to Balak that he was not to go and prophesy a curse on Israel. After further offers of reward, however, Balaam inquired again of God to see if there was not some way he could go. God told Balaam that he could go if the men came for him again. Yet there is no indication in the scriptural text that this confirmation came before Balaam saddled up his donkey to go to Balak to prophesy against Israel.

A self-willed prophet takes a mile when God gives an inch. God was angered because Balaam went ahead anyhow. He sent an angel to cause a breakdown in the prophet's transportation so that he would be stopped. The donkey saw God's angel of providential restriction, but the prophet Balaam was too blinded by his self-will to see that God was involved in his frustrating situation.

A Point for Prophets to Ponder:

Judging from Balaam's story, even a donkey can discern the spiritual world and God's divine restrictions better than a prophet blinded by lust for riches, power and promotion. Prophets with the sinful character flaws of Balaam allow the potential rewards of riches to influence them toward displeasing God in their striving to please people in hopes of earthly gain.

Balaam tried to please God and serve Mammon at the same time. He had the root problem that Apostle Paul calls the root of all evil, the love of money (1 Tim. 6:10). Indications are that Balaam held a secret resentment in his heart toward Jehovah for not allowing him to prophesy anything that Balak desired he prophesy against Israel--thus causing him to lose all of Balak's promised riches and promotion.

Balaam could not prophesy anything except what God told him, but he finally by-passed that restriction by not prophesying in the name of Jehovah. Instead, he pulled upon his prophetic insight and gave counsel to the Moabites and Midianites about how they could destroy the Israelites by causing them to sin against God by adultery and idolatry (Rev. 2:14; Num.25:1-13). By doing so, Balaam finally received the riches and position he wanted, but he was also destroyed with the Midianites under the judgment of God (Josh. 13:22).

SEEING PROPHETS AS GOD SEES THEM

When we read the account of Balaam in Numbers, he does not look like a false or wrongly motivated prophet. Only in light of Peter's, Jude's and Jesus' comments about Balaam do we begin to see him as God saw him. If we were to judge this prophet only by the accuracy of his prophecies, we would have to declare him a true prophet. The average minister today would have him on their television programs and brag on his accuracy as a prophet and his integrity as a man of God.

Balaam prophesied only what God spoke to him even though he was offered great riches to prophesy differently. The references in Numbers make him look like a man of integrity in the prophetic ministry who resisted all temptations. In fact, he gives the only Messianic prophecy in the book of Numbers, *"A Star shall come out of Jacob; A Scepter shall rise out of Israel."* Balaam prophesied the scripture that we all love to quote, *"God is not a man that He should lie, nor a son of man that He should repent. Has He said, and will He not do? Or has He spoken and will He not make it good?* He also prophesied that when God's people had no iniquity or wickedness and the shout of the King was in their midst, they could not be cursed. He was the greatest prophet among his peers. He had a reputation which extended for hundreds of miles that those he blessed were blessed and those he cursed were cursed. "I know that he whom you bless is blessed, and he whom you curse is cursed." Nu.22:6.

So on what basis does the New Testament declare Balaam to be a false prophet? His false status is only perceived by God's Spirit of discernment, which searches the heart and motive. The Scriptures declare that human beings judge by outward looks and performances, but God judges the heart, weighs the spirit and identifies the motive behind the performance (1 Sam. 16:7; Prov. 16:2).

Motive Plus Action Equals Deed:

The book of Revelation says that every person's eternal reward and destiny will be determined by his or her deeds/works... The "works" by which all people will be judged are not just actions but are a combination of the act and the motive behind it. So in judging whether someone is a true or false minister, God evaluates the person's motive as well as ministry, the person, and the performance.

Several incidents recorded in Scripture show people who seem to be right nevertheless giving false prophecies and then being judged as false prophets. But Balaam is the only one who portrays the reality that a prophet can give accurate prophecies and yet be a wrong enough person on the inside to be judged a false prophet. Sadly enough, most Christians would not realize that a Balaam type prophet is a false prophet. Most of them only know the passage in Deuteronomy (18:22) that declares a person's "true prophet" status is determined by whether the word that a person gives is accurate and comes to pass.

Balaam spoke only God-directed words, and they came to pass. But the New Testament uses him as an example of what a prophet should not be and do. God is more concerned about the purity of His prophets than the accuracy of their prophecies; He values the men and women themselves and their motives as well as their message and ministry.

WOLVES IN SHEEP'S CLOTHING

Listen to the words of Jesus concerning inward spirit and motivation: "Beware of false prophets which come to you in sheep's clothing, but inwardly they are ravening wolves. Ye shall know them by their fruits....Not everyone that saith unto me, Lord, Lord, shall enter into the kingdom of heaven: but he that doeth the will of my Father, which is in heaven. Many will say to me in that day, Lord, Lord, have we not given true prophecies in your name? And in thy name have cast out devils? And in thy name done many wonderful works? But Jesus will say to those who had great ministry on the outside but were not righteous on the inside, depart from me, ye that work iniquity" (Matt. 7:15,16, 21-23).The preachers that Jesus is speaking these word to are ministers with accurate teaching, prophesying and preaching, and some with even miraculous, but at the same time they are workers of iniquity.

Jesus said a prophet or any minister can have the outward clothing and ministry of a sheep but the inward spirit and motivation of a wolf. Though they do the works that Jesus promised believers could do, yet they are not righteous--not right inside. Jesus actually said He would not allow them into heaven.

Being Intimate With God Required.

The verb "to know" is used in the Hebrew of the Old Testament to convey the intimate relationship between husband and wife, as in "Adam knew his wife Eve" (Gen 4:1). I think Jesus' use of the word "know" here conveys a similar meaning in a metaphorical sense.

When speaking of these false ministers, Jesus says that at one time, they went through the spiritual "legal ceremony" of being married to Him by being born again and called to the ministry. They took the power of attorney of their "husband" (Christ) and wrote checks on the bank of heaven, signing it with the name of Jesus. Now they prophesy and work wonderful works by God's grace, faith, and divine enablement. But they never allow Jesus' life and motive to become their motivation and purpose for ministry. So on that day, Jesus will say to them that He never knew them.

All Christian Ministers must guard against self-deception, self-justification, and improper motivation. So we need others to help us see ourselves in areas where we have blind spots. The book of Proverbs tells us that "all the ways of a man are clean in his own eyes" (Pr. 16:2), and the prophet Jeremiah said, "The heart is deceitful above all things, and desperately wicked; who can know it?" (Jer. 17:9).

For that reason, every fivefold minister needs to submit to someone whom he or she respects enough to be willing to listen when the other person provides instruction and correction. That is why in our Christian International Apostolic Network of ministers of which I am the founder and Bishop Apostolic Overseer, we have established a structure of accountability: Bishop Bill Hamon is accountable to some senior apostles outside his organization and also to his Board of Directors; the CIAN ministers are accountable to the Bishop and His apostolic Team of senior leaders over the Network. Everyone needs to be a member of a ministerial association with workable and trusting relationship and accountable and not a loner separated off to himself. The following scripture gives insight concerning why a minister would isolate himself from other ministers. "A man who isolates himself seeks his own desire; He rages against all wise judgment." Pro.18:1. The old analogy statement is so true for this type of person---the banana that gets separated from the bunch is the one that gets peeled and devoured.

Every Minister and Christian who stands before God will hear one of two statements:

"Well done good and faithful servant!"
or
"Depart from me you worker of iniquity!"

Chapter 6
Achan and the "My Ministry Syndrome"

Why the Severity of God's Judgment on Achan? This is a living demonstration of one of God's people yielding to the lust of the eyes, lust of the flesh and the pride of life. Achan confessed to Joshua that he SAW a beautiful Babylonian garment, the gold and the silver, and he took them, and hid them in his tent.

Achan's outward sin was to take from the conquered city of Jericho a Babylonian garment, a two-pound bar of gold, and about eight pounds of silver (Joshua 6:17-19; 7:1-26). The sin was serious because God had explicitly declared that all the gold, silver, bronze and iron was devoted to God's treasury. He had further said that if any soldiers took it for themselves, they would be accursed and would incur God's curse on all Israel as well.

Everything else, including all humans and animals in Jericho, were to be killed and then destroyed by fire. If any broke God's commandment, they would receive the same judgment decreed for Jericho. Achan did just that, so he and his family and animals were stoned to death by the Israelites, then burned and covered with a heap of stones.

A NEW PLACE IS A DANGEROUS PLACE

God's severest judgments are manifest when He is establishing His people in a new place of restoration truth and ministry. For that same reason, He struck Ananias and Sapphira dead for being deceitful when He was establishing the New Testament Church (Acts 5:1-11).

The Lord's purpose in such severity is to produce the reverential fear of God within the people and to let all know that God is serious about the principles He is establishing for His new movement.

The Prophetic-Apostolic Movement brought the Church "across Jordan" in its restoration journey to possess its promised Canaan land. The Church has now entered its Third & Final Reformation which has engaged the Body of Christ into its "Army of the Lord" warfare just as Joshua and his army of the Lord engaged in the first battle of Canaan against Jericho. If this is a divinely established fact, then that means judgment has begun with the house of God, and His severity in judging all disobedience has begun to be manifest in the Church since the 3rd Reformation's beginning on earth was divinely decreed in 2008. The full beginning and God's purpose for the 3rd Reformation is in my twelfth book, "Prophetic Scriptures Yet To Be Fulfilled."

ACHAN'S SINFUL CHARACTER FLAW AND PITFALL

What caused Achan to sin as he did when thousands of his fellow Israelite soldiers resisted the temptation? When Joshua asked Achan for his reasons, he replied, "I saw, I coveted, I took, I put it in my tent." Clearly, his root problem was selfishness which produced pride that caused him to rebel against God's commands given by Joshua. In the English language, the middle letter in SIN is "I". When you crucify the self-life of "I" and reduce it to "O" it changes SIN into SON True sonship in Jesus Christ is accomplished by us dying to self and allowing the life of Christ to be made manifest in our mortal bodies (2 Cor. 4:10-11; Gal. 2:20).

If we fail to move through the Seventh chapter of Romans, which is the chapter revealing Christians in bondage to the "self-life; and enter into the eighth chapter of Romans which reveals saints living "In the Spirit," then we will end up praying the prayer that Paul prayed at the end of chapter seven: "Oh, wretched man that I am! Who shall deliver me from [this self-oriented life] of death?" (Rom. 7:24).

"My Ministry Syndrome."

This is the sinful character flaw I call the "My Ministry Syndrome." Achan's weed seed attitude was selfishness and concern only for "me and mine" with no concern for others with similar needs and opportunities. Achan was self-promoting and possessive without regard for directions given by the leadership. He was a loner without the team ministry concept. Christians with the "Achan spirit and attitude" are destined to commit a serious sin that will cause their destruction as it did for Achan.

The other 600,000 soldiers had also spent time in the wilderness (parallel to our preparation for ministry); made sacrifices (times of financial lack and small offerings); gone without change of raiment (lack of new ministry opportunities); and avoided the temptation to grab the gold and silver (bigger offerings or salary). They had endured the same apprenticeship training for warfare in the desert. Even Joshua, the commander-in-chief, did not manifest a presumptuous attitude as Achan did. Nor did Caleb, who had twice as many years of ministry and many more reasons to think and reason, like Achan.

The Achan syndrome will make people feel they are exempt from divine directives and have special privileges to enjoy the material things on which God has placed restrictions. When ministers and Christian leaders start thinking they deserve more recognition and offerings, or focus only on their own desires, possessions and ministry, then the seed of the Achan spirit is in their heart. When they press for personal promotion, take the gold that belongs to God's treasury and put it in their own "tent" (ministry), then the destructive Johnson grass roots have intertwined with the roots of their good cornstalk.

When Christians lose the greater vision for the success of the whole Body of Christ, then the Achan seed has sprouted into a plant of self-destruction. They have taken of the accursed thing that God hates--the pride, selfishness and self-promotion that caused the fall of God's heavenly minister of music, Lucifer (Is. 14:12-15).

God's Overall Purpose Our Primary Goal:

Any of us who are a fivefold minister---apostle, prophet evangelist, pastor or teacher must constantly remind ourselves that our primary goal should be the fulfillment of God's overall purpose for His Church, not our possessing the most or making our ministry the greatest. For example, Christ's purpose for my particular ministry as an individual apostolic prophet is to fulfill His greater purpose in raising up a last-days company of prophets. This international company is then called to the greater purpose of colaboring with Christ to fulfill God's plans for His universal Church. Christ's Church is then called to colabor with God in fulfilling His purposes for planet earth. And the perfected Church on the redeemed earth is destined to fulfill that even greater eternal purpose which God purposed in Christ Jesus, the Lord of heaven and earth. Rom.8:17; Eph.1:10; 3:11; 4:11.

Most all of the root problems and sinful attitudes of ministers and other church members would be eliminated if we had the proper perspective on God's purpose for our position in the Body of Christ. The apostle Paul portrayed this truth when he used the analogy of the human body to describe the Church, declaring, "Now ye are the Body of Christ, and members in particular" (1 Cor. 12:27). Though there are many members, there is only one Body with one overall purpose.

Interdependent, Not Independent:

We are not independent ministries, but interdependent upon one another and upon the Body's headship directives. When I first started raising up the company of prophets in the late 1970s most had the concept that a prophet was related and subject to no one but God. I discovered that when a person had the old perspective that insists the prophet is a loner, functioning independently of the rest of the Church, then that made him subject to the pitfall of selfishness and the potential of self-deception. It is the lone sheep which separates from the flock that gets devoured by the wolves.

For that reason, each member has the responsibility to fulfill his/her own function and to stay properly related to the Head, Jesus Christ. The ministry and success of any individual member is not an end in itself; rather, it exists to contribute to the function and fulfillment of the whole Body. And the whole Body was formed and now functions to fulfill the desires and directives of its Head. This is the reason the sins we commit that affect the whole Body of Christ are more serious with God.

Six Things God HATES---The Seventh is an Abomination!

In Proverbs sixth chapter, it lists six things that GOD HATES, and a seventh that He really hates with a passion. In fact, it says that it is an abomination to God. The six are:

1. A proud look--pride,
2. A lying tongue--deception,
3. Hands that shed innocent blood--character assassination,
4. A heart that devises wicked plans--wrong motive,
5. Feet that are swift in running to evil--responds quicker to evil than to God,
6. A false witness who speaks lies--deceiver and talebearer.
7. Anyone who sows discord among brethren--causes strife and division within the Church and between churches... Sinning against the Body of Christ can get a Christian in serious trouble with God.

Achan committed a sin against the body of Israel, and it cost him his life, family, and possessions. In the New Testament, Christian are not killed physically for committing this sin, but it does cost them and affects their personal life, family and possessions.

CAN'T WIN BATTLES WITH SIN IN THE CAMP!

After Achan had sinned and Joshua did not yet know about it; Israel fought against their next enemies, but they were defeated and 36 Israelis soldiers were killed. (These are the only soldiers the Bible mentions being killed during Israel's following seven-year military campaign.) When that happened, Joshua cried out to God, Why? He fell on his face before the ark of the Lord until evening. Then for the first and only time Joshua questioned God and complained. "Alas, LORD God, Why have You brought these people over the Jordan at all---to deliver us into the hand of the Amorites, to destroy us? Oh, that we had been content, and dwelt on the other side of the Jordan! O Lord, what shall I say when Israel turns its back before its enemies?" God answered. Why? Because Israel has sinned, by taking of the accursed thing that I told them not to take. Notice, God did not say someone or one of the soldiers has sinned, but Israel has sinned. God included the whole army. Achan was not a leader in Israel, but just a soldier in the Israeli army but his sin affected the whole army.

What to do About Sinning Church Members:

Sometimes a local church is stalemated and not winning victories because one member in the church is committing serious sin before God. I am sure it would bring the reverential fear of God to the congregation if God told the pastor to bring all the members one by one before the whole congregation and the guilty person would be excommunicated and turned over to Satan for the destruction of the flesh.

Apostle Paul actually instructed the Corinthian church leaders to do that to the person who was committing a horrible sin. "It is actually reported that there is sexual immorality among you, and such sexual immorality as is not even named among the Gentiles---that a man has his father's wife! I have already judged him who is doing this deed. Now, I command you in the name and power of our Lord Jesus Christ to deliver this person over to Satan for the destruction of the flesh that his spirit may be saved in the day of the Lord Jesus."

There is a teaching circulating in the Church world that Jesus Christ never judges anyone, and there is no judgment for Christians. This man was a member of the Corinthian church, a N.T. Christian. Let us look at the Apostle's thinking on these matters, who wrote 14 of the N.T. books of the Bible. The following quotation from 1 Corinthians chapter five is from the Living Bible. Please take note of Paul's instructions concerning what is God's thoughts on it and what should be our attitude toward Christians who are committing sins, especially when it is publicly known:

> "Everyone is talking about the terrible thing that is
> happening there among you, something so evil that even
> the heathen don't do it: you have a man in your church,
> who is living in sin with his father's wife. And are you

still so conceited, so 'spiritual'? Why aren't you mourning in sorrow and shame, and seeing to it that this man is removed from your membership?

"Although I am not there with you, I have been thinking a lot about this, and in the name of the Lord Jesus Christ I have already decided what to do, just as though I were there. You are to call a meeting of the church – and the power of the Lord Jesus will be with you as you meet, and I will be there in spirit – and cast out this man from the fellowship of the church, and into Satan's hands, to punish him, in the hope that his soul will be saved when our Lord Jesus Christ returns.

"What a terrible thing it is that you are boasting about your purity, and yet you let this sort of thing go on. Don't you realize that if even one person is allowed to go on sinning, soon all will be affected? Remove this evil cancer – this wicked person – from among you, so that you can stay pure. Christ, God's Lamb, has been slain for us. So let us feast upon him and grow strong in the Christian life, leaving entirely behind us the cancerous old life with all its hatreds and wickedness. Let us feast instead upon the pure bread of honor and sincerity and truth.

"When I wrote to you before, I said not to mix with evil people. But when I said that, I wasn't talking about unbelievers who live in sexual sin, or are greedy cheats and thieves and idol worshipers. For you can't live in this world without being with people like that. What I meant was that you are not to keep company with anyone who claims to be a brother Christian but indulges in sexual sins or is greedy, or is a swindler, or worships idols, or is a drunkard, or abusive. Don't even eat lunch with such a person.

"It isn't our job to judge outsiders. But it certainly is our job to judge and deal strongly with those who are

members of the church, and who are sinning in these ways. God alone is the judge of those on the outside. But you yourselves must deal with this man and put him out of your church." (1 Cor.5:1-13LB).

What To Do When SIN is In The Camp?

"So the LORD said to Joshua: 'Get up! Why do you lie thus on your face? (complaining). Israel has sinned, and they have also transgressed my covenant which I commanded them. For they have even taken some of the accursed things, and have both stolen and deceived; and they have also put it among their own stuff. Therefore, the children of Israel could not stand before their enemies, but turned their backs before their enemies, because they have become doomed to destruction. Neither will I be with you anymore, unless you destroy the accursed from among you. 'Get up, sanctify the people and say, sanctify yourselves for tomorrow, because thus says the Lord God of Israel: there is an accursed thing in your midst, O Israel; you cannot stand before your enemies until you take away the accursed thing from among you".

God then told Joshua to find the guilty person by the process of elimination probably by the Urim and Thummim flashing when the twelve tribes passed by, it indicated that the sin was in the tribe of Judah. Then by families, households, man by man until Achan was pointed out to be the guilty person. God had decreed that the one found guilty was to be killed by stoning and burned with fire, he and all his family and all possessions, "because he has transgressed the covenant of the LORD, and because he has done a disgraceful thing in Israel." "So all Israel stoned them with stones, and they burned them with fire after they had stoned them with stones." The anger of the Lord was burning hot against the Children of Israel because they had taken of the accursed things. But when Joshua executed God's Judgments on the matter; *"Then the LORD turned from the fierceness of His anger."* **Jos.7:1-26.**

The sin was so serious with God that He said He would not be with Israel any more unless they destroyed the accursed from among them. God had given a command through Joshua; *"Israelites, by all means abstain from the accursed things, lest you become accursed when you take of the accursed things, and make the camp of Israel a curse and trouble it."* What made the gold, silver, bronze and brass an accursed thing for any Israelite to take it for himself? Because God had said it was consecrated to the LORD and was to go into the treasury in the house of the LORD. It was the firstfruits of their first battle taking the first city in their military conquest of Canaan. Jericho was to be the tithe of their total conquest of Canaan. Every living thing breathing in Jericho human and animal was to be killed. Everything that could burn was to be consumed with fire. All metals were to be purified by fire and dedicated to the treasury of the LORD.

Achan took that which was to be given into God's treasury and put it in his own tent. God had already established through Moses His claim on one-tenth (tithe) of all the income of the Children of Israel. The tithe was to be consumed, burned as an offering on the altar of sacrifice or destroyed; So, if one put their tithe in with the ninety percent then all 100 percent was accursed and doomed to destruction; because they had taken what was to be dedicated to God and used it for themselves. They were robbing from God if they did not pay the tithe. That is why God had Prophet Malachi prophesy to the nation of Israel; "Will a man rob God? Yet you have robbed Me! But you say, in what way have we robbed You? In tithes and offerings, you are cursed with a curse, for you have robbed Me, even this whole nation. Bring all the tithes into the storehouse (God's treasury)." This is one reason that Achan's sin was so serious and required total destruction of all he was and had; he robbed from God's treasury.

THE LORD IS ONE GOD AND CHANGES NOT

Some reading this book might have the tendency to think we are using illustrations in the Old Testament and the dealings of the God of the Old Testament. The God of the Old and the God of the New Testament is the same God who never changes and is the same yesterday today and forever. There is one Eternal God in the Bible but two covenants. Whatever Jehovah God said was contrary to His will, nature, and what is right and wrong to Him in the O.T. is still the same to Him in the N.T. God the Father, The Son of God and the Holy Spirit are the same in every area of their nature, standards, character and conviction of what is right and wrong in the human race.

Some say that the O.T. God was an angry God who demanded righteousness and was quick to execute judgment on wrong doers. But the Son of God of the N.T. was longsuffering, full of mercy and came to bring love, peace and joy to the human race and didn't judge or condemn anyone. They overlook the reality that it was the O.T. Jehovah God who sent His Son to provide redemption for mankind because He SO LOVED the world. The scriptures say that God is love and talks about the love of God. You would think if their concept of two different God's were true then the N.T. would speak of the love of Jesus Christ and Jesus is love. The Bible does say that Jesus was God manifest in the flesh; the brightness of His glory and the express image of the person of God. Jesus said, if you have seen Me, you have seen the Father for Me and My Father are one. Jesus did come to save, heal and bless humanity, but Jesus received all of His attributes, Spirit and loving nature from His Father God, who has always had that nature and character. Jehovah God has always been who He is and will always be the same from eternity past to eternity future. Jehovah God the Eternal does not need to change for He is complete in Himself having and being everything He needs to be to meet the needs and fulfill every being in His eternal universe. He is the one and only true God, who has always been and always will be the same for endless eternity.

THE SIN OF A MINISTER BEING EXCLUSIVE AND SECLUSIVE

Apostle Paul used the illustration of the human body to reveal how the Church is the Body of Christ. Christ is the head of the Body, and all true Christians are the body. It is one body but with many members like the human body. The members and their ministries differ as much as the heart and the mouth, the eye, and the hand. No member functions independently of the body. Each member functions, not just for itself, but for the functioning of the whole body and so it is with members of the Body of Christ. The Body may be able to function without certain members, but no member can function apart from the Body. A member that gets separated from the Body withers and dies unless it is put on some sort of artificial life support system.

But God is now in the process of pulling the plug on the life support system of every ministry that is not properly related to the Body of Christ. Every member of the Body diseased with the cancerous cells of exclusiveness, seclusiveness and independence will be surgically removed by God. The root system of the "my ministry and my needs first" syndrome will be plowed upside down and exposed for what it is, then raked and burned in God's purifying fire (Mal. 3:1-3; 1 Cor. 3:12-15).

"The son of man will send out His Angels, and they will gather out of His kingdom all things that offend, and those who practice lawlessness, and will cast them into the furnace of fire. There will be wailing and gnashing of teeth." (Matt.13:41-42)

The Achan spirit manifests itself when ministers become so wrapped up in their own needs, desires and ministry that they think they have the right to take special privileges and possessions beyond that of their fellow ministers. Such a spirit is a seed of self-deception that will cause ministers to become a law unto themselves with an attitude that insists, "I deserve greater offerings and more opportunities. If I don't take, I won't get. If I don't promote my own ministry, no one else will." We must not let the enemy come during the night of temptation and sow such Achan seeds in the field of our hearts (Matt.13:24-26).

Remember, all that was recorded about what Israel did and how God dealt with them was not just written for the history of Israel, but for instructions, understanding God's Word, will and ways, warnings and admonitions to the Church. Especially to you and I who are living in the consummation of the ages. *"Now all these things happened to them (Children of Israel) as examples, and they were written for our (The Church's) admonition, upon whom the ends of the ages have come."*

(1 Cor.10:11).

The Amplified Bible gives greater amplification to this scripture:

"Now these things befell them (Israel) by way of a figure [as an example and warning to us]; they were written to admonish and fit us for right action by good instruction, we in whose days the ages have reached their climax (their consummation and concluding period)."

God rejected His children of Israel when they sinned and rejected Him. Jesus will reject those who willfully practice sinning and reject the life of Christ. Apostle John in his epistle declared that God would reject those who willfully practiced major sinning. The Old Testament declares that God changes not, and the New Testament declares that Jesus is the same yesterday, today and forever. The scriptures declare that Jesus was the full expression of the nature, character, and heart of God. He also declared that all that He spoke were the very words of God. So how can someone say that God the Father and Jesus the Son were two different Gods with completely different temperaments, characteristics, and motivations. God executed vengeance on sin and Jesus executes vengeance on sin. All sin that has not been forgiven and cleansed by the blood of Jesus will receive Father God's wrath.

Chapter 7
Judas' Root Problem and Character Flaw:
"Desire to be Rewarded for Every Service"

Judas and Achan had a kindred spirit and the same root problem. Judas's outward sin was the betrayal of his Lord when he sold Jesus out to the enemy. But the thinking and attitude that caused Judas to take this action was the root problem. I am quite familiar with the problem, because in my years as bishop of the Christian International Apostolic Network of prophetic ministers (CIAN), I have had occasion to counsel and deal with some "Judas" ministers with a similar character flaw.

DISAPPOINTMENT IN PERSONAL AMBITIONS

Judging from what I have seen in these cases, Judas's thoughts probably went something like this: "I've forsaken my business and sacrificed my opportunities to advance myself in position and possessions over the last three years by following Jesus day and night. Now I get the impression from what Jesus is saying and doing that He won't fulfill my dream. I thought following Jesus would advance my position, power, and prestige, but I was wrong."

In this way, Judas probably built up in his own mind a case for feeling justified for taking the actions he did. He began to interpret and apply the prophetic promises Jesus had made to the Twelve in a way that was different from the Lord's intent. The motivation for the prophetic promise of Jesus came from the incident with the rich young man who asked Jesus what he must do to inherit eternal life. Jesus told him to keep the commandments, and the man said that he had been doing that faithfully all his life. Jesus told him that if he wanted God's best then give his wealth away to the poor and then he could follow Him as one of His disciples. The thought of giving up all his wealth was too much for him so he left. Jesus said it was easier for a Camel to go through the eye of the needle than for a rich person to enter the kingdom. That shocked and puzzled the Apostles causing them to ask the question, who then can be saved? Jesus said, with men this is impossible, but with God all things are possible. Then Peter declared we have left everything to follow you what are we going to get for forsaking all to be Your disciples? Jesus gave the following prophetic promise as an answer to Peter's question. "Then Jesus said to them, Truly I say to you, in the new age (the Messianic rebirth of the world), when the Son of Man shall sit down on the throne of His glory, you who have [become My disciples, sided with my party and] followed Me will also sit on twelve thrones and judge the twelve tribes of Israel." Mt.19:28AMP.

Notice, Jesus said all twelve would sit on twelve thrones judging the twelve tribes of Israel. This prophetic promise was given to all twelve which included Judas. The idea of setting on a throne like a king as a judge and ruler of one of the tribes of Israel evidently became the main motivation of Judas to remain a disciple of Jesus. Judas was looking forward to being a ruler over one of the tribes of Israel, but at the end of three years Jesus began talking about the Son of man being crucified, dying and leaving this world. (Mt.20:17-19).

It looked to Judas as if Jesus had misled him and would not fulfill His word to them of being rulers in Israel. The Jewish concept of the Messiah was that He would come and restore Israel as it was in the days of King David and Solomon. Judas began to get discouraged and disillusioned about Jesus and beginning to doubt whether He was the true Messiah. So he probably reasoned, "I could have made at least thirty pieces of silver profit during these past three years. I deserve something for the years of sacrifice and service I have given to Jesus, especially since it sounds like He is not going to fulfill His prophetic promise He made to me of a high position in Israel."

STEPS IN SATAN'S DECEPTION

Satan's first step in developing the Judas spirit in people is to convince them that the leadership they have been serving, and to whom they have been related and accountable, is not living up to the promises they have made to them. These "promises" may even be personal prophecies they received or prophecies they once heard the leadership give to the church or ministry as a group. The people who are disappointed in this way typically make a private (and wrong) interpretation and application of the leader's promises or prophetic statements which causes them to conclude that the leaders have not fulfilled their word.

Such a Judas type of thinking allows a sense of self-justification for betraying friendship and selling out to the enemy for personal gain. This action consequently makes those who take it feel judged by others for what they have done. So self-deception must then come to convince them that the leadership and others are neither understanding nor beneficial.

Pride and an exalted sense of self-importance come next to convince them to do what Lucifer did--to pull away and head up their own ministry. They leave the fellowship and refuse to allow their overseer to have input into their lives. By then, the spirit of self-delusion has invented a dozen arguments why they are "justified" in their every attitude and action. "Every way of a man is right in his own eyes," says Proverbs, "but the Lord weighs the hearts" (Prov. 21:2).

The Judas spirit starts in seed form with the feeling that we must be rewarded immediately for every service rendered and given recognition or a higher position for time and money spent to participate in and propagate the ministry. It begins with the attitude that says, "God owes me for services rendered. I deserve better. I deserve more offerings and honor than I am receiving. They should recognize me and have me speak more often." This is where it starts; but if we do not allow God and the leaders over us to correct this character flaw and adjust this attitude; we will hang ourselves and our ministry just as surely as Judas hung himself on a tree.

NO RIGHTS TO SELF-PROMOTION OR SELF-PRESERVATION

Ministers and Saints must take on the ministry attitude of the Spirit of Christ, which does not demand the right of self-promotion and self-preservation. Jesus did not demand that the Father promote Him and give Him a good reputation. Instead, Jesus made Himself of no reputation (Phil. 2:7). He could have called for an angelic host to help Him (Matt. 26:53), but He laid down His rights and His life for His brethren. He let others hang Him on a tree. Yet this seeming act of self-destruction actually led to His preservation, because the Father raised Him from the dead and promoted His ministry to the right hand of the throne of heaven.

Jesus was dealing with this weed seed attitude in His disciples when He declared that "except a corn of wheat fall into the ground and die, it abides alone: but if it dies, it brings forth much fruit" (John 12:24). Those who desire to be true and mature ministers must die to self-ambition, self-promotion, and self-interest. If they don't allow the "death to self" process to take place, they are destined eventually to sell out their relationship with Jesus, as Judas did, for the sake of worldly goods and carnal desires.

The bottom line is this: Selfishness is the root problem of ninety-nine percent of all unscriptural attitudes and actions. Self-centeredness is what gives power to the three sources of all sin--the lust of the flesh, the lust of the eyes, and the pride of life (1 John 2:16). All outward sins come from one of these three sources, and they receive their right and power to function in an individual through his or her unsanctified self-life.

That's why in dealing with ministerial downfalls and prophetic pitfalls, we must lay the axe of truth to the root of the tree rather than wasting our time merely pruning back the branches. The self-life out of order is the root of the tree; individual sins, the breaking of the Ten Commandments and works of the flesh, are simply the branches of the tree. Or to use our earlier illustration, adultery, lying, dishonesty, anger and other sinful manifestations are the blades of the "Johnson grass" growing above ground. But selfishness is the root system underground. We may cut away the blades of grass, but they will grow back again and again until the underlying root system is destroyed.

Test of God's Seeming Failure to Fulfill:

During the years that Judas served as an apostle–minister of Jesus Christ, there were several indicators that everything was not quite right with him. He was appointed treasurer of the group. Scriptures state that Judas was dishonest and deceptive in his position for he took money from the treasury for his own personal use. *"Judas Iscariot, one of his disciples, and even then getting ready to betray Jesus, said, why wasn't this oil sold and the money given to the poor? It would have easily brought 300 silver pieces. He said this, not because he cared two cents about the poor, but because he was a thief. He was in charge of their common funds, but also embezzled them."* Jn.12:6 Mess.

This scripture reveals that Judas's "M" of money was out of order. This was further confirmed when Judas wanted money from the Jewish Sanhedrin for his betrayal of Jesus. Judas also criticized Jesus, his apostolic overseer for allowing Mary to take the expensive ointment and anoint the feet of Jesus. His motivation was because he wanted more money in the bag so that he could embezzle more for himself.

When a church member who may even be an elder is quick to criticize the actions and decisions of the pastor, or a minister is quick to criticize his apostolic overseer, it shows a root problem which could cause them to betray their leader as Judas betrayed Jesus. Judas also questioned the integrity and truthfulness of Jesus when it sounded like Jesus was not going to fulfill His prophetic promise to make him a ruler over one of the tribes of Israel.

Disappointment over God seemingly not fulfilling His promise to you is one of the greatest tests of your character, confidence in God and the degree of your unlimited commitment to Jesus Christ. I have gone through several of those in my 64 years of Christianity. I saw my son and daughter-in-law, Tom and Jane Hamon, go through that test. Their son Jason was born with a severe bi-lateral cleft palate February 17, 1987. Everyone was praying for a miracle of healing and Jane believed with her whole being that her son was going to be healed at Easter. But Easter came and went, and he was not healed. It was emotionally devastating, but they did not let it cause them to lose faith in God and His will to heal or lessen their commitment to serve God. They took the attitude that Job took, and I have taken several times in such experiences, "Though God slay me yet will I trust Him." Job 13:15.

Responding Like Peter or Judas Iscariot:

Apostle Peter faced circumstances similar to those of Judas. He left his fishing business and his family to follow Jesus. When Jesus was arrested, he also became discouraged, disillusioned and confused, even to the point of denying His leader and Lord. Yet Peter repented when he realized he had spoken foolishly and immaturely and had acted wrongly toward Jesus. Like the prodigal son in Jesus' parable, he turned away from the attitude that says give me wealth, fame and freedom, and took on instead the attitude that says make me a servant of my Father. Luke 15:12,19.

We all have said and done or will someday say and do foolish things under great pressure, fear and confusion, especially when--like the Twelve--we see all our hopes, dreams and ministry falling apart all around us. When that happens, do we follow the example of Peter or of Judas? Like Peter, we must be willing to admit wrongdoing and then change. If we become divinely flexible and adjustable, God can restore us and cause our ministry to become more effective than we ever dreamed possible just as He did for Apostle Peter.

The result of their choices determined their destiny. Judas lost his apostleship with Jesus Christ. He did not repent of his sin of betrayal but went out and committed suicide by hanging himself thereby sending his soul to hell to burn in the Lake of Fire forever.

Peter realized he had sinned by his denial of the Lord three times. He knew that lying was a sin and was greatly ashamed that he had not fulfilled his promise to Jesus that he would die for him. Peter repented and recommitted his life to Jesus Christ and went on to become one of the 12 Apostles of the Lamb of God. What a difference our choices make!

Chapter 8
Ministers & False Doctrine:
The Originator & The Origination

In an earlier chapter we covered the origination of sin. We found that it originated in Lucifer who became Satan-the Devil who becomes the originator of all that is false, evil, deceptive, false doctrine and all things that are contrary to who God is. He is the root of all that is contrary to God's word, will, and way. There was nothing contrary to God in His eternal heavenly universe until Lucifer developed pride, self-exaltation and rebellion against God.

Sin originated in the Human Race when Eve believed the falsehood of Lucifer and was deceived into eating the forbidden fruit. Adam ate knowing that he was breaking God's command of "Thou shall not." We discovered that an abbreviated definition of sin is doing that which is contrary to God's word, will and way, whether it is a sin of omission or commission.

The Creative Power of Man's Imagination:

Man was created in God's own image and likeness. That includes the ability to create ideas through the imagination of man apart from the devil or God. Every thought of man is not from the devil or God. Therefore, false concepts of God and man can originate in man's own imagination. This is illustrated in man's creation of science fiction movies, inventions of all modern transportation and electronic communication. The devil always wants to add some of his thoughts and philosophies into movies to bring subtle deception as he did to Eve in the Garden of Eden. God seeks to add what He can and especially in Christian movies. Of course, the devil is always available and anxious to deceive man into believing and teaching things that are contrary to God so that more humans will end up in hell with him. However, man is still capable of creating his own thoughts. Every thought of man originates from one of three sources---God's spirit, the evil spirit or man's own spirit. Most often 90% of man's thoughts originate from his own spirit and creative imagination. Therefore, false doctrine can originate in the creative and imaginative mind of man even in a Christian minister.

The Devil and Human Beings:

The devil hates all human beings, even those who are his greatest disciples. He is incapable of doing anything for humans which would be good for them. He hates with a vengeance those who believe in Jesus Christ and are saints of the Most High God. Jesus said that the whole motivation of the devil coming to the human race is to steal, kill and destroy, whereas the whole motivation of Jesus coming to the human race is "that they may have life and that they may have it more abundantly." Even when the devil helps people become successful and popular, it is a means to an end to destroy them. When Satan sees a minister with the seeds of pride and self-exaltation he lets them become successful and increase in the pride of Lucifer so that they become more susceptible to his deception and introduction to false doctrine, in order for more people to be indoctrinated in the counterfeit.

HOW FALSE DOCTRINE ORIGINATES

There are several ways. One being that Satan appears to a particular person or an ordained Christian minister as an Angel of light. The angel (Satan) gives them a new message to preach to the Church that is supposed to be a revelation from God. They declare they are "Sent Ones," which is the meaning of "Apostle." These apostles transform themselves into the Apostles of Christ and seduce many Christians into believing their false doctrine.. Paul warned the Church about these apostles.

"For such are false apostles, deceitful workers, transforming themselves into apostles of Christ. And no wonder! For Satan himself transforms himself into an angel of light. Therefore it is no great thing if Satan's ministers also transform themselves into ministers of righteousness, whose end will be according to their works." 2Cor.11:13-15.

For instance, Mohammed testifies that at 40 years of age he went to a cave to think and pray and In a vision the Angel Gabriel appeared to him and gave him the Islamic religion to propagate. At first Mohammed and his followers tried to make converts by preaching with friendly persuasion, but after being rejected and persecuted they converted to the sword as a means of converting individuals but whole nations. With their fanatic zeal caused by their teaching that the highest reward in heaven for them was killing anyone who would not convert to the Muslim religion enabled them to conquer North Africa, Western Asia and the Middle East, including Jerusalem. They believe they are the chosen people of God destined to rule the whole world. Mohammed's passion was to deliver mankind from the idolatrous worship of the Dark age Church, mainly Catholicism, had imposed upon the people. He and his army of followers destroyed over 360 idols in Mecca. That year, A.D. 622 is recognized as the year of the birth of Islam.

Mohammed appeared at a time when the church had become paganized with the worship of images, relics, martyrs, Mary, and the Saints. In a sense, Islam was a revolt against the idolatry of the "Christian" world. It did deliver the people from certain bad conditions but put them into bondage of a worse, more religiously controlling nature. Within 110 years, the followers of Islam had swept nation after nation under their control until they tried to conquer Constantinople, the gate way to Europe. The Muslim March was stopped by an army led by Emperor Leo 11. Muslims then tried to enter Europe through Spain and France, but were stopped at the city of Tours. They retreated to the Arabian dominated world where the Moslem faith has been the controlling religion to the present day. The Muslim faith produced a religious, hard, dominating spirit and fanatical followers. They were motivated more by hatred of the unbelievers of Islam than love for the souls of man of nonbelievers. Their religion was propagated by the sword and encouraged slavery, harems, and the degradation of womanhood. Islam's greatest error, and proof that it is not a faith born of God, is the fact that it views Jesus as no more than a Jewish prophet, inferior in every respect to Mohammed. The Muslims claim that they believe in the one true God (Allah in Arabic) of the Old Testament. But their concept of God is a fearless, relentless dictator, with no love for humanity outside the followers of the prophet Mohammed.

Joseph Smith founder of Mormonism, according to his account, while praying Joseph was visited by two "personages" who identified themselves as God the Father and Jesus Christ. He was told not to join any of the churches. In 1823, Joseph Smith said he was visited by an Angel named Moroni, who told him of an ancient recording containing God's dealings with the former inhabitants of the American continent. In 1827, Joseph retrieved this record, inscribed on thin golden plates, and shortly after began translating its words by the "gift of God." The resulting manuscript, the Book of Mormon, was published in March 1830 and on April 6, 1830, Joseph Smith organized The Church of Jesus Christ of Latter-day Saints and became its first president.

Please take note that both Mohammed and Joseph Smith were seemingly sincerely seeking God for answers. How do we know that these were false representations of heavenly beings, even the devil transforming himself into an angel of light and impersonating Jesus Christ? The main reason is that both of these religions make Jesus Christ less than God. The Muslim's religion does not believe that Jesus was the Son of God but just one of the prophets. Both developed a book that they make coequal with the Bible, the Koran and the Book of Mormon.

What Makes Some People Susceptible to Deception?

The Scriptures teach that several things can make a person susceptible to believing and teaching false doctrine. For instance, the pride of Lucifer; they know and preach truth but are unrighteous in their lives which make them subject to deception. (Rom.1:18), Jesus Christ and Apostle James stated that if people are hearers of the Word and not doers of the Word they open themselves to self-deception. James 1:22. Self-righteousness can cause deception—"If we say that we have no sin we deceive ourselves." Apostle Paul writing to the Thessalonian Christians declared that those who are subject to deception are those who *"do not receive the love of the truth that they should be saved. And for this reason God will send them strong delusion that they should believe the lie that they all may be condemned who did not believe the truth, but had pleasure in unrighteousness."* 2 Thess.2:10-12. We must keep a love for truth as revealed in the Word of God about ourselves and the true teachings of the Bible. Our greatest safeguard against deception, in believing and teaching false doctrine, is true honesty, humility, integrity, counsel and correction from mature ministers and self-examination with the Word of God. Let a man examine himself and in the multitude of counsel there is safety. 1 Cor.11:28

THE DEVELOPMENT OF FALSE DOCTRNE

Jesus Knew It Would Happen.

Jesus said, "Many false prophets will rise up and deceive many, and because of lawlessness the love of many will grow cold." "False christs and false prophets will arise and show great signs and wonders to deceive if possible, even the elect. See, I have told you beforehand." "Take heed that no one deceives you. For many will come in My name, saying, 'I am He,' and will deceive many." (Mt.24:11,12,24; Mk.13:5,6)

The true church started out in unity on the day of Pentecost and maintained oneness of doctrine, power, and purpose for several years. It gradually grew into many varied teachings, concepts, and practices concerning Christ and His Church, just as it has today in modern Christendom. Before listing the "isms" that developed in the first few centuries of the Church, it is necessary to examine a few of the Biblical accounts that predicted this development.

The "Great Falling Away" During the "Dark Age" of the Church

Paul wrote, " *Now the spirit expressively says that in the latter times some will depart from the faith, giving heed to seducing spirits, and doctrines of demons, speaking lies in hypocrisy; having their own conscience seared with a hot iron"* (1 Tim.4:1,2). An example of "seducing spirits, and doctrines of demons" is given in first Timothy 4:3, which says; "*Forbidding marrying, and commanding to abstain from foods which God created to be received with thanksgiving by those who believe and know the truth.*"

For the time will come when they will not endure sound doctrine, but according to their own desires...they will turn their ears away from the truth and be turned aside to fables (2 Tim.4:3-4)

Beware, brethren, lest there be in any of you an evil heart of unbelief, in departing from the living God (Heb.3:12)

There will be false teachers among you, who will secretly bring in destructive heresies, even denying the Lord who bought them, and many will follow their destructive ways, because of whom the way of truth will be blasphemed. By covetousness, they will exploit you with deceptive words.

Peter also stated that men would arise who lack spiritual understanding and who would misinterpret Scripture and apply it wrongly.

"Our beloved brother Paul, according to the wisdom given to him, has written to you, as also in all his epistles, speaking in them of these things, in which are some things hard to understand, which those who are untaught and unstable twist to their own destruction, as they do also the rest of the Scriptures. You, therefore, beloved, since you know these things beforehand, beware lest you also fall from your own steadfastness, being led away with the era of the wicked" (2 Peter 3:15-17).

Apostle Paul declared there would come a "falling away" first, before the coming of the Lord took place; that a man would arise who would sit as God in the temple of God. This system would lead them into strong delusions and cause them to believe a lie. God will allow this to happen because they did not receive the love of the truth that they might be saved.

Falling Away Fulfilled:

The great apostasy of the dark ages with its one world church system fulfilled these Scriptures in a general way. They may also be fulfilled in a personal and intensified way at the end of the Church Age. But in terms of the Church as a whole, these Scriptures have already come to pass. Thank God the true spiritual Church, the Body of Christ, has had its prophesied Apostasy and great Falling Away during the Dark Age 500AD – 1500AD. Then the Second Reformation began and it would have nine major restoration movements over the next 500 years to restore back into the Church all that the First Generation Church had as manifested in the Book of Acts (1517AD-2007AD. In 2008, The Third & Final Church Reformation began and will continue until all prophetic Scriptures are fulfilled. Acts 3:21; Heb.10:13; Mt.24:14; Dan.7:14,18,22,27; Eph.4:ii-13.

The Church Birthed Out of Judaism:

The major struggle of the baby Church born on the Day of Pentecost was separating the Church from Judaism. It took the early Apostles ten years to cut the umbilical cord, and another ten years before it was officially separated from Judaism. It was officially done at the first Church Council at Jerusalem, which most Church historians agree was about AD 50, 20 years after the birth of the Church. Peters' experience ten years before at Cornelius's house demonstrated to him that God did not require any requirements of the Law for Gentiles to be born again and filled with the Holy Spirit. Paul received revelation from God that the Law and all of its ceremonial requirements including circumcision, the tabernacle of Moses, in fact all Jewish things were types and shadows of the Church.

"Do not let anyone criticize you for what you eat or drink, or for not celebrating Jewish holidays and feasts or new moon ceremonies or Sabbaths. For these were only temporary rules that ended when Christ came. They were only shadows of the real thing – of Christ Himself." Col.2:16-18.

The Councils decision was that Peter's experience and Paul's revelation were of God and were true doctrine and practices for the New Testament Church. Paul had taught the Gentile and Jewish Christians for years what he later wrote especially in Romans, Galatians, Ephesians, Colossians and in Hebrews, so the Christians were thoroughly founded on the fundamentals of the Christian faith but then some ministers came down from Judea teaching that they had to still keep the Laws of Moses and the Abrahamic covenant of circumcision to be saved. They were of the group that evolved into the Ebionites who just added Christ to traditional Judaism. Paul was highly offended at their teaching and disputed their doctrine vehemently. They decided to take the issue to the Apostles in Jerusalem which instigated the Council at Jerusalem.

The official letter containing the decisions of the Council was delivered to Antioch by Paul and Barnabas accompanied by two prophets from Jerusalem---Judas and Silas. Acts 15:22,32. Being as they were already founded in good Christian doctrine based on the teachings of Apostle Paul and the Elders at Antioch, they only stated the following in the Letter: "Since we have heard that some who went out from us have troubled you with words, unsettling your souls, saying, You must be circumcised and keep the law---to whom we gave no such commandment.....But it seemed good to the Holy Spirit , and to us, to lay upon you no greater burden than these necessary things: That you abstain from things offered to idols; from blood, from strangled animals, and from sexual immorality. If you keep yourselves from these things, you will do well. Farewell." Gen 9:4; Acts 15:1-35.

They did not require the Antioch Christians to keep any of the ceremonies in the Abrahamic Covenant or the Mosaic Covenant. That was required by the Old Covenant/Testament, but none of it was required in the New Testament/Covenant for salvation.

There were many doctrinal controversies in the first three centuries. They mainly dealt with the deity of Christ; whether He was less than God, co-equal with God or God manifest in a human body. There were more than twelve major "isms" in the Early Church. We list two as an example; one that was false and one that was true.

1. Montanism: It would have its modern-day counterpart in the Pentecostal and Charismatic churches of today. They believed in the gift of the Holy Spirit with speaking in tongues, supernatural manifestations of the gifts of the Holy Spirit, and most of their doctrines were in line with the fundamentals of the faith.

2. Gnosticism: Their modern day counterpart would be Jehovah Witnesses, Christian Science, and Unitarianism. Their teaching no doubt influenced Masons and New Agers. They glorified knowledge and personified the spirit of exclusivism, and the pride of Lucifer.

Development of the Roman Catholic Church:

During the Dark Age of the Church, there were only two major Christian denominations recognized in Christendom---The Roman Catholic Church and the Eastern Orthodox Church. No "ism" term is readily available to describe these two representations of Christianity, yet they also developed doctrines and practices sanctioned by its councils and bishops, that were adverse to the doctrines and practices of the early apostolic church of the Book of Acts. The Church that existed between A.D. 300 and A.D. 500 is more closely identified with the modern Historic Protestant churches in doctrine and practice. After the year A.D. 500, it correlates more to the present Roman Catholic Church. Many of the teachings and practices, such as penance as a sacrament, indulgences, purgatory, and the Papacy, were not in the Church prior to that time.

The word Catholic means throughout the whole; general, universal, all-inclusive. For this reason, the word Catholic was used when making reference to the Church throughout the world. A common statement made by theologians was wherever Jesus Christ is, there is the Catholic Church. Local churches were normally identified by saying the church in Alexander or Antioch, or Rome, etc.

Through the centuries, the bishops of Rome worked toward acquiring the leadership of the Church and making their city the headquarters of the general, universal assembly of believers. Therefore, during the Middle Ages the "Catholic" worldwide church developed into the Roman Catholic Church. In A.D. 1054 a schism was finally declared between the Western and Eastern churches, effectively dividing Christendom. The Eastern or Byzantine churches became the Greek Orthodox, Russian Orthodox, etc. The Western church became known as the Roman Catholic Church.

The Church Loses most of its Spiritual Ministry and True Doctrine.

The Emperor Constantine accepted Christianity in AD 313, and for the first time made it possible for Christians to become citizens of Rome. Constantine encouraged his constituents to become Christians, but 70 years later Emperor Theodosius made it compulsory, when he made Christianity the state religion of the Roman Empire. His decree forced all Roman Empire subjects to formally accept Christianity in order to maintain their citizenship, hold office, and carry on business. (What a reversal, for just 100 years prior Emperor Septimius Severus decreed that he would destroy all Christianity from Rome. His seven years of persecution (303-310) was so severe that the Christians declared him to be the Antichrist.) The political Christianization of Rome was the final blow to the message of repentance, conviction of sin, spiritual rebirth, and the need for a transformed life in order to become a Christian. Prior to this time conversion had been voluntary and marked by a genuine change of heart and life. Christ had designed the Church to conquer by purely spiritual and supernatural means. Theodosius not only demanded adherence to Christianity, but he undertook the forcible suppression of all other religions and prohibited idol worship. Under his decree, heathen temples were torn down, and there was much bloodshed among the heathen priests and worshipers. The structural part of the Church was enhanced when Christians became politically dominant. The world was also blessed in its physical, moral, and social life. Slavery, gladiators fights, killing of unwelcome children, and crucifixion as a form of execution were abolished with the Christianization of the Roman Empire. Many humanitarian societies were established by the state, through the influence of the church. However, when the Spiritual Church was in control In apostolic days, these humanitarian needs were met by the Church without state support or control.

"Isms" of the Structural, Accepted, Popular Dark Age Church:

Because of the Old Catholic Church involvement with heathen customs, and its desire for political and material gain its primary "ism" problems were paganism, materialism, ritualism, and formalism plus many doctrines that were contrary to biblical truth.

The Christians of the first few centuries battled not only against a persecuting heathen world, but also against all the "isms" and "schisms" within their own fold. The old Catholic Church became more and more formal, ritualistic, a religion of the mind, and an intellectual faith requiring belief in a hard, fast system of doctrine. Emphasis was laid on correct belief and on obedience to the dogmas of the religious hierarchy rather than on the Bible and inner spiritual life.

Early Church Ministries, Manifestations and Doctrines:

The Spiritual Church of the Book of Acts practiced being justified by faith, cleansed from sin by the blood of Jesus, and relating personally to Jesus Christ through a born-again, salvation experience. Water baptism was more than a formality, it brought identification with the death of Christ, a life of separation unto God in holy and virtuous living motivated by the love and grace of God.

Christians received the gift of the Holy Spirit and prayed frequently in their own supernatural spirit language. Their ministers and leaders were not appointed by men for political reasons, but were called, anointed, enabled, and appointed by the Holy Spirit. The minister did not "lord it" over the flock but ministered to then the living word, supernatural healings and miraculous deliverances by the gifts of the Spirit. They manifested the life and liberty in the worship as portrayed in the worship book of the New Testament Church, the book of Psalms.

Communion was given without elaborate formal ceremonies. The Presbytery laid hands on the Christians for healing, the Holy Spirit's gift of one's own spirit language, and for the revealing of their call and ministry in the body of Christ. They lived in expectancy of the second coming of Christ in their day. They really believed that the wicked who died in their sins would suffer forever in hell while the righteous would be eternally rewarded. In the very beginning, they had such love and unity that they had all things in common

From Newborn to Full Grown:

The newly born Church was not mature in all its doctrines and performances, but it was the new baby Church, which had all the elements and parts that would be a perfected part of the mature Church at the end of the Church Age. Just as a baby boy has all that a grown man has, but is not mature. However, after 500 years of existence, the Church had lost all these experiential truths and had gone into its winter season of sleep and the Dark Age. (Thank God, the Church would awakening 1000 years later and start on its journey again. Nothing will stop the Church until we are fully prepared as a Bride for her Bridegroom.) Mt.16:18; Eph.4:11-13; 5:27; Rev.21:2.

Restoration of Truth or Reactivation of Error or New False Doctrine:

The restoration of the Church which is called the Second Reformation began in AD 1517 and continued until 2007. Keep in mind that everything taught and manifested during each of the restoration periods is either a restoration of biblical truth and spiritual ministries or a reactivation of a false doctrine that developed during the deterioration of the early Church. Most of the cults that claim to be Christian developed because a restoration minister received a false revelation that he or she preached, moved away from mainline Christianity and developed their own denomination. This is the reason that everything we hear and experience must be examined in the light of the whole Bible, especially the New Testament, which is the history, pattern, and instruction for the universal Body of Christ.

Everything new and different is not necessarily of the Holy Spirit. It must measure up to the Word of God, biblical hermeneutics (the science of biblical interpretation), Holy Spirit enlightenment, and divine wisdom (spiritual common sense). To stay balanced and from getting involved in false doctrine---Stay in the word and trust the Holy Spirit to lead you into all truth, be teachable, but not gullible. Hunger and thirst after righteousness and maintain a love for the truth, and you will go from glory to glory and from faith to faith. The Holy Spirit will lead you into all truth until you are fully established in the present truth and grow up in all things into Him, who is the head, even Christ Jesus. Eph.4:15; 2 Cor.3:18; Jn.16:13; Mt.6:33.

Chapter 9
The 21st Century Church—False & Strange Teachings

RECOGNIZING FALSE & STRANGE DOCTRINES

False teachings are more easily recognized by biblical scholars and ministers. However the average Christian who is not grounded in a balanced understanding of God's Word, His ways of doing things and the type of life that God wants man to live are more susceptible to false teaching and strange ways. Why is this? Because the false and counterfeit has to be so much like the real that only the experts can tell the difference.

Characteristics of False Doctrine & Strange Teachings:
This can be illustrated by the ingredients in rat poison. When you read the label on a package of rat poison, it reveals that less than 1% is poison, and the more than 99% is tasty, nutritious food for the rat. However that 1% is enough poison to kill the rat if he eats it for a short period of time. Most of the rat killing food must be real food and appealing to the rat in order to get him to accept and eat the part that is poison. False doctrine must have enough biblical truth to sound biblical in order to entice a Christian to accept the false part. It can be 99% accurate Biblical truth, but the one percent false can be enough to kill the spiritual life of the person who believes it and begins to practice it. As an example the Seventh Day Adventist (SDA) denomination teaches the same as an evangelical would on being born again, baptized in water, living a sanctified life, second coming of Christ, resurrection of the dead and an eternal heaven and hell. They were established

before the Pentecostal Movement in early 1900s, so they do not include the baptism of the Holy Spirit. But they add the 1% of teaching; that keeping Saturday as the Sabbath day of worship is essential for salvation and that keeping the Sabbath is God's "Seal" for a person's salvation. After believing and practicing this doctrine for a while members of this organization start trusting their keeping of the Sabbath as their guarantee of heaven instead of the 99% of fundamental truth. Jesus no longer becomes the central truth and salvation but the keeping of the Sabbath.

In the first years of my pastoring in the mid-1950s I debated with SDA ministers. We would always come to the crucial point-they would make the seventh day the "Seal" and I would declare the Seal to be the Holy Spirit. The seal of God is like the State Seal on a document, it makes it legitimate and guaranteed by the government. It means the approval, authorization, and guarantee of your salvation by the government of heaven... *"You are **sealed** with the Holy Spirit of Promise, who is the guarantee of our inheritance until the redemption of the purchased possession." "Do not grieve the Holy Spirit of God, by whom you were **sealed** for the day of redemption." Eph.1:14; 4:30.*

False teachings can also be compared to counterfeit money. It has to look and feel like the real government published money in order for people to accept it as real money. The counterfeit is made up of the same things as the real---a certain type of paper, colors and designs, etc. It looks and feels so much like the real that it takes those trained to recognize the counterfeit to realize that it is not genuine. There can be no counterfeit unless there is the real in existence. For example, no one would accept a thirteen dollar bill because there is no government produced thirteen dollar bills. There cannot be false Christ's unless there is a real Christ, false prophets unless there are real prophets alive and active in the world.

It is also like the 10 M's. How many of the 10 M's being out of order does it take to make a person false? How many "Christian" denomination doctrines have to be false to make them a cult or non-mainline Christian Organization. For the SDA denomination, it only took one. The 10 M's are like the steel links of a chain. If you were hanging over a 3000 foot cliff on the end of a chain with 10 links and one of the links started cracking and breaking---how many links have to break before you plunge to your destruction on the rocks below? It does no good to brag about the nine that are in good shape if the one breaks. There are many examples in the Bible that illustrates this truth. For instance, Jesus told His disciples to *beware of the leaven of the Pharisees and the Sadducees...then the apostles understood that Jesus was talking about their doctrine."* Mt.16:6-12. Jesus used the illustration of leaven (yeast) to show how one false doctrine can affect the whole of the rest of the doctrines of a person, local church or denomination. It only takes a minute amount of yeast to permeate an entire loaf of bread. Apostle Paul wrote to the Galatian and Corinthian Christians about a doctrine that some were introducing into their midst that would put them back under the law and cause them to *"fall from the grace of God"* thereby affecting their entire Christianity. *"A little leaven leavens the whole lump."* Gal.5:9. Some say it is just one person sinning in the church or its just one teaching that is questionable. One person sinning or one doctrine that is contrary to God's truth, nature, and character can have a devastating effect on any group of people. Listen to Paul's admonition to the Corinthian Church in the Message translation. *"Your flip and callous arrogance in these things bothers me. You pass it off as a small thing, but it's anything but that. Yeast, too, is a 'small thing' but it works its way through a whole batch of bread dough pretty fast. So get rid of this' yeast'."* 1 Cor.5:6. A sin or a false doctrine is no small thing to the Lord. The Living Bible translates this scripture: *"Don't you realize that if even one person is allowed to go on sinning, soon all will be affected."* We can see from all of these scriptures that one sin or one false doctrine can affect the whole assembly just as Achan's one sin affected the whole nation of Israel.

There is one more quick illustration that makes this truth so real and serious. My wife's mother and father lived with us for several years before her father died of colon cancer. The physician explained it this way. One cell in the colon changed from a life giving cell to a death delivering cell. It grew undetected until, when they did exploratory surgery, they found the one cancer cell had multiplied until it had broken out of the colon and had invaded all his internal vital organs. They just sewed him up and sent him home to die six weeks later. One cell becoming a false cell brought death to the whole body. Most organizations and individuals that start teaching false doctrine do not detect it as being false doctrine, which was accepted because of the deceiving *spirit of error*. That spirit of error to the organization is like the minute amount of yeast that invades the dough for the loaf of bread. It is like the cancer cell undetected and unchecked that brings death to the rest of the members of the body.

Strange Doctrine And False Doctrine:

There are false doctrines that can move a person or organization away from the mainstream of God's true Church. There is also what the Bible calls various and **strange** doctrines, Heb.13:9 *"Do not be carried away with various and strange doctrines."*

The Old Testament talks about putting away strange gods and not to make offerings with strange fire. Some other translations use the word "Profane" and "unholy" for the word "strange." *"But Nadab and Abihu, the sons of Aaron, placed strange fire in their censers, laid incense on the fire, and offered the incense before the Lord---contrary to what the Lord had commanded them! So fire blazed from the presence of the Lord and destroyed them."* Lev.10:1,2LB; Nu.3:4; 26:61

No doubt Paul used the word "strange doctrine" based on the story of what happened to Aaron's two eldest sons who offered "Strange Fire" in the incense offering. God had Moses consecrate Aaron's four sons to the Priestly ministry to offer animal sacrifices and incense offerings. There were some sacrifices and incense offerings that only Aaron was to offer. Aaron's four sons were to perform the sacrifices and offerings that the Levites were not allowed to do. Their sacrifices and offerings were to be done at a specific time and in a particular way. The two older brothers took fire from the common area and not from the special place consecrated for that purpose and offered an incense offering that Moses had not commanded them to offer. The "strange fire" offering was contrary to God's will and way for when

— 172 —

and how it was to be done. It was so offensive to God that He killed them right in the Sanctuary as they were making the offering.

WHY DID GOD KILL THEM?

It sounds mysterious why God would kill Nadab and Abihu for what they did. What made it so serious that God would kill them by striking them with a lightning bolt of fire? In Matthew Henry's Commentary on this scripture, he uses several pages to explain the many possible reasons why God did it.

They were guilty of doing that which the Lord had not commanded them to do. They committed the sin of presumption, performing their work before their time and offering the wrong sacrifice at the wrong time. They began doing that which only their father Aaron was supposed to do. Prior to this act, they had been offering the sacrifices they were supposed to do according to the commandment of Moses. God had told Moses that only Aaron could offer the sacrifices of atonement, and his four sons were to offer sacrifices that the Levites could not offer. There is also the indication that they had drank too much of the wine used in some of the offerings outside the Tabernacle, but inside the fence as you enter through the gate. This is likely what motivated God to give the following ordinance to Aaron and the priests immediately after this incident.. *"Do not drink wine or intoxicating drink, you, nor your sons with you, when you go into the tabernacle of meeting, lest you die, that you may distinguish between the holy and unholy, and between the clean and unclean."* Lev.10:8. This may be one reason Paul wrote that bishops should not drink wine or any intoxicating drink. (1 Tim.3:3) Being drunk when they entered the holy Tabernacle of God, and failing to offer the right sacrifice at God's timing and divine order, showed their lack of respect for God's holy place and His commandments. They had been emphatically directed to do everything according to the divine order and pattern that God was giving to Moses, but they did not. *"So fire went out from the Lord and devoured them, and they died before the Lord."* God spoke immediately through Moses to Aaron as he was gazing upon the charred dead bodies of his two eldest sons. *"By those who come near me I must be regarded as holy; and before all the people I must be glorified." Lev.10:3*

It would be very wise for every saint of God and Christian minister to take seriously God's attitude toward those who minister His sacred word and perform His spiritual ministries as revealed in the previous scripture. It is good to know that Jesus is our friend and God is our Heavenly Father, but some during the Charismatic movement came close to being disrespectful by acting and saying things like God is good ole Dad and we hang out together making it sound like God is just like one of their buddies. Some did not dress up to go to God's house of worship as much as they did going to a party or banquet celebrating some earthly dignitary. I know to the modern day generation this sounds old fashion. But all the examples in the Bible reveals that God is not pleased when people come lightly and loosely before His presence in His holy Sanctuary. The Holy Spirit is restoring the reverential fear of God back into His Church in this day and hour.

THE VALUABLE REVERENTIAL FEAR OF GOD

Notice what the following Scripture Phrases say about the reverential fear of God: "The fear of the Lord is the beginning of wisdom...serve the Lord with fear and rejoice...You that fear the Lord praise Him...The Lord is with them that fear Him...Angel of the Lord encamps round about those that fear God...Fear the Lord you saints...No want to them that fear God...The fear of the Lord prolongs your days and is a fountain of life...Do not fear man but fear God who can destroy both body and soul in hell...serve God with reverence and godly fear...cleanse yourself from all filthiness of your flesh and spirit perfecting holiness in the fear of God...submit one to another in the fear of God...Fear God and give glory to His name...Then those who feared the Lord spoke one to another and a book of remembrance was written before God for those who fear the Lord; they shall be Mine, saith the Lord of Hosts, on the day that I make them My jewels."

God Is Stricter When Establishing The New

One major reason this was such a serious sin to God, is that God was in the process of establishing the Dispensation of the Law with all of its sacrifices and offerings. All of these things were to be temporary means for people to be forgiven of their sins. All of these were to be types and shadows and illustrations of the coming Christ who would be the true forgiver of all sins of mankind. *"God took our list of sins and destroyed them by nailing them to Christ's cross. In this way God took away Satan's power to accuse you of sin, and God openly displayed to the whole world Christ's triumph at the cross where your sins were all taken away. So don't let anyone criticize you for what you eat or drink, or for not celebrating Jewish holidays and feasts or new moon ceremonies or Sabbaths.* **For these were only temporary rules that ended when Christ came. They were only shadows of the real thing – of Christ himself."** *Col.2:14-17LB; Heb.8:5; 10:1.*

Because everything was to be a type and shadow of Christ and His Church is the reason God was so strict and detailed with Moses telling him to do everything exactly as He commanded him without any deviation from the original pattern. God is much stricter and more judgmental when He is establishing a new divine order. That is why God was so strict and seemingly merciless with Achan when He was establishing Israel in the Land of Canaan; and why God was so severe with two members of the New Testament Church, Ananias and Sapphira (by killing them when they lied to the Holy Spirit), because He was in the process of establishing His divine order for the New Testament Church.

God is now in the process of establishing His new divine order for the Third and Final Church Reformation. We, who are founders and proclaimers of God's timely purpose on earth; revealing His word, will and way for His new divine order; we have to be very diligent, reverential and holy during this time in our life and work, especially while Jesus Christ is in the process of establishing His Third Reformation purpose for His Church.

Strange gods, strange fire and strange doctrines are those things people start teaching and practicing that is non-biblical, contrary to the context and spirit of the Word of God and not compatible with God's nature, character and ways. It may not be damnable heresies, but it is things that God would call foolish, ridiculous and things that greatly displease the Lord Jesus.

As an example of this, in 1959, I was traveling in ministry, and I preached at a church pastored by a friend of mine. He asked me to stay for a month and pastor his church while he and his wife went on vacation. He asked if I would visit this house meeting where some of his members were visiting and evaluate what the minister was teaching. I discovered he was teaching some "strange doctrine." He was saying that God revealed to him that our rewards in heaven will be thus and so. Those who just make it into heaven would be less than five feet tall and have black hair and no breasts. Each new level of overcomers would increase in height, their hair would grow lighter and breasts would be bigger. Those who were the greatest overcomers would be over six feet tall, snow white hair and large sized breasts. He tried to authorize his teachings by saying that an angel had taken him to heaven and shown him the saints who manifest the overcome rewards. The members who were attending asked me if this was deep teaching. I said no, it's not deep, but a strange doctrine coming from the vain imaginations of a ridiculously unbalanced preacher.

"Do not let anyone declare you lost when you refuse to worship angels, as they say you must. They have seen a vision, they say, and know you should. These proud men (though they claim to be so humble) have a very clever imagination. But they are not connected to Christ, the head." Col. 2:18,19LB

MOST RECENT STRANGE DOCTRINE

There was another strange doctrine being propagated on the Internet as recent as 2014. One of my ministers told me about it and pulled it up on his computer. It showed the person who originated the concept and was propagating this teaching. He called it "Grave Sucking" and had several young people lying on the grave of a historic anointed man of God, supposedly soaking up the anointing from the grave. The leader spoke all the language of Charismatic, Prophetic, Apostolic, and Kingdom terminology. At the end of the presentation, the leader and the people were throwing their arms out toward the camera implying they were throwing the anointing from the man of God's body in the grave to the viewers.

They base their authority for doing "Grave Sucking" on the story of the dead man being thrown into the grave of Elisha and coming back alive. The problem of that is there is no record of the man receiving the anointing of Elisha and carrying on his ministry. There is no biblical record or inference that any of the New Testament apostles or saints laid on the grave of Abraham, David, Isaiah or any of the anointed prophets or Patriarchs. Not only are there no examples of such a thing happening, it is not in the spirit, biblical context or content of the Church of our Lord Jesus Christ. It is usually the wild concoctions and imagination of a minister who wants to sound like he has a new sensational revelation that makes him look knowledgeable and special. But also, it is what Apostle Paul calls "strange doctrine" that is to be rejected and avoided. One meaning of divine wisdom is spiritual common sense. When something is ridiculous and nonsensical, and there are no scriptures even suggesting the practice and no biblical examples of it being done, then it is "strange doctrine."

There are things that the scriptures tell Christian to do and examples of saints practicing it that may look strange and ridiculous to the world. For instance, "speaking in tongues" to the natural mind of the world it may look ridiculous and sound nonsensical. But Christians have scriptures showing that Jesus instituted "speaking in other tongues" on the Day of Pentecost and examples of the apostles praying for people to receive the ability to pray in "other tongues." Apostle Paul dedicates two chapters to the proper use of tongues and the benefits of praying in a spirit language that the natural mind does not understand. That is one reason I wrote the book, "Seventy Reasons For Speaking in Tongues," to give understanding of God's many purposes for giving the saints their own spirit language when He birthed the Church on the Day of Pentecost. Also praying, believing and worshipping an unseen God may look and sound strange to the world, but it is not strange doctrine for it is biblically true and proven workable by millions of Christians and it is true doctrine for Christians to believe and practice.

SOUL MATES AND SPIRITUAL SPOUSES

In the early days of the Later Rain movement (1950s), there were many truths and ministries restored back into the Church. However like every move of God there are those who are immature, unsanctified, lacking scriptural knowledge and biblical wisdom who cannot discern between the thoughts that come from God, and those that come from their own imagination or suggestions from Satan. A woman minister came up with the "revelation" that married Christians have "soul mates" which may not be the person they married. Especially those whose mate is not saved and does not attend church with them, they would need to find their soul mate from among the church members. What would start out being a "soul mate" or "spiritual spouse" usually ended up in sexual immorality. She preached this "strange doctrine" as being a direct revelation from God. I was surprised to find when I was itinerating in ministry in Europe in 2010 that this same strange doctrine had surfaced in some of the churches in those nations. I cover this subject in my book "Prophets---Principles to Practice & Pitfalls to Avoid" pages 29,30:

> **The Deception of "Ministerial Mates":** In my years as a bishop over many ministers, I have had to deal with a number of deceptions that lead ministers to destruction. Over the last several decades, one deception I have often heard is the concept of a "ministerial mate" or a "spiritual spouse." This "strange doctrine" keeps reappearing in Christendom and has even crept into the Charismatic and Prophetic-Apostolic Movements. In fact, it seems to have made greater inroads into those circles where there are claims of revelation knowledge and prophetic direction.

A "*ministerial mate*" or "*spiritual spouse*" is anyone a married minister (or any Christian person) allows to become a closer companion than his or her true spouse, especially when that person is of the opposite sex. It is usually an associate minister, secretary, worship leader or youth minister. For a married person to cultivate romantic feelings or actions or sexual involvement with someone other than his or her marriage partner is sin in God's sight. So this kind of inappropriate closeness is dangerous because it usually leads to romance and finally to sexual immorality.

A Gradual Process of Bonding and Deception: Of course, this situation does not happen overnight. Typically, a minister and an associate or secretary work closely together over months and years until a "soul tie" develops--that is, a close emotional bonding. The minister's spouse ceases to be his or her closest friend, counselor, sounding board and co-laborer in the ministry. The minister begins to spend more time with the associate at the office and out of town at conferences than with the spouse at home.

As this deception takes root within the minister, he or she takes further actions to fulfill its ultimate purpose. The minister's spouse is manipulated out of active ministry with the minister and the church, with an accompanying alienation of affections within the marriage. The minister justifies himself in such actions by claiming that the "ministerial mate" is more understanding and appreciative than the spouse. The "mate" seems patient, kind, sweet and trusting, while the spouse appears as fussy and demanding, always questioning why the minister has to be away from home so much and spends so little time with the family.

The Spouse Must Take Action. Sin and lust are deceitful, blinding a person to reality until the deception leads to its final result: an adulterous affair that destroys the minister's marriage, ministry and character. So a minister's spouse who senses such a situation developing needs to bring it to the attention of the spouse-minister. If the minister responds with understanding, begins immediately to adjust the situation, and works toward restoring a proper relationship with the family, then the spouse need mention it to no one else.

On the other hand, if the minister responds with resentment, accusing the spouse of jealousy, lack of commitment, or failure to understand ministerial responsibilities, then the spouse's obligation is to go immediately to their spiritual overseer, telling all and getting the overseer involved in the situation. The spouse must not be stopped by threats or a spirit of intimidation intended to keep them from getting help. The situation will not improve simply by being ignored or by the spouse's keeping silent in hopes that time will work it out. Prayer will help, but this particular situation is usually not resolved without proper outside help.

Remember: Revealing this problem to a spiritual overseer does not mean someone is betraying confidence, failing to stand by his or her spouse, or failing to cover the sin with love. In this case, the scriptural command "Open rebuke is better than secret love" (Prov. 27:5) supersedes the scriptural principle "Love covers a multitude of sins" (1 Pet. 4:8). This principle is like the law of aerodynamics superseding the law of gravity. It does not do away with the law of gravity; it just supersedes it for a time to accomplish a higher purpose. I have talked to many wives of ministers who have been kept in bondage by the misuse and abuse of this scripture. The longer a spouse waits to get help, the more the situation will deteriorate, increasing the possibility that both the marriage and the ministry will be dissolved.

Avoid this prophetic pitfall and character flaw at all costs. When all things are in divine order, then the proper priorities and responsibilities are these: first God, then family and ministry. All other areas should be taken care of only after these three areas of responsibility are fulfilled. I have seen this process take place in many ministers. If you happen to be in this process act on these principles and believe God for resolution and restoration.

CHARACTERISTICS OF CULTS

A "Cult" is a perversion, a distortion of biblical Christianity and/or a rejection of the historic teachings of the mainline Christian churches. A cult, then, is a group of people polarized around someone's interpretation of the Bible and is characterized by major deviations from Orthodox Christianity relative to the cardinal doctrines of the Christian faith, particularly the fact that God became man in Jesus Christ, and Jesus is Deity and one of the three in one Godhead.

The purpose of this book is not to cover all the different religions and "Christian" cults. There are many books written that cover all the religions of the world. The one that I used the most in research was the "Handbook of Today's Religions" authored by Josh McDowell and Don Stewart, published by Thomas Nelson Publishers. They cover all the religions that do not use the Bible as a basis for their beliefs, such as the teachings and beliefs of Hinduism, Buddhism, Confucianism, Shintoism and a few others. They also give 20 examples of the Occult practiced by individuals and groups.

The majority of the "Christian" Cults such as, Jehovah Witnesses, Mormons, Christian Science, Christian Universalist Association and others originated from a minister who was originally a part of a mainline Christian denomination. Most of them originated during the 1700s & 1800s. All of them claimed divine revelation for their beliefs and several claimed supernatural visitations of Jesus or heavenly angels. All the founders come across as wholly dedicated to God with an intense desire to get answers, to know which denomination has all the truth, and if not, what other truth there was to be revealed. (It becomes a counterfeit of the Holy Spirit bringing the Church to the restoration of all truth and ministries of Jesus Christ. Acts 3:21; Eph.4:11-15). Most of their strange and false doctrine came from reading some of the teaching of Church leaders and Philosophers of the first three centuries of the Church. The majority of the strange and false teachings of the 21st century are an extension of the Christian cults that were formed during the Church Restoration time of the Holiness Movement. The warning to present day ministers is the fact that most of the ministers who founded these cults were one-time members or ministers of Historic Protestant and Holiness Movement churches. We all need to heed the guidelines I gave in an earlier chapter on fortifying ourselves against the spirit of error and receiving and preaching false doctrine.

21ST CENTURY FRUIT FROM THE ROOT OF UNIVERSALISM

The teachings and practices of many groups, today received their teachings and practices from Universalism, such as the extreme grace teaching. Liberal theology in the modernistic Christian denominations, cults such as Christian Science, Unitarianism, New Agers, extreme left-wing political views and all groups which put more emphasis on intellectualism and exclusivism.

During the Latter Rain Movement during the 1950some ministers started teaching the doctrine propagated by the Universalist. That is, that Jesus died to save everyone, and that includes the devil and all his fallen angels and every human being who has ever lived on planet earth. Every being that God had ever created would be in heaven with Jesus. He taught that God's love and grace were so infinite that it included the ultimate reconciliation of all things.

REACTIVATION OF ERROR:

During the latter part of the 20th Century a Pentecostal preacher that pastored a large Charismatic church started teaching a version of the false doctrine known as universalism and ultimate reconciliation. It is referred to as the "Inclusion" doctrine. He started teaching that all human beings are saved, but they don't know yet that Jesus has saved them, however, they will discover it when they get to heaven. He declared that no human being would go to hell for it was only prepared for the devil and his angels. This is a prominent Pentecostal preacher who for years was mainline church doctrinally sound and could preach fundamental truths with anointing and zeal. What made him go astray? It is the same thing that has caused most of the cults within Christendom to do away with the doctrine of an eternal hell. You find out your best friend or someone you greatly admire and respect is a homosexual or is practicing some other horrible sin. A close relative like a parent or child dies without ever accepting Christ as their personal Savior, and you cannot accept the idea that they would go to hell and suffer eternally. I heard this preacher testifying on TV that he just could not accept the idea that his unsaved loved ones would go to hell, so he invented the inclusion doctrine and to him that put them in heaven and made him feel better. When a person starts resenting some truth of God's Word and begins to think that it is not just or right they open themselves up to the spirit of error and deception that causes them to believe and preach a false doctrine. When a person is deceived, they will propagate the false with the same conviction and zeal as they do when preaching the truth.

PERSONAL EXPOSURE TO EXTREME GRACE

Before I went to Bible College in 1953, I was attending an independent church that was filled with people who had come from Pentecostal denominations. They all were still practicing the anti-worldliness teachings of the Holiness and Pentecostal movement that believed all sports and world entertainment such as movies were sinful. The women could not wear lipstick, ear rings, or jeans but had to wear long dresses with long sleeves and their hair long. When I came back from Bible College, I was shocked at what I saw. The women were dressed like the rest of the women in the world dressed. They wore earrings and lipstick, had their hair cut short and even wore jeans to church. I was deeply ingrained in the Pentecostal customs at that time; in fact, it wasn't until our 25th wedding anniversary that I allowed my wife to get her ears pierced or to wear earrings. The present day Charismatic Christians that do not have a holiness background do not realize the challenge it was for us to make the transition from everything being worldly except going to church.

The minister that came in taught on the "Grace" of God and against what he called Pentecostal legalism and self works for right standing with God. What he taught delivered the saints from their legalism "clothesline" holiness, but he taught beyond that saying that the flesh profits nothing, only what is done in the spirit. That is a true statement but the application he put to it was not. He also quoted the scripture, *"to the pure all things are pure."* Interpreting it to mean that Christians are pure and whatever they do is purified by their purity, and it doesn't make any difference what they do in their flesh as long as their spirit is pure. Many of the church members began doing everything the ungodly did. A year later it was exposed that the married pastor was committing adultery with the female worship leader. One sister said, I always thought we could have all that God wants us to have and also enjoy all the world has to offer.

I cried out to God, asking what is happening in the Church. That is when God spoke to me that I would find His answer in Duet.13:1-4. "If a prophet arises among you, or a dreamer of dreams, and gives you a sign or wonder, and the sign or the wonder he foretells to you comes to pass, and if he says, let us go after other gods---gods (doctrines) you have not known---and let us serve them, you shall not listen to the words of that prophet or to that dreamer of dreams. For the Lord, your **God is testing you** to **know** whether you love the Lord your God with all your mind and heart and with your entire being. You shall walk after the Lord your God, and [reverently] fear Him, and keep His commandments and obey His voice, and you shall serve Him alone and cling to Him."

"The Lord tests the righteous."

Ps.11:5. The Lord revealed to me that what was happening, God was testing His people to see if their hearts were in alignment and agreement with His first and utmost commandment, to love the Lord their God with all their heart, soul, mind and strength. The pastor and many of the saints failed God's test. God testing His people to determine those who are entirely His is one application to Apostle Paul's statement in 1 Cor.11:19, *"For there must be also heresies among you, that they which are approved may be manifest among you."* God allows His children to be exposed to all kinds of doctrines and false preachers to see whether they will yield to the Spirit of truth or the spirit of error. If the first and greatest commandment that Jesus gave is in control of their life then they will yield to and be directed by the Spirit of truth.

There is a very popular Charismatic preacher preaching a doctrine that has the potential of being the first step of leading a Christian into the second step which would be the inclusion doctrine and that would lead them into the 3rd step which would be the Universalist doctrine of ultimate reconciliation. Saints who are insecure, legalistic and perfectionist need a lot of grace teaching. But grace taken to the extreme becomes very dangerous. This Charismatic preacher may have only this one percent that is unscriptural, but that one percent can activate the spirit of error and lead some Christians to a false belief that gives them a false security in their sins being forgiven when they may not be. It is the teaching that our future sins are already forgiven before we ever commit them. Therefore, we do not have to ask forgiveness for them. The blood of Jesus and God's grace is available and sufficient to forgive and cleanse us from any sin we might commit, but nowhere in scripture does it say or imply that sins are automatically forgiven without ASKING for forgiveness. Apostle John declared, *"**IF** we **CONFESS** our sin He is faithful and just to forgive."* James said that we had not because we ASK not. Jesus said "ASK and you shall receive." There is no forgiveness of sin without asking Jesus to forgive.

SIMILAR TEACHING AS UNIVERSALIST

The present day teaching that there is no need to confess our sins as they are already forgiven is a lighter version of the inclusion doctrine which says all mankind is already forgiven by Jesus but they just don't know it and haven't acknowledged it. This teaching is similar to what Universalism teaches concerning the blood of Jesus. They teach that the blood of Jesus was holy and able to cleanse from sin before it was shed upon the cross. Therefore, the crucifixion of Jesus was useless and needless. They teach that we should not talk about the cross, rather just glorify the blood of Jesus.

In all the offerings for sin in the Old Testament it was insufficient for the animals to walk by the altar with the blood still flowing through their veins, the Lamb's throat had to be sliced open, the blood poured into a container and sprinkled on the sacrifice and sometimes the person being sanctified. The blood had to be shed and applied. *"Without the shedding of blood there is no remission of sins."* Heb.9:22.

Jesus had to be crucified, and His blood shed for His blood to cleanse us from sin. All mankind is not automatically saved just because the blood of Jesus was shed for the whole human race. Jesus said that it is only the "whosoever" of the human race who believes in Jesus and confesses their sins to Jesus for forgiveness that are cleansed from their sins and made a child of God. Not one person in the human race has forgiveness of sins unless they have believed on the Lord Jesus and asked for forgiveness of their sins.

The doctrine of forgiveness of future sins without asking for forgiveness from Jesus may seem like a small insignificant doctrine, but when it is contrary to the teaching of the Bible it becomes a spirit of error. It is like the minute amount of yeast that affects the whole loaf of bread. It only takes one cell in the body to be activated into a cancer cell, and if not recognized as a false cell it can multiply and contaminate the whole body. Sinning and false doctrine are not small trespasses to Jesus. He was the Truth and gave us the Holy Spirit of Truth to keep us from believing the false. He shed His life's blood to cleanse us from all sin and His grace to give us power to live victorious over sin. The ultimate reconciliation and inclusion doctrines magnify the grace of God and declare it covers all the sins of mankind, just as the forgiveness of sins without confession is covered by God's grace. That type of teaching is what mainline Christianity calls "Extreme Grace." God's grace does not cover unconfessed sins.

"If we confess our sins He is faithful and just to forgive us our sins and to cleanse us from all unrighteousness." "The GRACE of God that brings salvation has appeared to all men, teaching us that denying ungodliness and worldly lusts, we should live soberly, righteously, and godly in the present age." God's grace is more than "God's unmerited favor." A fuller definition of divine grace is "God's unmerited divine enablement." By grace---God's divine enablement---we are saved through faith and that not of ourselves; it is the gift of God. Wherever sin abounds God's unearned powerful enablement to live victorious over sin abounds even more. God's grace enables us to be born again, not practice sinning, manifest the supernatural miracles of God and able to do all things through Christ who strengthens us by His enabling grace. All this grace is available to us, but sad to say, we Christians do not draw upon all of God's grace that is available to us which causes us to sin and come short of the glory of God. But Jesus our great mediator and advocate knowing humanity made provision for our occasional failures. *"My little children, these things I write to you, so that you may not sin. And if anyone sins, we (Christians) have an advocate with the Father, Jesus Christ the righteous. And if we will confess our sins Jesus is faithful and just to forgive us our sins." 1Jn.2:1; 1:9.*

Chapter 10
THEN & NOW

RESTORATION OF TRUTH VS. REACTIVATION OF ERROR

All **new teachings** that have developed over the last 500 years have been the restoration of truth back into the Church that was lost during the Dark Age of the Church or the re-emphasis of a false doctrine. The majority of times, it was a minister within a mainline protestant denomination that began teaching the false doctrine and started a church that went astray from the fundamentals of the New Testament Church. For instance, the approximate 100 years of the Protestant Movement (1520-1620) were the first beginning of many of the present non-mainline Christian organizations. I want to deal with one of them because a modern day apostle who was part of the pioneering of the restoration of the Prophetic and Apostolic took up the teaching of one of those groups, called "Preterism".

After doing intensive research, I found the background for the beginning of this teaching. It began during the peak of the Protestant Movement. Martin Luther was the main pioneer of the Protestant Movement. The Lutheran Church was named after Luther and was one of the mainline Protestant Movement church organizations. The Catholic Church excommunicated Luther and declared him a heretic. Martin Luther counteracted by declaring that the Catholic Church was the Mother Harlot mentioned in the book of Revelation and the Pope was the Antichrist. The Catholic hierarchy raised up a group of theologians called the Jesuits. To counter the accusations of Luther the Jesuits developed two teachings: one put all prophecies in the book of

Revelation to be fulfilled during a 7-year period at the end of the Christian dispensation. The other teaching declared that all the prophecies in the book of Revelation were fulfilled before the Catholic Church was officially formed. Both views were to prove that the Pope could not be the Antichrist and the Mother Harlot for all those prophecies had been fulfilled, or they were yet to be fulfilled at the end of the Church Age.

The following statements by G.S. Hitchcock, a Catholic writer, and Dean Henry Alford a Protestant theologian both in different writings attribute these two concepts to the same source: "The Futurist School, founded by the Jesuit Ribera in 1591 looks for Antichrist, Babylon, and a rebuilt temple in Jerusalem, during a 7-year period at the end of the Christian dispensation." "The Preterist School, founded by the Jesuit Alcasar in 1614, explains the Book of Revelation prophecies were all fulfilled by the fall of Jerusalem in 70 AD, or the fall of Pagan Rome in 410 AD."

The Present Truth Protestant Movement Churches, the main ones being Lutheran, Anglican and Presbyterian rejected the teaching of Preterism. The word "Preter" means past time and already fulfilled. Preterism teaches that every future event prophesied in the New Testament was fulfilled during and sometime after 70AD when Jerusalem was destroyed by the Romans. The prophecy Jesus gave concerning the Temple being torn down and not one stone left upon another was fulfilled.

Fundamental Truth Vs. Eschatology:

There are many errors and strange doctrines in Preterism, but the one that is the most serious does not deal with eschatology but one of the foundation stones of the Christian Faith---the future resurrection of the dead. They declare that 1 Cor.15:51, 52 and 1Thess.4:17,18 has already been fulfilled and also everything in the Book of Revelation. These two Scriptures are the main ones Evangelicals use to explain the "Rapture" of the Church. They both speak of the bodies of the departed saints being resurrected, and the bodies of the living saints being translated and transformed in a moment in the twinkling of an eye into immortal bodies.

Some have asked why there needs to be a resurrection of the earthly physical body. There are several reasons. The main reason is the simple fact that Jesus promised His children that He would make sure they received a resurrected human body just like His. Phil.3:21. Jesus has the same human body He had while on earth. His resurrected flesh and bone body was changed into an immortal flesh and bone body which is now seated at the right hand of God. The body of Jesus that was born of the Virgin Mary, walked the shores of Galilee and hung on the cross of Calvary is the same body that was resurrected into a glorious, immortal, indestructible, eternal mankind flesh and bone body. He did not discard His earth-body or have it swallowed up by a spirit body from heaven as Preterism teaches, nor dissolved and a new body made out of some heavenly material as Jehovah Witnesses teach. The reason some question the resurrection and restoration of the human body is because they cannot figure out with their natural mind how it can be done when the dust of your body has been scattered to the four winds or absorbed into some plant. My answer is that the Almighty Scientist who stated He was going to do it knows exactly how it will be done. I tell some maybe it is like the way the bodies of the animals in the movie Jurassic Park were reformed. Maybe the angels take one genetic cell from each human body and when the archangel sounds that special trumpet and Jesus gives that shout all human bodies which have died are resurrected-reformed, and at the same time the living saints bodies are immediately changed to be just like Jesus's body in heaven and the bodies of the saints who had just been resurrected. Then God's eternal mankind Church members will be like He originally made man---spirit, soul, and body. We do not have to understand how it all works. Just know and believe that Jesus said it, and He will do it. I don't understand how the red blood of Jesus cleanses my blackened soul and makes it white as snow, nor how Jesus gives me a born again experience making me a new creation in Christ. I just believe, receive and have all my sins removed and become a new creation child of Father God..

IMPORTANCE OF THE FUTURE RESURRECTION OF DEAD

The future resurrection of the dead is one of the central foundational doctrines of true Christianity. Apostle Paul declared that if there is no general resurrection of every human being who has ever lived on planet earth, then Christ was not resurrected from the grave. And if Christ was not raised from the dead then that nullifies our Christianity. It was not enough for Jesus to die on the cross and be buried; He had to be resurrected. Paul taught, if Christ had not risen from the dead then our Christian faith would be futile, and we would still be in our sins. *"Jesus Christ was declared to be the Son of God by the resurrection from the dead." Rom.1:4.* The proof that Jesus is the real Son of God is the fact that He rose from the dead. That is the reason Apostle Paul said Jesus was declared to be the Son of God **BY** His resurrection from the dead. Notice the importance that Apostle Paul puts on the truth, necessity and reality of the resurrection of the dead in the following scriptures.

> *"Now if Christ is preached that He has been raised from the dead, how do some among you say that there is no resurrection of the dead? But if there is no resurrection of the dead, then Christ is not risen. And if Christ is not arisen, then our preaching is empty and your faith is also empty. Yes, and we are found, false witnesses of God, because we have testified of God that he raised up Christ, whom he did not raise up-if in fact the dead do not rise. For if the dead do not rise, then Christ is not risen. And if Christ is not risen, your faith is futile; you are still in your sins! Then also those who have fallen asleep in Christ have perished. But now Christ is risen from the dead and has become the firstfruits of those who have fallen asleep." 1 Cor.15:12-20.*

The truth of the resurrection of the dead is so fundamental and essential to Christianity that it needs to be read in two or three present English translations. Let these two translations in present-day terminology expand your understanding and stamp the importance of the resurrection within your heart.

The Living Bible:

"But tell me this! Since you believe what we preach, that Christ rose from the dead, why are some of you saying that dead people will never come back to life again? For if there is no resurrection of the dead, then Christ must still be dead. And if he is still dead, then all our preaching is useless and your trust in God is empty, worthless, hopeless; and we apostles are all liars because we have said that God raised Christ from the grave, and of course, that isn't true. If the dead do not come back to life again. If they don't, then Christ is still dead, and you are very foolish to keep on trusting God to save you, and you are still under condemnation for your sins; In that case all Christians who have died are lost! And if being a Christian is of value to us only now in this life we are the most miserable of creatures. But the fact is that Christ did actually rise from the dead, and has become the first of multi-millions who will come back to life again some day."

The Message:

"Now, let me ask you something profound yet troubling. If you became believers because you trusted the proclamation that Christ is alive, risen from the dead, how can you let people say that there is no such thing as a resurrection? If there's no resurrection, there is no living Christ. And face it – if there's no resurrection for Christ, everything we've told you is smoke and mirrors, and everything you've staked your life on is smoke and mirrors. Not only that, but we would be guilty of telling a string of barefaced lies about God, all these affidavits we pass on to you verifying that God raised up Christ – sheer fabrications, if there's no resurrection. If corpses

can't be raised, then Christ wasn't, because he was indeed dead. And if Christ weren't raised, then all you're doing is wandering about in the dark, as lost as ever. It's even worse for those who died hoping in Christ and resurrection, because they're already in their graves. If all we get out of Christ is a little inspiration for a few short years, we're a pretty sorry lot. But the truth is, that Christ has been raised up, the first in a long legacy of those who are going to leave the cemeteries."

This False Doctrine Started in the Day of Apostle Paul:

Paul wrote to Timothy that a couple of their fellow Church ministers had strayed from the truth and had started teaching some false doctrine.   He said their message would spread like cancer. *"Hymenaeus and Philetus are of this sort, who have strayed from the truth, saying that the resurrection is already past, and they overthrow the faith of some."* 2 Tim.2:15-18.   The books of Matthew, Mark, and Luke record Jesus rebuking the Sadducees and telling them they did not understand the Scriptures nor the power of God. He showed them by Scripture that they were in error for not believing in the immortality of the soul and the resurrection of the dead. Paul declared in his defense before Governor Felix. *"I believe there will be a resurrection of the dead, both of the just and the unjust."* The resurrection of the dead is one of the six foundational doctrines of Christ's Church listed in Hebrew 6:1,2NKJ. 1. Repentance from dead Works, 2. Faith toward God,   3. Doctrine of baptisms,   4. Laying on of Hands,   5. **Resurrection of the dead,** 6. Eternal Judgment. The statement, I believe in the Resurrection of the Dead, is also in the Apostles Creed of Christendom.

Problems with False Doctrine & Spirit of Error:

A fellow minister asked me if I would have this apostle who is propagating Preterism preach in my conference again. I replied that I love and appreciate the brother, but I would not, even though he can preach deliverance, prophetic, apostolic and kingdom greatly and fairly accurately. However, when the spirit of error comes and is accepted as truth it causes a person to preach a false doctrine with the same persuasive power that he preaches the truth. Because of his past and present reputation of preaching the truth, the average church member assumes the error must be true because the other messages he preaches are true. That 1% of poisonous false doctrine becomes the small amount of yeast that can spread through the whole church. As Apostle Paul declared, it overthrows and pollutes the faith of some. A minister can have 99% good biblical doctrine but if that 1% of poison-doctrine is preached in a church it is like weed seeds that are sown in a garden which begins to spring up and choke out the good plants. Also believing a false doctrine opens a person to the spirit of error. When a person even preaches the truth, but they have the spirit of error, it can be transferred to those who are susceptible to it. It is the same as when a person preaches in a church and at the same time is living in adultery, he releases an immoral and divorcing spirit into the congregation even though his words may be speaking truth. I have witnessed this happening in many churches during the last 60 years. I have talked to many pastors who testified after a minister that had these problems preached in his church; he would have to deal with an abundance of these same problems among the members of his local church.

False Doctrine Can Cause an Eternal Problem:

Remember that rat poison has to be mostly nutritional tasty food in order to entice the rat to eat the poison that is camouflaged in the good ingredients. And counterfeit money must have all the ingredients of government printed money in order to get the public to accept it.

We do not know how much false doctrine a minister must believe and preach before he loses his right standing with God. We do know the attitude of Jesus Christ concerning anyone who removes vital truth from His holy Word, the Bible. We derive this from some of the final words of Jesus in Revelation 22:19, the last chapter and one of the last three verses in His holy Book. *"If anyone takes away from the words of the book of this prophecy, God shall take away his part from the Book of Life."* The potential consequences of doing away with foundational truth and preaching a false doctrine should make ALL saints and ministers fully examine themselves and submit themselves to proven and mature ministers to make sure that any new thing they start believing and teaching is solid biblical truth. Even Apostle Paul submitted his new teaching to the apostles at Jerusalem and received their approval that his new revelation was according to Scripture and the witness of the Holy Spirit.

Beliefs That Lead to Immorality:

During the centuries of the Church, there have been many teachings by "Christian" ministers that led them and their followers into sexual immorality. In the New Testament, the standard was that a man was to be the husband of one wife according to the original pattern God established in the beginning with Adam and Eve. If there was ever a time that it would have been good for a man to have many wives, it would have been the time of Adam. He was told to populate the earth and he could have done that much faster if he had many wives, but God only gave him one and declared when they were joined together in marriage they would be one flesh. Jesus established it that way because it was best for the human race. Also, it was to be an illustration of a person being joined to the Lord and becoming one spirit with Christ Jesus. Also a type of Jesus being joined in one Body with His Church. Christ is the Head of the Church, and the saints are the individual members of the one Body of Christ. Eph.1:22,23; 5:30-32 1 Cor.6:17; 1 Tim.3:2.

A Few Examples From the Many:

Joseph Smith, the founder of the Mormon religion, added the teaching of multiple wives. The New Testament is emphatic that a man having sexual relations with another woman other than his one official wife is committing adultery, which is a sin of sexual immorality according to God's word. Jesus declared that all the sexually immoral would spend their eternity in the Lake of Fire. Rev.21:8.

During the 1950s there was an evangelist privately teaching to women in the Church that we are all in the Body of Christ, and we are all one like husband and wife are one. He used this teaching to get single and married women to have sex with him. He had a wife at home, but he was having sexual relations with other women in almost every church he preached. It is hard to grasp that Christian women would fall for that teaching and commit adultery with the preacher, but Lucifer who deceived Eve is a master deceiver and manipulator.

"For such are false apostles, deceitful workers, transforming themselves into apostles of Christ. And no wonder! For Satan himself transforms himself into an angel of light. Therefore, it is no great thing if his ministers also transform themselves into ministers of righteousness, whose end will be according to their works." 2 Cor.11:13-15.

There was a charismatic pastor in the 1990s that privately taught some women in his church a doctrine that led to sexual immorality. He told them that it was their duty before God to minister to God's man with sexual favors. Over a dozen women testified that this minister had sex with them. One of the lead female singers and worshippers testified that the minister had been having sex with her for 15 years. Her husband was an elder in the church, but he never knew it was going on until the end. This was not going on in the backwoods of Tennessee, but in a major city in the United States. The Pastor had a church of thousands, wrote many books, national television program, and was an Apostle-Overseer of a ministerial network with hundreds of ministers and churches.

Now is The Time To Be Cleansed and Delivered:

These examples are just a few of the many that are taking place within Christendom in all denominations from Catholic to Charismatic. A whole book could be written revealing all the sinning, deception and various and strange doctrines that are taught and practiced within Christendom, but that would not be edifying and beneficial to the Body of Christ. I just want to give a minimal number of examples to reveal that they really exist. We also want to examine what kind and how much false doctrine does a minister have to teach before God rejects him, from being one of His ministers. One thing we need to consider is the fact that there is no scripture that even implies that death cleanses our soul of unforgiven sins and our mind of false teachings. If we do not have scriptures and Bible examples explaining and demonstrating what happens at death concerning these areas then it remains somewhat of a mystery, and we cannot establish a definite teaching on it.

We need to understand that any teachers that make sin less than what God declares it to be are guilty of teaching "Strange" doctrine. Any teaching that leads, deceives and manipulates Christians into sexual immorality does not come from God, but from the mind of carnal man and Lucifer the deceiver.

Nothing in all of God's nature, character, and Holy Spirit or His written Word allows or approves of sexual immorality. Any sexual activity committed in mind or body outside of marriage to one person is declared to be sin according to God's Word. Sexual immorality is described as works of the flesh, perversion, motivated by lust of the flesh and declared to be an ungodly sin whether committed by a non-Christian or a professing Christian or a minister in Christ's Church. A person guilty of sexual immorality that has not been forgiven and cleansed by the blood of Jesus has the door to heaven shut to him, and the gate to the Lake of Fire opened wide.

Saved By Pre-Knowledge:

One reason I am sharing this information is to prevent you from being seduced by these strange doctrines of men. While teaching in a Bible college in the 1960s, I shared with the class about the fact that ministers could be guilty of adultery, homosexuality, etc. Some of the students had never heard of such a possibility and complained to the president of the College that I should not share such things with them. One of the young men in the class was invited by a pastor that came and spoke at the college, to go with him on a mission trip. This minister was the pastor of a large church and was head of a great network of ministers. He was married with three teenage children. While they were on the trip the minister tried to get the student to commit a homosexual act with him. The student told me when he returned that If I had not told him about these things and what to do if put in that position, that he would have left the Bible College and probably not gone into the ministry. Thank God he did graduate from Bible College and became a national minister and is still ministering.

What Does God's Love, Mercy, and Grace Cover?

All mainline Christian theologians agree that God's **love** is great enough to love and redeem the most wretched and wicked man on earth. God's **grace** which is God's unmerited divine enablement is sufficient to give a Christian the power to resist any temptation and live victorious over all kinds of sin. In the first three centuries of the Church God's grace gave millions of Christians the ability to go through great persecution, suffering and martyrdom. God's **mercy** is available to all generations, and His mercy extends to the vilest of ungodly sinners.

But mainline Christian theologians also agree that God's mercy, love, and grace never ever condones sin as being allowable for Christians to commit. God's righteous and holy nature of love, mercy and grace cannot and will not ever allow sin, ungodliness and pride into His holy Heaven. People with a life of unforgiven sins, ungodly living and the selfish pride of Lucifer will not be allowed into heaven, regardless of whether they are uncivilized heathens, ungodly sinners or professing Christians. There is a line in a song we sang in Church right after I got saved that says, "Heaven is a holy place, filled with glory and with grace, sin can never enter there."

HEAVENLY VISITATIONS NOT ENOUGH & NO GUARANTEE

Supernatural Experiences Insufficient:

Most of the Christian cults and even the founder of Islam make claims to angelic visitations and visits to Heaven and Holy Spirit revelations. Nevertheless, they did not maintain true doctrine. Most were members or ministers of a mainline restoration church but started studying other writings that sowed the seed of their revelation of their false teaching. Others claimed direct revelation from Jesus, angels or supernatural visions.

The Bible is full of people having visions, revelations, and angelic visitations. God promised that when he brought forth His Church it would be marked by the supernatural. Sons and daughters would prophesy, young men see visions, old men dream dreams, many would prophesy, and God would show wonders in the heavens and signs on the earth. Ezekiel received many heavenly visions in the Old Testament. Apostle Paul received a heavenly visitation of Jesus Christ at his conversion and one heavenly trip to heaven during his ministry. Apostle John received one long heavenly visit and angelic visitations that revealed all the visions in the Book of Revelation. Apostle Peter had one vision that helped him know that Gentiles could be saved without keeping the covenants and doing the sacrifices of the Jewish religion. Daniel had about 10 visions, dreams and supernatural experiences in his 70 years of ministry. Abraham received eleven personal prophecies from God and one divine visit from God and two angels in the form of men during his 175 years of life. David, the only man that God declared was a man after His own heart, received no divine visitations of angels or visions or trips to heaven. *"I have found David, a man after My own heart, who will do all My will."* I always wanted to have many angelic visitations and heavenly experience or spiritual dreams, but I received very few in my lifetime. I complained to God, and He reminded me that when I was pastoring at the age of 19 He told me that my life would be patterned after David and I would be a David to him. I restudied the life of David and discovered that he had very few divine visitations but he was led by the Spirit, moved in revelation and was inspired to write most of the Psalms, many of which are the pre-prayed prayers that Jesus prayed while on earth. (Psalm 22 being one example).

The devil seeks to counterfeit everything God has and does such as appear to people as an angel of light or a minister of Jesus Christ. Apostle Paul warned the Corinthian Christians concerning those who falsely claim to be mighty men of God and even Satan masquerading as an angel of light. *"I will cut out the ground from under the feet of those who boast that they are doing God's work in just the same way we are. God never sent those men at all; they are "phonies" who have fooled you into thinking they are Christ's apostles. Yet I am not surprised! Satan can change himself into an angel of light, so it is no wonder his servants can do it too, and seem like godly ministers."* 2 Cor.11:12-14.

Some of the following experiences the founders of new religions had with angels could have been Satan appearing to them as one of God's angels.

Mohammed, The Originator of Islam:

Reportedly when Mohammed first came into contact with Christians in Syria, he was filled with horror at the quantity of idols in the church. It was recorded that when he was 40 years of age he went to a cave to think and pray. There, it is said that he had a vision. According to Mohammed's testimony, the *Angel Gabriel* appeared to him and told him that God wanted him to go and teach all his fellow Arabs his revelation. Those outside his immediate family and friends, rejected his new religion and tried to kill him. He fled to Medina, the same area to which Moses fled two millennial before. Mohammed started teaching his religion and building a following. The new religion was called *Islam*, meaning, submission and obedience to the will of God. At first Mohammed's followers had tried to make converts by friendly persuasion. After much rejection and persecution, they turned to the sword as a means of converting not only individuals but whole nations. With their fanatic zeal, they conquered North Africa, Western Asia, and the Middle East, including Jerusalem. Muslims were taught that the highest realm of heaven was reserved for those who died in military battle conquering "unbelievers" and giving them the option of converting to the Muslim religion or being killed. The Muslim faith produced a religious, hard, dominating spirit in its zealous followers. They were motivated more by hatred of the unbelievers of Islam than love for the souls of unbelievers. Their religion was propagated by the sword and encouraged slavery, harems, and the degradation of womanhood.

Islam's greatest error, and proof that it is not a faith born of God is the fact that it views Jesus Christ as no more than a Jewish prophet. They believe Jesus is inferior in every respect to Mohammed. The

Muslims claim that they believe in the one true God, (*Allah*, in Arabic) of the Old Testament. But their concept of God is a fearless, relentless dictator, with no love for humanity outside the followers of the prophet Mohammed.

Experience of A Founder and Leader of Universalism:

George de Benneville (1703-1793) was born to an aristocratic family who attended a Protestant church called the Huguenots. He attended university and became a physician. It is reported that while in Germany. He fell gravely ill and had a near death experience in which his spirit left his body, and he saw visions of heaven and hell. In hell, he felt such intense compassion that he states, "I took it so to heart that I believed my happiness would be incomplete while one creature remained miserable." In one of the visions, angelic beings clothed in garments as white as snow, proclaimed to him the good news of the restoration of all the human species, without exception. Dr. Bennevillee woke up in a coffin 42 hours after he had been declared dead, and he returned to life with confirmation of his mission; to preach the universal and everlasting gospel of boundless, universal love for the entire human race. After this miracle of returning from the dead, his preaching drew increasingly large crowds, and he was briefly imprisoned. His teaching stressed the unconditional love of God for all people, regardless of race, gender, creed, or culture. His universal teaching included the restoration of the devil and his angels and all mankind to heaven, with hell being eradicated.

Ellen White Major Founder of Seventh Day Adventist:

She lived most of her 87 years in the 19th Century (1827-1915). At age 12 she attended a Methodist camp and gave her heart to God and requested to be baptized by immersion. Seventh day Adventist believe that Mrs. White was more than a gifted writer; they believe she was appointed by God as a special messenger to draw the world's attention to the holy Scriptures and help prepare people for Christ's second advent. From the time she was 17 years old until she died 70 years later, God gave her approximate 2000 visions and dreams. The visions varied in length from less than a minute to nearly four hours.

She wrote 5000 periodical articles and 40 books. In some of the books, she describes what she saw and heard in her visions and visitations to heaven. She wrote books on spiritual gifts and prophecy. In one vision of being in heaven, she states that Jesus showed her a list of the 10 commandments with a halo over the fourth commandment. One of her most popular books, published worldwide was *The Great Controversy Between Christ and His Angels and Satan and his Angels*. Ellen White was given a vision of the relation of physical health to spirituality, of the importance of following right principles in diet and in the care of the body, and of the benefits of nature's remedies---clean air, sunshine, exercise and pure water. Though she blessed the Church and the world with much truth yet, there was enough error poison to cause the SDA denomination to be listed as a non-mainline Christian organization.

Joseph Smith, Founder of Mormonism, Church of Latter Day Saints.

In 1820 when Joseph Smith was 15 years old, he went into a secluded area to ask God which church he should join. According to his account, while praying Joseph was visited by two "personages" who identified themselves as God the Father and Jesus Christ. He was told not to join any of the churches.

In 1823, Joseph Smith said he was visited by an *Angel* named *Moroni,* who told him of an ancient record containing God's dealings with the former inhabitants of the American continent. In 1827, Joseph retrieved this record, inscribed on thin golden plates, and shortly afterward began translating its words by the "gift of God". The resulting manuscript, the *Book of Mormon*, was published in March 1830. On April 6, 1830, Joseph Smith, organized the Church of Jesus Christ of Latter-day Saints and became its first President. He established a governing body of five groups of which one consisted of twelve apostles. At the dedication of their temple in 1836, they reported that they participated in the prophesied endowment: a scene of visions, angelic visitations, prophesying, speaking and singing in tongues, and other spiritual experiences. In the summer of 1842, Smith revealed a plan to establish the millennial kingdom of God, which would eventually establish theocratic rule over the whole earth. There are many "various and strange" doctrines within the Mormon Church. They do not preach most of the doctrines of evangelical Christianity.

Mention is only made of the supernatural experiences of angelic visitations, prophesying and revelations to show further the reality that a few or many supernatural experiences does not guarantee that all taught by the group is a true doctrine. There are many non-biblical doctrines and practices in Mormonism too numerous to mention here.

1950s Healing Evangelist's Revelation From an "Angel"?

In the 1950s there was a healing Evangelist who became subject to deception which caused him to start preaching and practicing a false doctrine. One of the people who came before him in his healing line was a beautiful young woman. When he laid hands on her to pray for her, he felt a strange sensation go throughout his being. When he arrived back in his hotel room, he received a phone call. The caller described herself and asked if he remembered the strange feeling he had while praying for her. He said, yes. She replied; that was to give him witness that she was an angel sent from God to give him a new message for the Body of Christ and to establish a select people for God's purpose. She came to the hotel room and gave him many scriptures about the Body of Christ being one and joined to the Lord as man and woman being joined together. She would have sex with him which would appoint and authorize him to be the head of this new movement. The only way anyone could become a part of this special group was to be made one with him by having sex with him. He ended up having a church with over 200 people who had become members. He had a beautiful young lady who was supposed to be a 75-year old woman whom God had renewed her youth like Sarah. He had a bed in each side of the front of the Church, one where men were made members and one where women were made members.

The Evangelist had a great healing ministry, but when the "angel" told him he was specially chosen from among all others to produce this new elite company for Jesus Christ it appealed to his vanity and pride. Being told that he would be a special one above all others was the same Pride of Life tool that Lucifer used on Eve when he told her that she would be as wise as God if she ate of the forbidden fruit. The Lust of the Flesh convinced him that the method by which people had to become special members would be satisfying to him. The spirit of error with its three helpers deceived him just as Lucifer deceived Eve, the mother of the human race.

There were several things which should have alerted him that this was a lying spirit and false representation of one of God's angels. Angels do not have to call you on the phone they can just appear in the room. No angel ever appeared to God's man as a woman. Any "angel" appearing as a woman would be an angel of Satan regardless of how bright she might be or what seemingly great message she was bringing to the person. The only reference in the Bible of women with wings, were the two mentioned who were carrying the basket of wickedness to Babylon. They had the wings of a stork which Scripture declares as unclean. Zech. 5:5-11; Lev.11:19. Also, he should have known he would be committing adultery whether she was an angel or a human

Trips to Heaven and Spirit traveling and ministry:

There are some in the modern day teaching that Christians can project themselves into the Third Heaven by imagination, concentration and believing for the Holy Spirit to take over and transport them to heaven. It sounds inviting and desirous to be able to take trips to heaven anytime you desired. However, there are no scriptural illustrations of anyone doing that, not even Jesus. If anyone should have been able to do that and have that privilege, Jesus Christ would be the number one candidate. Actually Jesus had very few heavenly visitations. There is no record of any supernatural experiences happening to Jesus until He was thirty and was being baptized by John the Baptist; God spoke loudly from heaven, "You are My beloved Son; in You I am well pleased." And the Holy Spirit descended in bodily form like a dove upon Him. Jesus had a visible direct encounter with Satan after He had fasted 40 days. And then angels came and ministered to Him Mt.4:1-11. Jesus had a heavenly visitation on the Mount of Transfiguration and later when He was praying in agony in the Garden of Gethsemane an angel appeared to Jesus from heaven and strengthened Him. Luke 22:43 Jesus did a lot of praying even all night at times, preached, cast out devils and healed the sick. But there is no record of Him making trips to heaven or doing spirit traveling and ministering apart from his body. All of those things may be possible, and some have testified of having those experiences, but they are not things Christians should be trying to project themselves into. Praise God, if heavenly visitations happen, but there are no scriptural examples or instructions on how to produce a heavenly visitation for yourself.

Why does God allow things like this to happen to ministers?

The answer is given in Duet.13:1-4 *"The Lord your God is testing you to know whether you love the Lord your God with all your heart and with all your soul."*

These are just a few historic illustrations and modern day examples revealing that supernatural experiences are not guarantees that all doctrine taught by the person receiving the experiences will be biblically accurate. Numerous other examples could be given but this should be sufficient to the honest Christian to prove that heavenly experiences do not prove that everything being taught is biblically correct or that the person's life is in complete order. Too many Charismatic Christians are too impressed by people who have supernatural experiences. We must remember that when the angels came before God that Lucifer slipped into the line. Sometimes when a person is receiving revelation Satan will slip his thoughts into the mix. Job 1:6. That is one reason Apostle Paul said that we must be diligent to separate error from truth. But one must have a thorough knowledge of the word of God to properly separate error from the truth. One must also know how to allow the Holy Spirit to witness to their spirit whether something is true or false. Understanding this principle gives us insight on why Paul wrote these words to the Galatian Christians: *"I am amazed that you are turning away so soon from God, who, in his love and mercy, invited you to share the eternal life He gives through Christ; you are already following a different 'way to heaven,' which really doesn't go to heaven at all. For there is no other way than the one we showed you; you are being fooled by those who twist and change the truth concerning Christ. Let God's curses fall on anyone, including myself, who preaches any other way to be saved than the one* *we told you about; yes, if **an Angel** comes from heaven and preaches any other message, let him be forever cursed. I will say it again: if anyone preaches any other gospel than the one you welcomed, let God's curse fall upon him."* Gal.1:6-9 LB *"Let no man deceive you by any means." "Little children, let no man deceive you. He that commits sin is of the devil, for the devil has sinned from the beginning."* (Lucifer was the originator of sin.) 2Thess.2:3; 1 Jn. 3:7

Chapter 11
Divine Progressive Preparation
for God's Pure & Mature Church

"I Will Build My Church:" Mt.16:18

Jesus declared that He would not only birth His Church but that He would build His Church until it becomes a glorious Church without spot or wrinkle.   He declared it would be more glorious and magnificent than the temple that Solomon built. His temple was made of the best wood and overlaid with silver and gold. It was one of the wonders of the world in its day. Jesus is building a spiritual temple made up of redeemed men and women who are the lively stones and building blocks of this spiritual temple. The Church of Jesus Christ is also called the Body of Christ. God planned the Church when He planned the Human Race. The Church is to fulfill God's eternal purpose for creating the earth and then creating man from the dust of the earth in God's own image and likeness.

The first book I wrote was titled "The Eternal Church" It was called the Eternal Church because the Church was planned in eternity past, birthed and built in earth time but will function now and forever in eternity future.   The book covers the origination and establishment of the Church (30AD-400AD); the great falling away of the Church called the 1000 year Dark Age of the Church (500AD-1500AD); the restoration of all truth and ministry back into the Church which is called the Second Reformation of the Church (1517AD-2007AD); the fifth division in the book covers the end time ministry and destiny of the Church in fulfilling God's eternal purpose for creating the human race. (2008-Christ's Second Coming). Satan has desperately tried to stop God's Church from being the pure and mature Church. He knows that when the Church becomes all that it is supposed to be that Jesus will return with His saints and bind the devil, all his host of evil spirits including all of his wicked human followers, and cast them into the Lake of Fire. Satan is doing everything he can to pervert the Church in it doctrines and way of life to keep it from having the pure truth and life of Christ. The last generation of the mortal Church will have, be and do all that Christ has destined it to.

During the last 500 years of Church restoration, all truths and ministries that were lost during the Dark age of the Church have been restored back into the Church. The period of the restoration of the Church prepared the way for the launching of the Third and Final Church Reformation, which was decreed from heaven in 2008. The Third Reformation will bring about the final maturing and ministry of the mortal Church. The Army of the Lord is about to be activated into manifesting with great power the Kingdom of God until God's prophetic decree in Revelation 11:15 is fulfilled. The devil knows his time is very short, and he is intensifying his assault on the Church with strange doctrines and false teachings. He wants to drag every human he can to his hellish eternity. He has invented numerous false teachings to get people to believe there is no devil or hell, and that they can get into heaven without Jesus Christ. He has invented doctrines to make people think they can live ungodly, immoral lives and still enter heaven.

We have listed many of those demonic and false religious teachings in other chapters. In this closing chapter, I want to reveal the way to stay in the middle of the stream of God's progressive Church. If the devil cannot get a Christian into false doctrine, then he seeks to make them ineffective by getting them off the main path of God's purpose for His Church by going to extremes left or right.

Extreme Swings in the Pendulum of Restored Truth.

When truth is in the process of being restored to the Church, it usually swings extremely to the right, then to the left, and finally hangs straight with a balanced message, like the pendulum of a grandfather clock, in the middle of the two extremes. Those who get stuck out on the extreme left become cultic in their doctrines and practices. Those who don't make it back from the extreme right become an exclusive group who separate themselves from the rest of the Body of Christ. Then there is the group who bring themselves together from both extremes to maintain a balance in proper biblical doctrine and practice as God originally intended it to be restored within the Church.

A restoration movement may also be compared to the times when heavy rains come and cause a river to flood over its banks. Some of the water gets stuck out on the right side of the river and forms little ponds where a few fish stay. Some of the water on the left never makes it back to the river but forms bayous and swamps where all kinds of slimy and poisonous creatures dwell. As the flood waters recede, the main body of water flows between the river banks of wisdom and maturity in ministering the restored truths and spiritual experiences

It's like the story Jesus used about casting the fishing net and drawing all the fish into the boat. After the fish are in the boat where they can be seen and examined, the bad fish are separated from the good fish. The boat then continues on without all the non profitable fish aboard. Jesus also stated that tares should be allowed to grow with the wheat until harvest time and then the tares would be separated from the wheat and burned. Every restoration of truth goes through its sprouting forth time and then matures to the place where the movement leaders can properly separate the "tares" manifestations, teachings and practices from the true ones that the Holy Spirit birthed and brought forth. I have been going through that process as a pioneer and participant in the birthing and maturing of the Prophetic Movement and following Movements. I am just as committed to doing the same in the continuing restoration of Apostles and the Saints Movement to continue them into the present day Third & Final Church Reformation.

The "Balanced" Group May Lose the Anointing

A problem may also develop with the "balanced" group. They may become so protective of the truth and so reactionary toward the extremists that they keep the original truth yet lose the flow of the Holy Spirit. They may keep the purity of the doctrine yet lose the fresh anointing that restored those truths. They may maintain the proper preaching and practices yet lose God's mighty presence and power that originally accompanied their ministry. Sad to say, church history reveals that it is this balanced group that usually becomes the main persecutors of the next restorational movement of the Holy Spirit. They establish wineskins of doctrinal limitations with regard to what, when, where, who and how the truth can be ministered. Their wineskins become dry and set with such limitations that they cannot receive the new wine of restored truth that adds new truth and spiritual ministries to the Church. Those who understand the principles of restoration should never miss a new move of God. Most of the truths and ministries revealed and demonstrated in the Book of Acts is now active in the present restoration churches. During the Third Reformation, there are truths and ministries that have been in reserve to be manifest during the last generation of the mortal Church. The climax of the Third Reformation will be the return of Jesus with all His saints to cleanse the earth and the heavens of all evil and the negative results of the curse. Earth and its atmosphere will be cleansed by God's purifying fire producing what Apostle Peter said he was looking for, "New Earth where only righteousness dwells." 2Pet.3:13.

The Living Church is a Flowing River:

The Church of our Lord Jesus Christ is a river flowing with fresh water continually. It is not a pond of still water, but a river constantly flowing with fresh new water. Ezekiel 47 describes that river that gets deeper and wider as it continues to its destination. Christians who are in that river go from glory to glory, faith to faith, truth to truth until they come to the fullness of Jesus Christ, the way the truth and the life. For that reason, we must keep our wineskins flexible so that we can go from movement to movement of the Holy Spirit, incorporating into our personal lives and our churches all that God wants to restore to His Church (2Cor.3:18). At the same time, we must not become vulnerable to extremism and fanaticism. As the Apostle Peter declared, we must continually "be established in the present truth" without forsaking any of the truths and practices which have already been restored (2Pet.1:12). Jesus said that a wise scribe is one who brings out of his treasure chest treasure both old and new. The Church is not a water tank or salty Dead Sea, but a river of fresh flowing, life-giving water (Mt.13:52; Ez.47:1-12; Jn.7:38). Let us stay in the middle of God's stream of ongoing restoration

In my book, "Apostles, Prophets and The Coming Moves of God" I take 22 pages in chapter 12 to cover all the extremes that developed in all the restoration movements, and how to maintain a balance between the extremes. Truth taken to the extreme may not keep a church member or Christian minister out of heaven, but too much false doctrine and ungodly living can shut the gate to heaven for those who believe a lie and practice sinning. Jesus will not stop building His Church until He has the sufficient number of overcomers who are conformed to Christ's character and matured into the fullness of the stature of Christ Himself. Everyone whose sins are washed away by the blood of Jesus will enter heaven, but only the overcomers who have become kings and priests unto God will be placed in positions of ruling and reigning with Christ Jesus. There is no greater purpose in life than to love God with all your heart, soul, mind and strength; be conformed to Christ's image and likeness and be a victorious overcomer.

Most of the passages in the Bible contain the contrast between the blessings for obedience and the judgments for disobedience, from Adam and Eve in the Garden to the last chapter in the Bible. *"He who overcomes shall inherit all things, and I will be his God and he shall be My son, But the cowardly, unbelievers, abominable, murderers, sexually immoral, sorcerers, idolaters and all liars shall have their part in the lake which burns with fire and brimstone, which is the second death." Rev 21:7-8.*

The following prophecy given by a great man of God many years ago is so relevant to this message that I felt it would be greatly beneficial to you who are reading this book:

Coming Glory and Deceiving Spirits
by Stanley Frodsham

THIS PROPHECY was given at the Elim Bible Institute USA, in 1965 by the late Stanley Frodsham. Brother Frodsham was one of those who received his Baptism in the Holy Ghost at Sunderland in 1908 where the Pentecostal movement in Britain had its beginnings. He was a friend of Smith Wigglesworth, and this seems certainly relevant for us today.

Stanley Frodsham was also one of my teachers at the Bible College I attended 1953-54. He was the godliest minister I have ever known. He taught and imparted to me the ability to love the Lord Jesus in worship. He was very prophetic and loved the Lord like no one else I have ever known. You can receive with full assurance that His prophecy is a true prophetic flow from the heart and mind of God. Some of the old time prophets, such as Stanley Frodsham used to prophesy continuously for 30 or 40 minutes. Even though this is a long prophecy please read it thoughtfully and let it reemphasize to you many of the truths written within this book.

God's Prophetic Word to Christ's Church
By Stanley Frodsham

"When I visit My people in mighty revival power it is to prepare them for the darkness that lies ahead. With the glory shall come great darkness. For the glory is to prepare My people for that darkness. I will enable My people to go through because of a mighty visitation of My Spirit. Take heed to yourselves lest you be puffed up and think that you have already arrived. Many shall be puffed up in that hour as in the days of old. For many then did receive My message, but they did not continue in it. Did I not anoint Jehu? And yet the things I desired were not accomplished in his life.

Listen to the messengers that I will send, but do not hold any man's personality in admiration. For many whom I shall anoint mightily with signs and miracles and wonders shall become lifted up and put upon a pedestal, but they shall fall by the wayside. I do not do this willingly, for I have made provision that they might stand. I call many into this ministry and equip them, but remember many shall fall in that hour. For Babylon shall not stand. They shall be like bright lights, and the people shall delight in their ministries, but they shall be taken over by deceiving spirits and lead many of My people astray.

Hearken diligently concerning these things, for in the last days shall come seducing spirits. (1 Timothy 4: 1) They shall turn many of the anointed ones away. Many shall fall through diverse lusts, and because sin abounds in their lives. But, if you will seek Me diligently, I will put My Spirit within you. When one shall turn to the right hand, or one shall turn to the left hand, you shall not turn with them.

My people must be diligently warned concerning the days that lie ahead. Many shall turn after seducing and deceiving spirits. Many already are in the midst of the body seducing My people. It is those that do righteous that are righteous. Many cover their sins by their great theology and their great theological ways. But I warn you of seducing spirits who instruct My people in an evil way.

Many of these I shall anoint, that they may purify and sift My people, for I would have a holy people. Many shall come with seducing spirits and hold out lustful enticements. You will find, that after I evicted My people again, the way shall become more and more narrow, and few there are that shall walk therein. Be not deceived, it is the way of the righteous that is My way. For though Satan will come as an angel of light, hearken not unto him.

For those that perform miracles and speak not righteousness are not of Me. Those that have large crowds that follow them, but speak not of purifying and holiness are not of Me. I warn you, with great intensity, that I am going to judge My house, and have a Church without spot or wrinkle when I come. I desire to open your eyes and give you spiritual understanding that you may not be deceived, but may walk in uprightness of heart before Me, loving righteousness and hating and despising every evil way. Look unto Me and I will make you to perceive with the eyes of the Spirit the things that lurk in darkness. They are not visible to the human eye. Let Me lead you in this way, that you may precede the powers of darkness and battle against them. It is not a battle against flesh and blood, for if you battle in that way you will accomplish nothing.

But if you let Me take over and battle against the powers of darkness, then they are defeated and liberation is brought unto My people. I warn you to search the Scriptures diligently concerning these last days, for the things that are written shall indeed be manifested.

There shall come deceivers among My people, in increasing numbers, who speak for the truth and shall gain the favor and the hearts of the people.

For the people shall examine the Scriptures and say, "Is not what these men say true?" Then, when they have gained the hearts of the people, then and only then shall they bring out their wrong doctrines. Therefore I say unto you and warn you, 'Oh people, do not give your hearts to men, nor hold people in admiration, for by these very persons shall Satan enter into My people.' Watch for the seducers. Do you think a seducer will brandish a new heresy and flaunt it before the people? No, he will speak the words of righteousness and truth, and will appear as a minister of light declaring the Word.

And the people's hearts shall be won over by their words, then, when their hearts are won, they shall bring out their doctrines, and the people shall be deceived. The people shall say, 'Did he not speak this and that? Did we not examine it from the Word? Therefore, he is a minister of righteousness. This that he now has spoken, though we do not see it in the Word, it truly must be right, for everything else he has said is true.'

Be not deceived. For the deceiver will first work to gain the hearts of many, and then bring forth his false doctrines. You cannot discern those who are of Me and those who are not of Me when they start to preach, saith the Lord. But seek Me continuously, and when these doctrines are brought out, you shall have a witness within your heart that they are not of Me. Fear not, for I have warned you. Many will be deceived. But if you walk in holiness and uprightness before the Lord your God, your eyes shall be opened, and the Lord God shall protect you all the days of your life. If you will constantly look unto the Lord, you will know when the doctrine changes. And you will not be brought into this thing, if your heart is right, saith the Lord. I will keep you. And if you look constantly unto Me, I will uphold you. The minister of righteousness shall be on this wise, saith the Lord: his life shall agree with the Word, his lips shall give forth that which is holy truth, and it will be no mixture in his ministry. When the mixture appears, you will know that he is not a minister of righteousness. The deceivers speak first the truth and then error, to cover their own sins which they love.

Therefore, I exhort and command you, saith the Lord, to study the Scriptures relating to seducing spirits, for this is one of the greatest dangers for the Church in these last days. I desire you to be firmly established in My Word, not in the personalities or the ministries of men. You shall not be moved as many shall be moved. I would keep you in the paths of righteousness. Seek Me, diligently inquire of Me, that you may hear something, that you might know. I have come that you might have life, and have it more abundantly, and that you might triumph, even as I have triumphed. On the cross, I triumphed over all the power of Satan, and I have called you to walk in the same path. For those who will not minister the crucified life and cross of Jesus Christ, do not understand righteousness. It is when your life is on the cross that you shall have victory which I have experienced. As you are on the cross and seated in Me, you shall know the power of My resurrection. When I came in My glory, the principalities and powers in heavenly places were broken.

Fear not, for I have given you power whereby you may tread upon the powers of darkness and come forth victorious. It was on the cross that I triumphed over all things. My life shall flow through you as you enter into these precious truths. Look unto Me and appropriate My life. As your eyes and desires are towards Me, and you know what it is to be crucified with Me, then you shall also know what it is to be resurrected by Me. It was not in My life that I walked upon the earth, but it was in My life when I was upon the cross that I openly spoiled the principalities and powers of darkness.

I am showing you truths, that you shall come to know, that you too can be an overcomer to have power over the wicked one. This truth shall liberate you, and it will liberate those around you. You shall know also the fellowship of My suffering, saith the Lord. There is no way by which you can be partakers of the heavenly glory and reign with Me without drinking of the Cup of My suffering. If we suffer with Him, the Word says, then we shall also reign with Him. I desire to make these truths real within you. Have revelation given to you that you may have power to overcome the wicked one and bondages that are in your life. If you will indeed judge yourself, you shall not be judged. As you shall seek My Face and desire to be cleansed by Me, in all truth and sincerity of heart, I will judge you in the secret place. And the things that are in the secret place of your heart shall not be made manifest to others round about you. I shall do it in the secret place, and no other mind shall know it. And the shame that shall be seen on many faces in this last hour shall not be seen on your face.

Therefore, in love and mercy I am instructing you. And therefore, I have said that if a man judges himself, he will not be judged. It is not My good pleasure that the shame of My people be seen by all.

How can I judge the world if I judge not first My own house? Hearken unto these things which I tell you. If you will not hearken unto Me, then the shame shall be evident unto all. I would have you consider My life on earth: the anointing upon Me was great and yet, the temptation was great on every side. In one form and then in another, offering Me first the glory of the kingdoms of the earth, and then reviling and courting and intensifying on every point and persecuting Me. There will be great glory given to My people, and yet, I would have you to know that in this last hour, the temptations shall intensify on every side. The glory to My Church shall be great, and so shall be the temptation from the enemy to turn My people from the directed paths which I have ordained.

I warn you, that when the glory shall be manifested, the temptations shall be great, until very few that start shall finish the race. First, they shall be offered the great worldly possessions, prosperity and then reviling and unbelief shall overtake them. Consider your purpose in this last hour. At times, everyone shall rise up against and try with everything to turn you from that course of holiness. It is written of Me, that I set My face as a flint to go the direction My Father had prescribed for Me.

So, hear the Word of the Lord, if you are to finish the race with great victory and glory, you must determine to set your face as a flint with great determination. You must walk in the course laid before you.

Many of your loved ones and those who follow with you shall persecute you and even try to turn you from your course. With many words that seem right in the natural mind, they shall try to turn you. Did not Christ rebuke Peter who tried to turn Him off the course that God had prescribed for Him?

Understand these two things and meditate upon them solemnly in this last hour. The persecution and the darkness shall be as great as the glory, in order to try to turn the elect and the anointed ones from the path which the Lord God has laid down for them. Many shall start, but few shall be able to finish the course, because of the greatness of grace that shall be needed in that hour to endure to the end. The temptations and the persecution of your Lord were continuous. He was tempted by Satan in many forms through him, and He listened not, but He laid down His life upon the cross.

Think not that there shall be a time of no persecution. Think not that there will be a time of no temptation. For it shall be from the time of your anointing until the end of the course. Difficulties and great persecutions unto the end. The Lord must prepare you to be an overcomer in all things that you may be able to finish the course. The persecution shall increase, even as the anointing shall increase. Hear these words, 'My grace is sufficient for you' in that hour. In paths of justice and of righteousness shall the Lord God lead His people and bring them into a place which He has chosen for this time. For the Lord has chosen a place of righteousness. It is a place of holiness where He shall encamp round about them, and all who will be led of the Lord shall be brought into this holy place. For the Lord delights to dwell in His people. The Lord delights to manifest Himself through His people. The holiness of the Lord shall be manifested through His people. Let the Lord lead you into difficult places.

He led His people of old through a place where no man dwelt, where no man had passed through. It was a place of great danger and in the shadow of death. The Lord will indeed lead His people through such places, and yet, He will bring them into a place of great glory and victory. Understand that the way towards glory is great danger, but the Lord shall grace thee in that hour. Put your trust in Him and He will bring you into this place of holiness. For He desires to bring His people into this great joy and life. Put your trust in Him. Trust no man. It is a place where God will protect those from the voices that would try to turn them from the given path. He will bring them into a place where He will speak and lead His people. It is a place of great grace and glory. He will indeed camp round about them. Put your trust in Him, and He will surely bring you into this new place. Fear not the days to come. But fear only this: that you shall walk in a manner pleasing unto the Lord. It is a time I am ordering and setting up My Church. It shall indeed be without spot or wrinkle. I will do a work in My beloved that has not been seen since the foundations of the world.

I will show you these things that you might seek the Lord diligently, with all your heart, and that you may be preserving of His marvelous grace. Run not to this or to that one, for the Lord has so ordained thy salvation, it is in Him and in Him alone. You shall not turn to this shepherd or to that one, for there shall be a great scattering upon the earth.

Therefore look unto Jesus, for He will indeed make these things clear unto you. You shall not look here or there for wells that once held water, they shall be no more.

But, as you diligently seek Me, He shall increase your strength and your faith, and His grace and enable you to prepare you for the time that is to come. The truth that I have revealed unto you must become a part of you, not just an experience, but a part of your very nature. Is it not written that I demand truth in the innermost parts? It is a truth of the Lord expressed in your very being that shall hold you and sustain you. Many shall experience the truth, but the truth must become a part of you and your very life. As men and women look upon you, they will hear not only the voice, but see an expression of that truth in our innermost being. Many shall be overcome because they are not permitting the truth to become a part of them at all times. But I am showing you in these truths that they are to be a part of you, that you might be prepared and having done all, to stand, stand in this last hour. He that hath an ear, let him hear what the Spirit now speaks to His Church.'"[2]

[2] Frodsham, Stanley. "Coming Glory and Deceiving Spirits." *Visionary Advancement Strategies*. InJesus, 21 June 2008. Web. 25 June 2008.

Contact the Author

Questions? Comments? Contact the author!

Dr. Bill Hamon
CIAN-Global Network
Bishop & Founder

drbill@bishophamon.org
phone: 850-231-2600 x 657
fax: 850-231-5630
www.christianinternational.com

Additional Books by the Author

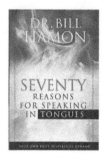
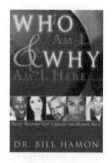
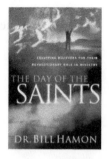

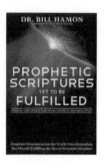
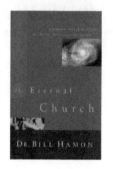
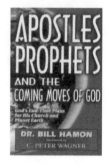

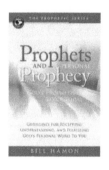

Books by Evelyn "Mom" Hamon

Evelyn Y. Hamon was raised in a Christian home and married her pastor (Bill Hamon) in 1955. For nearly 60 years she served alongside her husband in the ministry, from pastoring a small, rural church to overseeing a worldwide ministry. At the same time, she rasied three children in the fear and admonition of the Lord, who are now also in full-time ministry. Seeing her grandchildren serve God and her great-grandchildren raised in godliness was one of her greatest joys. Evelyn was gifted with a willingness to maintain a positive, overcoming attitude through life's challenges and an ability to impart that same attitude to others. Evelyn "Mom" Hamon went to be with Jesus on September 22, 2014.

Books by Jane Hamon

  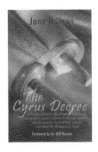